Sam Shepard
and the
American Theatre

SAM SHEPARD AND THE AMERICAN THEATRE

LESLIE A. WADE

Contributions in Drama and Theatre Studies, Number 76

LIVES OF THE THEATRE
JOSH BEER, CHRISTOPHER INNES, and SIMON WILLIAMS, Series Advisers

Greenwood Press
Westport, Connecticut • London

357774aa

Library of Congress Cataloging-in-Publication Data

Wade, Leslie A.
    Sam Shepard and the American theatre / Leslie A. Wade.
       p.   cm.—(Contributions in drama and theatre studies, ISSN
  0163–3821 ; no. 76. Lives of the theatre)
    Includes bibliographical references and index.
    ISBN 0–313–28944–1 (alk. paper)
    1. Shepard, Sam, 1943– —Criticism and interpretation.
  2. Theater—United States—History—20th century. I. Title.
  II. Series: Contributions in drama and theatre studies ; no. 76.
  III. Series: Contributions in drama and theatre studies. Lives of
  the theatre.
  PS3569.H394Z97   1997
  812'.54—dc21   96–47537

British Library Cataloguing in Publication Data is available.

A paperback edition of *Sam Shepard and the American Theatre* is available from
Praeger Publishers, an imprint of Greenwood Publishing Group, Inc.
(ISBN 0–275–94584–7).

Library of Congress Catalog Card Number: 96–47537
ISBN: 0–313–28944–1
ISSN: 0163–3821

First published in 1997

Greenwood Press, 88 Post Road West, Westport, CT 06881
An imprint of Greenwood Publishing Group, Inc.

Printed in the United States of America

The paper used in this book complies with the
Permanent Paper Standard issued by the National
Information Standards Organization (Z39.48–1984).

10 9 8 7 6 5 4 3 2 1

98 0544

Special thanks to
Simon Williams, Gresdna Doty, and Bill Harbin

Contents

Series Foreword

Lives of the Theatre is designed to provide scholarly introductions to important periods and movements in the history of world theatre from the earliest instances of recorded performance through to the twentieth century, viewing the theatre consistently through the lives of representative theatrical practitioners. Although many of the volumes will be centred upon playwrights, other important theatre people, such as actors and directors, will also be prominent in the series. The subjects have been chosen not simply for their individual importance, but because their lives in the theatre can well serve to provide a major perspective on the theatrical trends of their eras. They are therefore either representative of their time, figures whom their contemporaries recognised as vital presences in the theatre, or they are people whose work was to have a fundamental influence on the development of theatre, not only in their lifetimes but after their deaths as well. While the discussion of verbal and written scripts will inevitably be a central concern in any volume that is about about an artist who wrote for the theatre, these scripts will always be considered in their function as a basis for performance.

The rubric "Lives of the Theatre" is therefore intended to suggest both biographies of people who created theatre as an institution and as a medium of performance and of the life of the theatre itself. This dual focus will be illustrated through the titles of the individual volumes, such as *Christopher Marlowe and the Renaissance of Tragedy, George Bernard Shaw and the Socialist Theatre,* and *Richard Wagner and Festival Theatre,* to name just a few. At the same time, although the focus of each volume will be different, depending on the particular subject, appropriate emphasis will be given to the cultural and political context within which the theatre of any given time is set. Theatre itself can be seen to have a palpable effect upon the social world around it, as it both reflects the life of its time and helps to form that life by feeding it images, epitomes, and alternative versions of itself. Hence, we hope that this series will also contribute to an understanding of the broader social life of the period of which the theatre that is the subject of each volume was a part.

Lives of the Theatre grew out of an idea that Josh Beer put to Christopher Innes and Peter Arnott. Sadly, Peter Arnott did not live to see the inauguration of the series. Simon Williams kindly agreed to replace him as one of the series editors and has played a full part in its preparation. In commemoration, the editors wish to acknowledge Peter's own rich contribution to the life of the theatre.

Josh Beer
Christopher Innes
Simon Williams

Introduction: Sam Shepard and the Narration of Nation

No playwright in the recent history of the American theatre has garnered more attention and acclaim than Sam Shepard. From his early experiments in the Off-Off Broadway avant-garde to his widely renowned family plays, he has fascinated audiences with an effulgent, often hypnotic drama of American anxiety and ambition. With a career that has spanned three decades, Shepard has achieved the rank and stature accorded such figures as Eugene O'Neill, Tennessee Williams, and Arthur Miller. The leading dramatist of his generation, Sam Shepard has become the latest Great American Playwright.

As a volume in the "Lives of the Theatre" subseries of the Greenwood Press "Contributions in Drama and Theatre Studies" series, this study surveys the life and art of Sam Shepard. It also attempts to situate his work in postwar U.S. theatre and its shifting conditions of production. Given Martin Esslin's contention that "Sam Shepard *is* contemporary American theatre,"[1] perhaps no figure is better suited for such service. Since his debut as a playwright at Theatre Genesis in 1964, Shepard has seen his work staged in the leading Off- (and Off-Off) Broadway, regional, and university theatres of the nation. He has worked with many of the country's noted directors, actors, and producers. The production history of his plays—and its glaring want of Broadway credits—reveals much about the institutions of American theatre, its production modes, its aesthetics, economics, and ideologies. His involvement in film as actor, writer, and director, moreover, testifies to the heavy interchange between stage and screen and their respective positions in the American entertainment industry.

Shepard's longevity in the American theatre also makes his career valuable as a vehicle for cultural critique; his writing dates from the early sixties and the counterculture rumblings of lower Manhattan through the new conservatism of the Clinton/Gingrich era. His plays may be viewed as artifacts that document contemporary American history, and shifts in Shepard's aesthetic orientation often signal wider dislocations in the social and political landscape. That his works have continued to find audience throughout these many years further suggests that the playwright's appeal has not been based on innovative dramatic technique alone, but that his plays somehow speak to an American experience that lies deep within the nation's cultural memory.

Wynn Handman, artistic director of the American Place Theatre, once remarked that Shepard is "like a conduit that digs down into the American soil and what flows out of him is what we're all about."[2] Handman's observation implies that Shepard is somehow quintessentially American, and indeed throughout his career he has been heralded as the "most American" of our contemporary dramatists.[3] Drawing from the disparate image banks of rock and roll, detective fiction, B-movies, and Wild West adventure shows, his plays function as a storehouse of images, icons, and idioms that denote American culture and an American sensibility. If nothing else, his works act as a theatrical Smithsonian. This celebration of his "Americanness," however, invites speculation as to why Shepard bears this mantle, why he (and not Israel Horovitz, Adrienne Kennedy, or Ronald Tavel) has emerged from the legion of Off-Off Broadway writers to assume the role of Eugene O'Neill's heir apparent.[4]

This study attempts to answer the question of Shepard's prominence by viewing his work against the problems of identity besetting postwar American culture. From the Truman era to the present, the United States has been forced to confront economic upheaval, political realignment, demographic shifts, and increased diversification in its population. Shepard's designation as the playwright of the nation merits attention, since the very notion of national identity during this time has proven an ambiguous and often exclusionary concept. Analysis of his career (and his promotion in American theatre) thus introduces matters that bear upon consensus, community, and how the country has chosen to define itself over the last three decades.

Recent global reorganization (and ethnic violence) has brought increased attention to issues of nationalism and cultural identity. The work of Benedict Anderson is often cited for its discussion of "imagined communities,"[5] a phrase that suggests the constructed, even arbitrary nature of group affiliation, whether it be that of tribe, people, sect, or clan. In this light, a "nation" involves a set of beliefs or practices that, through the years, gain a metaphysical aura and the semblance of timelessness. According to Simon During, the idea of nation resides in the "battery" of social and aesthetic forms that define and "legitimate" the polity.[6] The theatrical life of a people thus takes on immense importance, for the determinants of community are frequently couched in a network of images, myths, and narratives depicted and purveyed in acts of performance.

Shepard's dramas deal heavily in the narratives that have helped fashion what has been termed "the American character," a concept that has been an issue of debate almost from the country's inception. Alexis de Tocqueville, one of the first to consider the nature of the American experience, argued in the 1830s that the United States was a rarity in modern history, a country whose origination took place for all the world to see (without appeal to blood lines, territory rights, or religious denomination). For Tocqueville, being American was a matter of citizenship. This conception of the American character has long held currency, giving rise to opinions such as "to be American is to be anonymous."[7] America in this view is not so much a heritage but a philosophy—a system of governance that defines and bestows rights and civil liberties. America, as Hans Kohn has described it, is a good idea, which one commits to by an act of volition.[8]

Such an understanding of America does not take into account the country's debt to the English legal system, the overwhelmingly European background of its early population, or the fact that not all inhabitants of the United States have had equal access to the rights of citizenship. The "know-nothings" of the 1850s, for example, preaching "America for Americans" in the face of rising Irish immigration, advanced the notion that some groups are more American than others, a perception that continues to find quarter today. As opposed to the view that America exists as a system of governance that operates from a position of neutrality, the nation may be seen as a "measure" of belonging, one fashioned by an ideological tug-of-war involving population groups, economic interests, and the negotiations of cultural power.

This study holds that the coherence of the nation owes much to the potency of its communal "stories," those myths given prominence in cultural consciousness. This examination thus finds the cultural/narrative theories of Mikhail Bakhtin a source of inspiration and directive. Bakhtin introduced the term *heteroglossia* to describe the plurality of voices and impulses at work in avant-garde art—pieces marked by randomness, eruption, and unconventional stylistic practices. Although Bakhtin's writing on this subject specifically addressed the novels of Dostoevsky, heteroglossia—and its implicit politics—may also be understood on a wider level, as a cultural phenomenon in which outbursts of anarchy, multiplicity, and difference challenge the dominant culture and its "legitimate" discursive forms.[9]

Against the voices of Otherness, Bakhtin saw the force of canonization, which works to regulate and institutionalize communal dialogue. In short, this model sees culture as ever shifting, activated by centrifugal energies that continually push outward, propelling cultural consciousness into unexplored forms and combinations, and centripetal forces that usurp, check, channel, and regularize.

This framework allows us to consider an artwork as a form of cultural conversation, which challenges or confirms the canonical voice; it also enjoins us to note the agencies that authorize, sanction, or censure aesthetic utterances. Bakhtin's insights are helpful to an examination of Shepard's art and its nationalistic implications, since we may view the American theatre and its institutional structures as a mode of governance, one that promotes (or critiques) America's canonical stories and their implicit definitions of national character.

Studies of this format are susceptible to the "great man and his works" mentality, underscoring the figure's genius, originality, and artistic triumphs (conquests). Recent trends in poststructuralist thought have conversely tended to discount the individual and to focus upon the systems that generate texts and the institutions that control them. This inquiry takes up an approach that, it is hoped, mediates the often dichotomized provinces of the subject and the system.

It should also be noted that this study views Shepard's art and his personal behavior in a similar light—both are understood as public gestures, as acts performed before the communal eye. Though Shepard has described his playwriting in terms of self-discovery, a point that underscores his theatre as a sort of ego-performance,[10] his plays, like those of any dramatist, are implicitly directed toward a spectator and thus enter into communal dialogue. His personal actions and postures also evince a rhetorical aspect. Even the tattoo he bears on his left wrist—the Hawk Moon—exists as a form of utterance, a revealing type of self-inscription that speaks to and calls for an audience.

In his essay on the politics of American performance, Joseph Roach advocates a culture-based criticism, suggesting that scholars need no longer pore over "Sam Shepard's spilled entrails."[11] While this study gives attention to the dramatist's family biography, his personal viewpoints, and choices as an artist, the work also attempts to understand his career in dialogic terms, that is, how the playwright has addressed the nation, and, perhaps more importantly, how the nation has deployed the playwright. Jack Kroll's claim that Shepard "has been the great, red, white, and blue hope of U.S. drama since he was barely out of his teens"[12] alerts us to Shepard's service as a cipher in the politics of communal desire. It also suggests that his rise to prominence, in part orchestrated by the institutions of the American theatre and the critical establishment, may be attributed to the national ethos of his work and its contribution to an American consensus.

It is revealing that Shepard has gained renown as an American playwright during a time in which the idea of American community has come under close review. On one side a figure such as Arthur Schlesinger laments the "disuniting of America" and argues for the conservation of American ideals.[13] To the contrary, African American scholar Molefi Kete Asante has written that "there is no common American culture as is claimed by the defenders of the status quo," that there is only a "hegemonic" culture "pushed as if it were."[14] Shepard speaks of America in his singular, often rollicking style, with an oeuvre that includes more than fifty stage and screen plays, four books of nondramatic writings, and over a dozen feature film performances. This study intends to trace and offer some explanation for the playwright's rise from Off-Off Broadway renegade to Hollywood leading man, from counterculture to cultural icon. It also seeks to address Shepard's evocation of the nation, and how his vision answers the heated and often divisive question central to current public debate: What does it mean to be an American?

NOTES

1. Martin Esslin, quoted in Stewart McBride, "Sam Shepard—Listener and Playwright," *Christian Science Monitor*, 23 December 1980, sec. B, p. 2.

2. Wynn Handman, quoted in Jack Kroll, Constance Guthrie, and Janet Huck, "Who's That Tall Dark Stranger?" *Newsweek*, 11 November 1985, 71.

3. Jack Kroll, "Crazy Henry," *Newsweek*, 8 May 1978, 94.

4. Lynda Hart raises this issue for consideration and argues that Shepard's recurrent designation as America's playwright "should give us pause." See "Sam Shepard's Pornographic Visions," *Studies in the Literary Imagination* 21, no. 2 (1988): 81.

5. For explanation of this term, see Benedict Anderson, *Imagined Communities* (London: Verso, 1983), 15.

6. Simon During, "Literature—Nationalism's Other?: The Case for Revision," in Homi K. Bhaba, ed., *Nation and Narration* (New York: Routledge, 1990), 138.

7. Michael Walzer, *What It Means to Be an American* (New York: Marsilio, 1992), 28.

8. Hans Kohn, *American Nationalism* (New York: Macmillan, 1957), 8.

9. For accounts of Bakhtin's theories, see Katerina Clark and Michael Holquist, *Mikhail Bakhtin* (Cambridge, MA: Harvard University Press, 1984); David K. Danow, *The Thought of Mikhail Bakhtin* (New York: St. Martin's Press, 1991); Gary Saul Morson and Caryl Emerson, *Mikhail Bakhtin* (Stanford: Stanford University Press, 1990); and Max Harris, *The Dialogical Theatre* (New York: St. Martin's Press, 1993).

10. Shepard, quoted in McBride, "Sam Shepard," sec. B, p. 3.

11. Joseph Roach, "Mardi Gras Indians and Others: The Cultural Politics of American Performance," 62. Delivered before the American Society for Theatre Research (November 1991). Subsequently published as "Mardi Gras Indians and Others: Genealogies of American Performance," *Theatre Journal* 44, no. 4 (1992): 461–83.

12. Jack Kroll, "High-Pressure Jazz," *Newsweek*, 8 November 1976, 109.

13. Arthur Schlesinger argues this point in *The Disuniting of America* (New York: W. W. Norton, 1992).

14. Molefi Kete Asante, "Multiculturalism Without Hierarchy," in Frances Beckwith and Michael Bauman, eds., *Are You Politically Correct?* (Buffalo: Prometheus Books, 1993), 191.

Chapter 1

Shepard and the Counterculture
Challenge

In his attempt to classify Sam Shepard, the critic Paul Berman distinguishes between those American writers who represent civilization and refinement—Henry James, for example—and those "naturalists" and "half-baked mystics" who write with abandon, of impulse and inspiration, like Walt Whitman.[1] Berman crowns Shepard the "primitivist" without peer. The playwright's 1971 program note to *Cowboy Mouth* seems to invite such an appraisal: "I like to yodel and dance and fuck a lot. Writing is neat because you do it on a very physical level. Just like rock and roll. A lot of people think playwrights are some special brand of intellectual fruitcake with special awareness to special problems that confront the world at large. I think that's a crock of shit."[2] Never to be mistaken for T. S. Eliot, Arthur Miller, or A. R. Gurney, Shepard in brazen fashion parades his antiintellectualism and his disdain of literary pretension. Berman's observation no doubt exposes something about the critical establishment and its cultural prejudices; nonetheless, Shepard's categorization as a wild-man rhapsodist is revealing, for he has been given (and has welcomed) the status of an outsider, a visionary on the edge of American civilization.

The curiosity of Shepard's career stems from the way in which this renegade of the sixties has gained mainstream acceptance and a position of elevation in the American theatre. He has been lionized as a writer of the American soil, the playwright who most ably captures the country's collective dreams, fears, and desires; he has recently been designated as a "national treasure."[3] Shepard's rise to prominence begs a very basic question: How (and why) has this Off-Off Broadway rebel become a hero of popular culture?

While the matter is not a simple one, the answer to this question in part lies in Shepard's vision of America and his response to select moments of

U.S. postwar history. To understand his emergence as a rogue playwright, one must in fact recognize the face of the nation in the 1950s and the country's rising sense of its own might and muscle.[4] A grasp of the decade is critical to an appreciation of Shepard's work, since the attitudes and apprehensions of this era would in large measure define his notion of modern America life, as a culture of encroachment, inimical to individuality and personal pursuit.

As a youth of the postwar era, Shepard grew up in a period most often regarded as a time of prosperity and national well-being. Following World War II and the defeat of the Axis powers, the country experienced an upsurge of patriotic fervor. These years mark the high point of America the nation-state, as the United States emerged as a global superpower, the defender of democratic principles (against Soviet aggression), in a new, bipolar world order. During this era the country prided itself on and defined itself by its civic culture, its political philosophy and capitalist industry, and sought to expand its ideology (and markets) throughout the world.

These years also brought a soaring postwar economy and unprecedented national productivity. Between 1940 and 1960 the U.S. Gross National Product (GNP) doubled.[5] The country's per-capita income rose 35 percent.[6] This economic boom transformed the United States into a profoundly consumer-oriented society, with climbing earning power, increased access to material goods (cars, dishwashers, toasters, and the like), and a dramatic rise in leisure time. Social commentaries of the day, including David Potter's *People of Plenty* (1954) and John Kenneth Galbraith's *The Affluent Society* (1958), documented America's abundance and the success of capitalism, which brought the country the world's highest standard of living.

The patina of health surrounding the fifties—given emblem in Dwight D. Eisenhower, the president as much noted for his golf game as his statesmanship—often diverts attention from the anxieties besetting the period. The early years of the Cold War brought the "Red scare," exploited by Senator Joseph McCarthy, who sought to purge government, education, and the media of Communist sympathizers. Such prominent figures as Lee J. Cobb, Leonard Bernstein, Aaron Copland, Burgess Meredith, and Orson Welles were all variously cited for "subversive" activities.[7] On the international level, attempts to halt the spread of Communism led to the Korean war, a "police action" that resulted in the deaths of over fifty thousand U.S. servicemen.

The decade nurtured a strident chauvinism, and the American way of life was held beyond reproach. These years saw the rise of television, and through such programs as "Ozzie and Harriet" and "Father Knows Best" the networks presented a sanitized America, free of dissent and diversity. Even though the 1954 *Brown v. Board of Education* Supreme Court decision had addressed segregation in the nation's schools, media representations of America remained exclusively white and middle-class. Poverty, sexism, and racism were rendered invisible. Throughout mainstream culture, that which controverted the American ideal received little notice, and the decade consequently earned repute as a time of consensus.

Writing during World War II, Margaret Mead claimed that Americans were all "third generation."[8] Mead delineated a melting-pot dynamic in which people of diverse origins became Americanized by "moving up" into middle-class culture (for instance, by buying cars and purchasing new homes). In the 1950s this assimilationist conception of American culture came to full flower. Boasting the world's most powerful military and most productive economy, the United States enjoyed a high degree of confidence and self-satisfaction. The structures of the government, military, and corporate economy served to define national identity and were by extension viewed as the repository of American values. The 1950s in essence fostered a centered national life. America had one culture, one identity, which invited participation through assimilation and acquiescence.

Shepard's early biography reflects many of the shifts and dynamics of American life following World War II.[9] Born in 1943 in Fort Sheridan, Illinois, the son of a military man, Sam Shepard Rogers VII (called Steve) spent his first years moving from base to base—from Illinois, to South Dakota, to Guam. Once discharged, Shepard's father moved the family to California, where he sought the heralded promise of the postwar economic boom. The fifties engendered a more transient population, and the Rogers family was only one of many who undertook a cross-country migration. California's robust economy, driven in large part by the military/aerospace complex, drew thousands of new arrivals, and by 1963 the state was the richest and most populous in the union.

After residing in Pasadena, Shepard's family settled in the small farming town of Duarte. Even though new developments and tract housing were working their way toward the working-class community, the Rogers did not enjoy "modern" suburban life; instead they resided in a converted greenhouse on an avocado ranch. Shepard's father struggled and often failed as a farmer and rancher.

California's bounty proved elusive for the Rogers family, which may in part account for Shepard's fond feelings for the family's ancestral home of Illinois and the heartland sensibility personified by his grandfather, "a redneck and staunch Harry Truman fan," who penned letters to the local newspaper under the name "Plain Dirt Farmer."[10] Much of Shepard's acclaim as an American playwright indeed springs from his basically agrarian outlook, which regarded the modernization of Southern California with suspicion and contempt. His plays draw heavily from his adolescence, his experience as a laborer, and work with livestock. He held membership in the local 4-H Club and for a time considered a career as a veterinarian.

Shepard once remarked that had he not moved to New York he would have "run a sheep ranch in Chino with a herd of 300 Southdowns."[11]

Although the writer perhaps aggrandizes his delinquency, he would admit to hating high school, drinking cheap liquor, drag racing, and fighting; he confessed to stealing cars and experimenting with drugs (he broke his high school's record for the 220-yard dash while on benzedrine). While rebellion is endemic to adolescence, the tensions Shepard experienced in his teenage years were deeply conflictive and often exacerbated by social insecurity. In *The Tooth of Crime*, the character Hoss recounts a high school occurrence in which he and two friends, an African American and a French Canadian, beat up their "rich kid" rivals in the parking lot of a Bob's Big Boy. Hoss attributes his animus to his outsider status, and in this character's anecdote Shepard betrays something of his own frustration and class consciousness. Often assumed as an American birthright, the abundance of middle-class life was for Shepard disputed by the realities of Duarte, and the youth consequently nurtured strong resentment toward social privilege and icons of the affluent.

This antipathy was further fueled by parental conflict, which activated in Shepard a transgressive attitude toward mainstream values and 1950s authoritarianism. His father was a man of considerable intellect and poetic inclination, who studied Spanish culture and literature. He also valued music—he played in a local Dixieland band—and amassed an extensive record collection. The father would, however, elicit much confusion and bitterness in his son, and even the most casual reader of Shepard's works recognizes the playwright's obsession with the role of the patriarch. Disturbed by his war memories as a pilot in Italy, Shepard's parent proved something of a martinet, a distant and demanding figure who found himself often at odds with his son. Never fully adjusting to the demands of the ranch and his household, the father estranged himself, sometimes through alcohol, other times through periods of actual abandonment. Like the paternal figures portrayed in *True West* and *A Lie of the Mind*, Shepard's own father finally renounced family life altogether and lived his last years in an alcoholic haze as a hermit in the desert of New Mexico.

When Shepard auditioned for the Bishop's Company Repertory Players, a touring theatre group sponsored by the Episcopal Church, his motives were not primarily aesthetic or religious. In the year and a half that he attended Mount San Antonio Junior College, he had acted in a handful of campus productions. Still, his stage experience was minimal, and, reflecting an egoism that surfaces throughout his playwriting career, he seized the Players' opportunity for self-serving reasons. The theatre, for Shepard, provided release from Duarte, release from parental dominance, and an avenue for his adolescent self-expression.

As Shepard began his life in the theatre, the country was experiencing a cultural sea change, and his first plays in a sense document America in the early sixties, a time of widespread exhilaration and exuberance. John F. Kennedy, the youngest American president, personified the idealism of an upcoming generation and called for a renewal of the national spirit. Against the complacency and consumerism of the 1950s, Kennedy espoused a vision of altruism and sacrifice, and indeed the early sixties exhibited a dramatic expansion of social awareness.

The 1960 sit-ins in Greensboro, North Carolina, where African American students protested segregated dining, served to awaken the civil rights movement. The status of American women also became a subject of national discussion, as evidenced in Betty Friedan's groundbreaking work, *The Feminine Mystique*. In 1962, Rachel Carson voiced an environmental warning in *The Silent Spring*, the same year the Students for a Democratic Society (SDS) held its first national conference. The assassination of Kennedy in November of 1963 would represent the first of many blows to the period's idealism; nevertheless, these years mark a radical shift in national consciousness and a movement away from the constricted worldview of the Eisenhower era.

This time also witnessed the emergence of a potent and highly vocal counterculture. Paul Goodman's classic work *Growing up Absurd* (1960) addressed the apprehensions spawned by an increasingly corporate American society, and great numbers of postwar youth proved unwilling to accede to the materialistic values of their parents. Though reared in an era of unprecedented prosperity, many sought an alternative social vision, one that advocated goals over material goods. By 1966, when *Time* magazine recognized the "under-25 generation" as the "Man of the Year,"[12] the baby boomers had emerged as a formidable demographic force and would question the very foundations of the American ethos.

After eight months of touring, Shepard quit the Bishop's Company Repertory Players in New York and decided to remain in the city. He searched out a high-school friend, Charles (Charlie) Mingus, Jr., an aspiring painter and son of the legendary jazz artist. The two shared a cold-water apartment on the Lower East Side and together sought adventure in the New York cityscape. The counterculture was in its ascendance at this time, and Shepard thrust himself into the youth revolution. Signifying a break with the past that was more personal than political, the nineteen year old dropped his patronym "Rogers"—his name had been in the family for seven generations—and entered one of the most tumultuous, exhilarating, and anxiety-ridden periods of his life.

According to Victor Turner, radical shifts in social or familial status are often attended by a "liminal" period, an interlude of antistructure, where the individual experiences an exploratory investigation of self, role play, and community.[13] The free play of Shepard's early experiences in New York, which, by his own account, was "like being a kid in a fun park,"[14] well corresponds to the liminal condition, as the youth followed a frank hedonism and pursuit of the new and exciting. His sex life during this period was active and indiscriminate. He also took part in the emerging drug culture. In his program note to *Red Cross*, the playwright explains how his use of "various plants and growths" had heightened his perceptions and had "led to myth discoveries in space and time."[15] Ralph Cook, director of Shepard's first productions, recalls that Shepard and Mingus frequently played cowboy-and-Indian games in the streets of Manhattan.[16] In this state of free-floating adventure, the young writer found excitement, euphoria, and more than a little bewilderment.

The counterculture's rejection of middle-class values evidenced itself not only in music, fashion, and alternative lifestyle choices but in avant-garde art practices. Abstract expressionism, made famous by the work of Jackson Pollock (whom Shepard deemed a model artist), had gained worldwide acclaim for the American avant-garde, and New York emerged after World War II as the world's leading international art center.[17] Young artists flocked to the city and took up the avant-garde attitude of defiance, renouncing the standards of traditional art and its formal apprentice/master training. Their desire to produce a new art (and a new culture) could be seen in a wide array of undertakings, from the films of Kenneth Anger, to the dance of Yvonne Rainer, to the pop art of Andy Warhol. Confident and ebullient, these artists advanced the work of such elder avant-garde figures as John Cage, Merce Cunningham, and Maya Deren, and produced a transgressive art characterized by spontaneity, playfulness, and stark originality. The boundaries between high art and popular culture were intentionally blurred, leading to artworks that combined various media and brought everyday objects and commonplace behavior into the realm of aesthetic experience. Andy Warhol's Campbell soup cans have become hallmarks of this period, as have the "happenings" championed by Allan Kaprow, Claes Oldenburg, and Jim Dine, where movement, sculpture, painting, and sound were blended into "nonmatrixed" collage events. Fueled by a self-assured radicalism, the avant-garde of the early sixties reconceptualized art practices, decentered aesthetic authority and sought, in the words of Oldenburg, "Rx art, 9.99 art, Now art, New art, How art, Fire Sale art, Last Chance art, Meat-o-Rama art."[18]

During the late fifties and early sixties, New York's Greenwich Village emerged as the epicenter of counterculture activity, and through his employment at a village jazz club Shepard made the acquaintance of numerous experimental musicians, painters, and performers. In essence, the youth found himself in the midst of a cultural explosion, and there he absorbed the aesthetic outlook and innovative strategies that would certify his early plays as bona fide products of a counterculture theatre.

Shepard debuted as a New York playwright on October 10, 1964, at the Theatre Genesis, where his one-act plays *The Rock Garden* and *Cowboys* were performed. The former depicts a young man of Shepard's age in a number of minimalistic, disjunctive actions involving a sister, mother, and father. Their noncommunicative exchanges indicate the household's sti-fling environment, which is exploded in the play's last scene. After the father expounds on the topic of rock gardens, the young man rejoins with an arrestingly graphic description of his sexual experiences. Described by Shepard as a play about "leaving my Mom and Dad,"[19] *The Rock Garden* functions as an aesthetic and personal declaration of independence; the shock effect of the closing passage moreover reveals the writer's willing-ness to shatter convention, to explore libidinal play, and to give expression to the irregular, the wayward, even the obscene.

Cowboys (later revised as *Cowboys #2*) further reflects Shepard's free-dom from family ties and his new life in New York. The action is set in a big-city environment where the central characters, Stu and Chet, play out cowboy scenarios (much like Shepard and Mingus in actuality). The piece follows no real story line but rather highlights the camaraderie of the buddies and their Wild West fiction making. Stu and Chet assume the cowboy roles of Mel and Clem and execute comic horseplay against the backdrop of an inhospitable urban expanse. As in its companion piece, *Cowboys* indicates the turbulent inner life of the young playwright and reveals the correspondence between Shepard's personal angst and his use of pointedly unconventional dramatic devices.

After a number of reviewers panned the one-acts, Shepard's disappoint-ment was checked by Michael Smith's favorable notice in the *Village Voice*.[20] Smith's confirmation underscores how important support can be for a beginning dramatist, especially since theatre, perhaps more than any other art form, requires community and collaboration. The critic's backing also draws attention to the institutional nature of American theatre and how a playwright's career is determined by material conditions that control and regulate performance possibilities (such as producers, theatre com-panies, funding sources, and the critical establishment).

Shepard has admitted his good fortune in arriving in New York just as the Off-Off Broadway movement was in the ascent, and without question his brand of playwriting (and its success) is linked to this specific historical moment in the American theatre. In one sense the Off-Off Broadway arenas vented Sam Shepard's wayward energetics and abetted his quest for self-actualization; the playwright correspondingly served the needs of the movement and became an avant-garde figurehead, riding the crest of a counterculture surge, fashioning arresting stage works that spoke to and drew from the experimental sensibility of Greenwich Village and the Lower East Side.

Prior to the 1960s, American dramatists were almost solely measured by Broadway success. The history of theatre in the United States is in large part an economic history, and the Broadway corridor in Manhattan has proved the mecca of American commercial theatre. This entrepreneurial theatre was perhaps never more popular than in the glittering era of the 1920s, when Broadway boasted more than eighty theatres and offered over 200 productions each season. After World II, however, inflation, union demands, real estate prices, and competition from film and television, began to weaken Broadway. By the mid-sixties only about forty Broadway theatres were in operation, producing fewer than seventy shows per season. At this time, a "straight play" cost between $75,000 and $100,000 to mount; a musical could require an investment of a quarter of a million dollars.[21] Given such financial stakes, the Broadway market grew increasingly dependent on commodity plays geared toward mass entertainment; in 1964, the hottest Broadway shows included *Hello, Dolly*, *Funny Girl*, and *Barefoot in the Park*.[22]

An alternative theatre had emerged in the 1950s known as "Off-Broadway."[23] This shift involved more than geography, as the smaller Off-Broadway houses aimed at placing aesthetics ahead of economics. The Circle in the Square Theatre proved the standard-bearer of the movement, and its 1952 production of Tennessee Williams's *Summer and Smoke* (which had failed on Broadway) was a resounding success. In fact, Off-Broadway gained much repute for its salvage efforts; it was the 1956 Circle in the Square revival of *The Iceman Cometh* that reestablished Eugene O'Neill as a major American dramatist. While Off-Broadway also showcased many works of Europe's foremost playwrights, including the absurdist writers Beckett, Ionesco, and Genet, its venues provided little encouragement to emerging American playwrights. By the mid-sixties Off-Broadway had become increasingly unionized, and productions ranged in cost from $10,000 to $40,000.[24] Many younger performers and writers felt that Off-Broadway had been seduced by the box office, that institutionalization had snuffed the movement's original spirit.

The counterculture energy of the sixties spurred a new order of performance practice that differed markedly from the work seen on Broadway and Off-Broadway stages. Considered under the umbrella term "Off-Off Broadway," this theatre did not emerge as a self-conscious, coherent movement but as the spontaneous blossoming of many diverse theatrical activities. The many Off-Off Broadway undertakings were nevertheless linked by a common radical outlook, one that dismissed commercial or establishment theatre and its middle-class fare. These theatre artists spurned the very idea of professionalism and thus viewed the Great White Way as an adversary to be traduced and toppled.

Joe Cino is largely credited with inaugurating the Off-Off Broadway movement, when in 1959 he began producing plays in the cramped confines of his coffee bar. In 1962 Ellen Stewart opened her Café La MaMa and likewise offered new playwrights a nurturing and low-budget platform for public performances. The initial emergence of the Off-Off Broadway movement depended upon a handful of strong-willed figures who sustained a performance space, and often a stable of favored writers, through shrewd resource management and passionate personal commitment. In the early 1960s a number of groups flourished under the guidance of several noted figures—including Al Carmines (Judson Poets' Theatre) and Ralph Cook (Theatre Genesis). The use of alternative spaces was common, as churches, cafés, galleries, lofts, and storefronts—almost any place that could accommodate an audience—were explored as performance sites. Unlike the commercial theatre and its high-figure production costs, Off-Off Broadway subsisted on shoe string budgets, and artists received little or no pay. A double bill of Joel Oppenheimer's *The Great American Dessert* and Apollinaire's *The Breasts of Tiresias* was, for example, staged at the Judson Poets' Theatre for $37.50.[25] Oftentimes, admission was the price of a cup of coffee. The environment was relaxed, low-key, and supportive; a patron of Caffe Cino once remarked, "You must go there and have their eggs. By the way, they do plays, also."[26]

Ralph Cook, who worked as a waiter with Shepard at the Village Gate, offered the playwright his first production opportunity with Theatre Genesis, housed in St. Mark's Church in the Bowery. Like Judson Memorial Church, St. Mark's functioned as a cultural arts center, and there the playwright saw artists as diverse as Sun Ra, William Burroughs, and the Fugs.[27] Shepard formed a special relationship with Theatre Genesis and would "hang out" at the church; he often ate and even slept there. Whereas the career of a Broadway writer has always been dependent on rave reviews and box office success, Theatre Genesis protected him from the boom-or-bust mentality of commercial theatre and allowed him the chance to experiment, to grow, and even at times to fail. Other writers—Lanford Wilson, Megan Terry, John Guare, Terrence McNally, Rochelle Owens, and Adrienne Kennedy, to name a few—likewise found Off-Off Broadway a sanctuary and stimulus to their innovative and sometimes idiosyncratic creations. Shepard would in fact later recall this environment as "a playwright's heaven."[28]

The early 1960s represent a complex yet fertile era in the life of the nation. The period's noted impulse toward liberation—clearly at work in the experimental theatre of the day—indicates a particular type of cultural moment (variously described as "liminal," "carnivalesque," or "heterotopian"). Enjoying a release from conventional hierarchies, this phenomenon involves the suspension of "official" culture and invites the exploration of recombined or alternative modes of outlook. Remembering his adventure in the New York counterculture, Shepard likened the time to a Mardi Gras and declared that in those years art was not a "cause" but an "active, playful thing, a way to inhabit a life."[29] This remark highlights the liminal nature of the Off-Off Broadway scene, its conditions of potentiality, and its upswell of creative activity (at its height the movement numbered well over a hundred theatre groups[30]). It moreover helps us see

Shepard's works as the by-products of such an environment, as anarchic, "unlicensed" performance pieces, spinning toward uncharted realms of consciousness and perception.

In January of 1964, Arthur Miller's *After the Fall* was presented as the inaugural production of the Lincoln Center Repertory Theatre and drew massive radio, television, and newspaper coverage. Much of this attention came from the fact that Miller had not written a play in nine years.[31] Viewed as a failure on most accounts, this event signaled the passing of the great American playwrights of the 1950s (the triumvirate of Miller, Tennessee Williams, and William Inge). This occasion also sent out a tacit invitation for new blood, for new forms and ideas to invigorate the American theatre.

While Shepard would in time be enlisted as the new hope of the American stage, he did not see himself as the inheritor of an American dramatic tradition. A self-styled iconoclast, in his early career he rejected the notion of playwriting-as-craft. To the contrary, he viewed writing as effusive overflow and practiced a type of "jazz sketching" advocated by Jack Kerouac, a sort of surrealistic automatic writing given over to impulses, drives, and associative chains of thought. Shepard saw revision as inherently dishonest. Many of his early plays were written hurriedly, often in a single sitting. This intuitive approach to dramatic writing reflects the egalitarian sensibility of the avant-garde and renounces the precepts of high art. It also reflects the multivalent impulse common to Off-Off Broadway theatre, a drive toward originality typified in a 1965 Café La MaMa benefit production aimed to help Ellen Stewart upgrade the theatre's electrical system, where experimental writers (Shepard among them) would present a spectrum of theatrical approaches—ranging from "non plays" to "outpourings"—in twenty-six different three-minute playlets.[32]

Following his debut at Theatre Genesis, Shepard wrote a flurry of one-acts and began to gain a modest reputation. He was invited to participate in the Playwrights Unit, a forum for emergent writers founded by Edward Albee; Shepard's *Up to Thursday* was consequently included in a Unit triple bill (November 23, 1964). Informed by the receipt of his draft notice (he avoided the draft by claiming to be a heroin addict), *Up to Thursday* thumbs its nose at images of authority; in one sequence two couples sitting in straight-back chairs engage in sexual banter and mindless, mechanical movements, while a youth in his jockey shorts lies under an American flag. Shepard shared billing with Paul Foster and Lanford Wilson, figures who would later also enjoy avant-garde acclaim. Highlighting the experimental nature of the undertaking, a reviewer from the *New York Times* called this presentation "an evening at the laboratory."[33]

Two minor pieces that have received scant critical attention—*Dog* and *Rocking Chair*—were presented at Café La MaMa on February 10, 1965. Admittedly influenced by Albee's *The Zoo Story*, *Dog* depicts a young man's immobilizing encounter with an intoxicated "negro." In *Rocking Chair* another young man listens from a rocker as a bedridden woman reads a short story. While these minor efforts in Shepard's oeuvre value novelty to a fault and risk charges of incoherence and banality, they may be regarded as the playwright's avant-garde calisthenics. The pieces were staged in a low-budget, low-tech production context, a situation that emphasized what the writer could accomplish with minimal means—a bed, a park bench, or a rocking chair, for example.

These early efforts mimic the European absurdists (perceived as rule breakers) and deal heavily in ellipses, non sequiturs, and repetitive physical movements. Beginning with *Chicago*, however, Shepard composed a series of one-acts that would herald the writer's singular outlook and visionary theatrical flair.

First performed on Good Friday in 1965 at Theatre Genesis, Shepard's *Chicago* was presented on a double bill with *The Customs Collector in Baggy Pants*, a piece by the Beat poet Lawrence Ferlinghetti. If any one feature of *Chicago* were to be singled out as illustrative of Shepard's emergent style, it would be the improvisatory nature of the work and its fascination with the phenomenon of *play* itself. *Chicago*'s anarchic progression is anchored by the prankish exchanges between Stu and his girlfriend Joy, who has been summoned for work in Chicago. Stu attempts to postpone her departure and speaks from his position in a bathtub, where he luxuriates, toying infantlike with his words: "Biscuits in the sun. And ya' run. And it's fun. Ya' have a gun."[34] Joy rejects Stu's entreaties but soon relents and joins her boyfriend in the tub, where the two enter a private playscape and enact nautical fantasies.

Chicago's effervescent, playful sequences are interrupted as visitors arrive and frustrate Stu's imaginative forays. He responds with a frenetic recitation that decries social relations and recounts the story of a seaside population's mass suicide. The intensity of the passage, however, is dissipated by the theatrical stunt that concludes the piece. As Joy waves goodbye, Joe, Myra, Sally and Jim, now with fishing poles, cross downstage and cast their lines into the house. Stu rises from the bathtub and leads the actors in a breathing exercise: "Outstanding air . . . What a gas. In your mouth and out your nose. Ladies and gentleman, it's fantastic!" (p. 59).

Shepard's next work, *4-H Club*, presented by Albee's Playwright's Unit at the Cherry Lane Theatre (September, 1965), likewise follows a nonlinear, associative movement. Reflective of Shepard's poverty during his life on the Lower East Side, the play's set is a trash-strewn apartment where its three inhabitants enact highly charged, male-oriented rituals. The play's opening exemplifies the bizarre and erratic nature of the work: after Joe drums at length on the apartment door with a broom handle, Bob and John smash coffee cups and gleefully kick the broken pieces back and forth to one another. Even though the play's title suggests the life of well-adjusted, hardworking farmboys, these characters know no bucolic peace but move from tedium to frenzied paranoia, improvising on topics that range from lawn care to wolverines. John concludes the play with a manic, incantatory description of carnivorous mandrills that is counterpointed by the screeching, screaming, and stomping of his cohorts.

Both *Chicago* and *4-H Club* reveal Shepard's dramaturgy as a sort of primal, often percussive, play therapy. Though he would avow no aesthetic school or philosophy and would often exaggerate his originality, the play-wright's direct and indirect debt to fellow workers in the avant-garde bears acknowledgement. Shepard's evolving style and its robust physicality indeed reflect a shift in performance aesthetics that prevailed in much Off-Off Broadway practice of the time.

Perhaps no group was more influential in the emergence of a counter-culture theatre than the Living Theatre, headed by Julian Beck and Judith Malina. Begun in 1947, the group initially produced poetic dramas (by Gertrude Stein, Garcia Lorca, Cocteau, and others) but by the late 1950s had moved toward a more militant experimentalism. Informed by the aesthetics of John Cage, the Living Theatre explored the random and the aleatory as performance variables. Beck and Malina's theatre was also one of the first to investigate the theories of French visionary Antonin Artaud, whose seminal text *The Theatre and Its Double* was published in English in 1958. Artaud's "theatre of cruelty" called for use of all theatrical elements (visual, aural, kinetic) in a ritualized performance aimed at delivering a series of shocks and jolts upon its audience. More visceral than intellectual, Artaud's prescriptions informed the Living Theatre's attempt at a vibratory theatre, one of spontaneity, urgency, and kinetic immediacy, and in such acclaimed productions as *The Connection* (1959) and *The Brig* (1963) we note the group's efforts to create nontraditional actor-audience relations and to dismantle the "fourth wall" illusionism that had for so long dominated the American theatre.

The counterculture theatre's impulse toward an unmediated—some would say "raw"—moment of plenitude and presence was continued in the work of Joseph Chaikin, a veteran of the Living Theatre, who wished to establish a training laboratory for alternative acting. Chaikin organized his own ensemble—The Open Theatre—and began his work in the fall of 1963 with seventeen actors and four writers. Renouncing the technically polished style of Broadway playing, he underscored that his actors were "not trying to groom" themselves for commercial theatre.[35] Rather, through game sequences and structured improvisations, Open Theatre participants sought an emblematic acting based in physical plasticity. Chaikin is perhaps best known for his use of the "transformation exercise," a direct challenge to Stanislavskian notions of fixed characters and "through lines," where actors would explore a series of emotions or conditions, attempting to discover appropriate "gestural or aural 'emblems' " for each successive emotional state.[36]

Shepard's involvement with the Open Theatre signals a direct link between the playwright and the aesthetic approaches current in the experimental theatre of the day. An original member of the ensemble, Joyce Aaron, who performed the role of Joy in *Chicago* and was for some time Shepard's lover, introduced the young writer to the Open Theatre in 1964. He took classes with Chaikin and would later work on such Open Theatre scripts as *Terminal, Re-Arrangements*, and *Nightwalk*. Shepard has frequently cited Chaikin as something of a mentor, and the Open Theatre's influence is clear in the spontaneous and fluid aspect of his writing. The two would enjoy a friendship and collaborative relationship that continues to today.

While devices and practices common to the counterculture theatre infiltrate much of Shepard's early writing, his following one-acts, *Icarus's Mother* and *Red Cross*, more pronouncedly display what may be considered an Artaudian fascination with the nonrational and hallucinatory. First performed in Caffe Cino in November of 1965, *Icarus's Mother* contains the playful stage antics that are common to Shepard's one-acts. It is however the piece's preoccupation with cabalistic knowledge that distinguishes the work. Inspired by an LSD trip,[37] the play exhibits a seething tension, exhilarating imagery, and a profound yearning for mystical, ecstatic experience.

The surface action of *Icarus's Mother* involves a group of friends (three males, two females) on a Fourth of July picnic, who in their postdining languor observe a plane overhead and muse upon the trail it leaves. Two of the men propound rational, quasi-scientific explanations; one of the women, however, takes a more poetic view and calls it "skywriting." Throughout the one-act, Frank and the female characters seem captivated by the idea of flight and its connotations of release; Bill and Howard, on the contrary, seek to delimit and bully. Upon returning from a walk on the beach, the women tell of a quirky moment of excitation occasioned by the reappearance of the plane. Jill explains: "we both went nuts or something and we took off our pants and ran right into the water yelling and screaming and waving."[38] In response, the plane takes ascent, scripts this message across the sky: "E equals MC squared" (p. 76), then nosedives into the ocean. Against the empirical outlook of the men, the pilot, as explorer of the outer regions, emerges as a holder of mysteries, conveyed in his cryptic Einsteinian hieroglyph. The play suggests that normative perception proves limiting and intimates that art should not simply "represent" reality but operate as a mode of passage to states beyond rational points of reference.

Red Cross, first staged at the Judson Poets' Theatre on January 20, 1966, also deals with heightened perception and the movement of consciousness that traverses (and produces) alternate and simultaneously existing worlds. Set in the all-white room of an anonymous resort or hotel, *Red Cross* follows an arbitrary series of involvements as Jim, a young man plagued with crab lice, converses first with his friend, Carol, and then with the maid who comes to change his bed linen. While the Red Cross emblem generally evokes associations of succor, safety, and solace, the image here suggests the wound of an ever-restive consciousness. At the play's outset, Carol pretends to ski while standing atop a bed. She concludes her recitation by claiming that her head has exploded, leaving only "a little red splotch of blood" in the snow.[39] This imagery is again employed in the play's closing. Carol returns with groceries, and after several moments of manic verbalization, she acknowledges Jim and discovers that a stream of blood is running down his forehead. Carol asks, "What happened!" Jim answers flatly: "When?" (p. 138).

In these early one-acts we can identify what would become distinctive features of Shepard's dramatic style and vision. With an approach to writing that values nonlinear action, associative image patterns, fluid characterization, and primitivistic appeals to the nonrational, these works confound conventional dramaturgy and give expression to an expansive, outward trajectory. One finds that these plays do not function just as verbal texts but as aural, kinetic, and visual experiences. Avant-garde work of this era witnessed the fruitful cross-fertilization of visual art, sculpture, dance, jazz, and film, and it was in fact the medium's eclectic nature that initially sparked Shepard's interest in theatre. As the writer once noted, one "can put anything in that space."[40] His multifaceted theatre has been interestingly compared to the "combines" of Robert Rauschenberg, whose highly original collage constructs are exemplified by his work *Monogram*, which utilized materials as diverse as a car tire, painted canvass, and a stuffed Angora goat.[41] This observation underscores the playful aspect of Shepard's work and reminds us that these early one-acts intended less to convey meaning than to create experience—to jolt, soothe, mesmerize, disturb, and ultimately transport.

The sixties counterculture often sought experiences that skewed perception and dislodged conventional frames of reference. Many people explored alternatives to Western thought, from Zen, to tarot, to the *I Ching*. The fevered theatrics found in avant-garde performance evidence the period's preoccupation with the paranormal and yearning for some sort of precultural purity. In writing on the evolutionary consciousness of the counterculture, Charles Reich championed this way of thinking as an escape from the overdetermined, technological rationality of the status quo. Reich described the new youth as one who "can say 'the full moon blew my mind' and is proud of it."[42] Shepard's aesthetics also value wonder, mystical states, and the expansion of consciousness, and we can conclude that his one-acts are less philosophical discussions or finely honed literary works than sensation-generating machines programmed for mind-blowing effects.

In just over a year, Shepard had eight plays produced and had become one of the leading figures of Off-Off Broadway theatre. The mainstream press, however, found his bizarre imagery, unstable characters, and provisional endings affrontive, almost beyond categorization. Stanley Kauffmann, writing on *Chicago*, called the piece an "anti-play" and asserted that its rather arbitrary conclusion "hurt" the work.[43] Edith Oliver's review in the *New Yorker* termed *Red Cross* "horrid" and "hateful" and labeled the play "absolutely unrecommendable."[44]

Yet it was the playwright's irreverence before conventional critical standards that endeared him to the youth culture: Shepard spoke the language of youth, his plays drew from the images and experience of youth. In his *Red Cross* program note the solidarity enjoyed between the playwright and his audience is clear: "Now settle back with a good cigarette, a fresh Orange Crush and don't be afraid of THE RED CROSS if it tends to drip on your lap. Bugaloo folks."[45]

Shepard's work thus became something of a rallying point for the counterculture, and the production of each new piece became a cause célèbre. The *Village Voice* in particular hyped his productions. Openly partisan in their backing, reviewers such as Michael Smith and Ross Wetzsteon—who would claim Shepard as "*our* playwright"[46]—cast the writer as the emblematic spearhead of an emerging alternative consciousness. *Chicago*, *Icarus's Mother*, and *Red Cross* all were honored with Obies, awards given annually by the *Village Voice* for Off- (and Off-Off) Broadway achievement. To date, no one in American theatre has received more Obies than Sam Shepard.

Along with new works by writers such as Maria Irene Fornés and Terrence McNally, Shepard's *Fourteen Hundred Thousand* was selected by the University of Minnesota's Office of Aid to Drama Research and subsequently staged in 1966 at Minneapolis's Firehouse Theatre. This effort marked the playwright's first production outside of New York's experimental theatre circles. Though thought a minor—even regressive—effort, the play also merits attention for its central thematic concern, that of social cohesion. This point bears underscoring, for if any one matter informs the entirety of Shepard's dramatic output it his obsession with community and its relation to the individual. This recurrent feature of Shepard's writing to a significant degree explains his subsequent popularity beyond the world of the avant-garde. Despite his youth-culture vogue and the Pop Art experimentalism that colors his work, the playwright might have earned no more than a footnote in theatre history texts had his plays not addressed in some compelling way the broader bonds (and breakdowns) of postwar American life.

Fourteen Hundred Thousand takes place in an urban apartment where

Ed and Tom are constructing a set of bookshelves. After Tom and his wife quarrel and splatter each other with paint, Mom and Pop arrive, declaring that fourteen hundred thousand books wait outside, ready to be walked up the apartment's eight flights of stairs. Farcical behaviors and absurdist exchanges carry the first half of the play. The work however concludes with an enigmatic discussion on civic planning and social engineering: Mom and Pop hypothesize about "Elevated cities suspended under vacuum air" and "vertical cities stretching north through Canada and south through Mexico."[47] At its end the play essentially asks: Is "community" possible?

Though Shepard does not deal in polemics or overt political commentary, his conception of community is very much colored by his notion of "nation." The playwright interestingly deploys nationalistic imagery throughout his one-acts: the youth in *Up to Thursday* sleeps under the American flag; *Chicago* opens with the Gettysburg Address; and *Icarus's Mother* takes place on the Fourth of July. In each instance, the image is used in a satiric fashion to debunk the idea of America, the righteous nation.

In his book *The Lonely Crowd*, David Reisman argued that the country's consumer economy and corporate structures had created the "other-directed" American, whose identity depended on the "mediation" of communal networks and mass communications.[48] In short, the economic prosperity and manufacturing boom of the 1950s (which fed American civic pride and chauvinism) had a downside, evidenced in its overbearing culture of conformity. As a teenager in the decade of consensus, Shepard cultivated an animus toward facile patriotism and communal allegiance. This antipathy toward systematization surfaces throughout his one-acts, which may indeed be regarded as rhetorical gestures of repudiation, aggressive utterances that target the regimentation of American society. The business-suited figures of *Cowboys #2* and the construction workers of *Up to Thursday* appear as villainous extensions of bureaucratic power. In *Chicago*, Shepard reveals his unease with group contexts (and their suffocation) when Stu tells of "some fat guy" who "stunk up" an entire train with his flatulence (p. 53). The trademark "manic monologues" of these plays may in this light be regarded as a social strategy, whereby hypnotic transport provides escape and social withdrawal. This phenomenon is evident at the conclusion of *4-H Club*, when John imaginatively exits his littered apartment and undergoes a sort of psychic levitation. Describing his passage to an exotic fantasyland, he intones: "You just float and stare at the sky."[49]

The pressures exerted by America's postwar mentality also inform Shepard's fascination with doomsday imagery. His habitual use of apocalyptic endings may in part stem from the nuclear anxieties of the fifties—the appearance of H-bombs, fallout shelters, and mutant-creature horror films.

This tendency seems more likely to issue from a personal source, from the dramatist's very real suspicion of social obligation, and instances of communal eradication are found not only in *Chicago* and *Fourteen Hundred Thousand* but in *Icarus's Mother*, where mothers, fathers, and kids in pajamas, standing en masse on the beach, are incinerated when the pilot's plane crashes in flames.

The element of explosion or disintegration, situated most prominently in *Icarus's Mother* though evident in other one-acts, suggests a way of understanding the coincidence of the political and the aesthetic in Shepard's work. It may be argued that Off-Off Broadway venues and the theatre they fostered gave expression to what Mikhail Bakhtin termed *heteroglossia*, the centrifugal impulse (that is, the outward explosion) of noncanonical art, which manifests itself through irreverence, eruptive expression, unconventional stylistic practices, and multiple positioning. Informing this dynamic is a fundamental politics of opposition, one that affronts and resists the conservative forces (and institutions) that regulate art and social conversation. If we thus view the work of the counterculture theatre as an expression of the heteroglossic, we see that its outbursts of anarchy challenged mainstream culture, disputing its narratives, values, and modes of production. In this light, Shepard's visceral theatrics and end-of-the-world scenarios appear to negate any assertion of cohesion or of centrism, and in his art we see the play of forces straining against the nation-state consensus and its media representations of the white middle class.

As the musicals *Walking Happy* and *You're a Good Man, Charlie Brown* were enjoying Broadway success, *La Turista*, Shepard's most anarchic and socially pointed work to that date, opened at the American Place Theatre (on March 4, 1967). The production signals a transitional move in Shepard's career, for the show represented a broadening of the playwright's audience base and inaugurated his association with a theatre outside the Village proper.[50] Cofounded by Wynn Handman and Reverend Sidney Lanier in 1964, the American Place Theatre operated out of St. Clement's Church and soon earned an esteemed position in New York theatre. The organization prized literary excellence and sought to advance the work of living American writers in an environment Handman described as "free from pressures of the 'market.' "[51] Unlike other groups with which Shepard had worked, the American Place Theatre was not chiefly counterculture in orientation. Over the years it would come to produce works by a wide range of writers, including Robert Penn Warren, Paul Goodman, Philip Roth, Ann Sexton, and Robert Lowell.

The American Place Theatre gave writers the option of barring critics from their productions—an option Shepard exercised. Despite Shepard's disregard of New York drama critics, *La Turista* marks a shift in Shepard's posture. The play is Shepard's first full-length, a work of expanded scope and self-conscious experimentation. The effort speaks to Shepard's ambition, and we see him moving beyond the one-act form to the more "respectable" two-act structure. *La Turista* is furthermore the first text that Shepard acknowledges revising. Shepard's willingness to consider his work outside the moment of creation testifies to his increasing awareness of dramatic form, and by extension his audience and the critical community.

Inspired by a trip to Mexico he took with Joyce Aaron, *La Turista* may be viewed as the culminating effort of Shepard's early playwriting career; the piece combines almost all of the writer's characteristic strategies and concerns. The first act of *La Turista* presents a hallucinogenic sequence of events in a Mexican hotel. Suffering from sunburn and Montezuma's revenge, an American couple—Kent and Salem (the couple was played by Joyce Aaron and Sam Waterston)—are approached by a Mexican boy who offers to shine Kent's shoes and then initiates a surrealistic father-son competition. After renouncing Salem's offer of cash, the boy spits in Kent's face (with impunity) and proceeds to undress and take Kent's place in bed, referring to Salem as "mother." Farcical body humor is also prominent, as Kent and Salem without reserve cross back and forth to the toilet, complaining of loose stools. Shepard's primitivist inclinations appear in a wildly theatrical spectacle in which a witch doctor attempts a bizarre cure that involves the slaughter of two chickens (whose blood is ritualistically poured upon Kent's back). The first act concludes with Shepard's now common "escape" imagery. The Mexican boy gives himself over to reverie and, reminiscent of John's final speech in *4-H Club*, tells of riding off to the Gulf of Mexico and his intent to "float to the other side."[52]

Set in a drab, plasticized American hotel room, *La Turista*'s second act lacks the vitality and visual brilliance of the first and conveys the tawdry, anesthetizing aspect of American mass culture. The action of Act Two curiously precedes the events in Act One. As the act begins, Kent is suffering from sleeping sickness, and a Doctor and his son (Sonny) have come at Salem's behest. Dressed like a Civil War–era physician, Doc attempts to keep Kent awake through talk, movement, and amphetamines. Kent's language borders on delirium. He and Doc enter into a lyrical duologue where the two play out a B-movie scenario, that of the mad scientist-creator and his human-beast progeny. The final sequence of the play enacts the monster's capture. However, as Doc, Sonny, and Salem move to secure Kent, Kent breaks free of his pursuers and crashes headlong through the motel wall, leaving a silhouette as evidence of his escape.

Touted as "the most experimental, far-out play in New York,"[53] *La Turista* without question exhibits a style that is expansive, explosive, and narcotic in its effect. Despite Shepard's protest that the play was simply meant "to be a theatrical event,"[54] *La Turista* appears more overt and incisive in its social commentary than the writer's previous works. Numerous details specifically invoke American culture. At the play's outset,

Kent and Salem are reading *Time* and *Life* magazines; American movies are parodied in Act One. Most telling are the character names, Kent and Salem, which refer to cigarette brands. In his depiction of the couple Shepard insinuates an element of incest as he more broadly critiques American big business and Madison Avenue advertising. While the work evinces a playfulness of spirit and avoids any heavy-handed moralizing, *La Turista* gestures at something seriously wrong in America's consumer society and expresses cynicism toward a culture programmed for the homogenization of thought, desires, and behavior.

If one looks at Shepard's early career from the vantage point of his renown in the 1980s, his image as an outsider—a seer into the American soul—owes much to his involvement in the iconoclastic American theatre of the sixties. During this period the playwright gained reputation as a counterculture holy man, a prophet decrying the tyrannies of postwar American life. Though he and his fellow Off-Off Broadway writers raised America up for critique and censure, their vitriol was in large part directed toward the structures and images of national life born of the 1950s. This point is key to Shepard's later success as an American playwright, as his denigration of corporate America and its various suppressions invites the evocation (and invocation) of an alternative vision of the nation, one born of myth and nostalgia.

Though Shepard was intimately involved in the sixties counterculture, he retained an individuality that would later prevent his easy categorization or dismissal as a hippie playwright. He denounced mainstream American life but also spurned the love-child fads, ascribing to no dissident ideology. His one-acts do not espouse Marxism or Maoism; rather, Shepard's plays evoke a fear of being pinioned, a paranoia of groupings, and a profound opposition to commitment. Edward Morgan has written that the sixties "reverberated with the quest for community,"[55] and indeed much of the renowned work of the avant-garde can be attributed to collective undertakings, evidenced most notably in the practices of the Living Theatre, the Open Theatre, and the Performance Group. In this regard Shepard was curiously out of sync with his generation: in his personal life and in his plays he did not advance any communal objective or identity. His one-acts do not envision any reconstituted social harmony or sense of *communitas*. Though associated with the Open Theatre and Theatre Genesis, the writer worked with various groups in an opportunistic fashion. He proved a guarded individual, often aloof, exhibiting a cowboy's maverick independence.

To explain Shepard's turn to the theatre and his participation in the counterculture, Kent's hurtle through the motel wall is worth recalling, for, like Kent, Shepard in his early career was governed by a compulsion to shatter, to break impositions (of parental authority, middle-class morality, and corporate conformity), to pursue his quest for freedom at any cost. The playwright's works of this period may thus be viewed as intense self-assertions, informed by an alternating sense of apprehension and bravado. Given his self-conscious cowboy posturing, the one-acts aim at maximizing stage energy, almost as a form of masculine display—a Lower East Side sort of barrel-racing or trick-roping. Sally Banes writes that in Greenwich Village "the terrain of artmaking was there, wide open for the taking"[56]; in this light, the Off-Off Broadway scene did not so much provide Shepard a community (or philosophy) but an open and pliant context for the staging of his intimate fears, aggressions, and emerging selfhood. Shepard was no groupie or revolutionary, but a counterculture cowboy seeking fame, fortune, and freedom on the frontier of the American theatre.

NOTES

1. Paul Berman, review of *A Lie of the Mind, Nation*, 22 February 1986, 215.

2. Program note found in Berman, review, 215.

3. Gordon Rogoff, "America Screened," *Village Voice*, 17 December 1985, 117.

4. For a historical survey of the 1950s, see J. Ronald Oakley, *God's Country: America in the Fifties* (New York: Dembner Books, 1986).

5. Cited in William E. Leuchtenburg, *A Troubled Feast: American Society Since 1945* (Boston: Little, Brown, 1979), 38.

6. Ibid., 6.

7. Cited in Oakley, *God's Country*, 71.

8. Margaret Mead, *And Keep Your Powder Dry* (New York: William Morrow, 1942), 27.

9. For biographical material on Shepard, see Vivian M. Patraka and Mark Siegel, *Sam Shepard* (Boise, ID: Boise State University Press, 1985); Martin Tucker, *Sam Shepard* (New York: Continuum, 1992); Ellen Oumano, *Sam Shepard: The Life and Work of an American Dreamer* (New York: St. Martin's Press, 1986); Don Shewey, *Sam Shepard* (New York: Dell, 1985); Robert Coe, "Saga of Sam Shepard," *New York Times Magazine*, 23 November 1980, 56–59, 118, 120, 122, 124; Robert Goldberg, "Sam Shepard, American Original," *Playboy*, March 1984, 90, 112, 192–93; and Michael ver Meulen, "Sam Shepard: Yes, Yes, Yes," *Esquire*, February 1980, 79–81, 85–86.

10. Shewey, *Sam Shepard*, 28.

11. Shepard, quoted in ver Meulen, "Sam Shepard," 80.

12. Cited in Edward P. Morgan, introductory chronology in *The 60s Experience: Hard Lessons About Modern America* (Philadelphia: Temple University Press, 1991), xix.

13. See Victor Turner, *The Ritual Process* (Ithaca: Cornell University Press, 1969) 95–96.

14. Shepard, quoted in Kenneth Chubb et al., "Metaphors, Mad Dogs, and Old Time Cowboys," in Bonnie Marranca, ed., *American Dreams: The Imagination of Sam Shepard* (New York: Performing Arts Journal Publications, 1981), 200.

15. Quoted in Robert J. Schroeder, ed., *The New Underground Theatre* (New York: Bantam Books, 1968), 80.

16. Cited in ver Meulen, "Sam Shepard," 80.

17. Sally Banes, *Greenwich Village 1963* (Durham, NC: Duke University Press, 1993), 4. This text provides an excellent analysis of the avant-garde in the early 1960s and serves as a prime reference source for my discussion of Shepard's early career in New York's counterculture theatre.

18. Claes Oldenburg, quoted in John Lahr and Jonathan Price, eds., *The Great American Life Show: 9 Plays from the Avant-Garde Theater* (New York: Bantam Books, 1974), 297–98.

19. Shepard, quoted in Coe, "Saga of Sam Shepard," 111.

20. See Michael Smith, "Theatre: *Cowboys* and *The Rock Garden*," *Village Voice*, 22 October 1964, 13.

21. Statistical figures on Broadway found in R. H. Gardner, *The Splintered Stage: The Decline of the American Theatre* (New York: Macmillan, 1965), 138–39.

22. Cited in Edward Parone, *New Theatre in America* (New York: Dell, 1965), 4.

23. For a history of Off-Broadway, see Stuart L. Little, *Off-Broadway* (New York: Coward, McCann & Geoghegan, 1972).

24. Cited in Michael Smith and Nick Orzel, eds., *Eight Plays from Off-Off Broadway* (New York: Bobbs-Merrill, 1966), 5.

25. Cited in Banes, *Greenwich Village 1963*, 45.

26. Patron of Caffe Cino, quoted in Smith and Orzel, *Eight Plays*, 54.

27. Cited in Jennifer Allen, "The Man on the High Horse," *Esquire*, November 1988, 146.

28. Shepard, quoted in *The Unseen Hand and Other Plays* (New York: Bantam Books, 1986), x.

29. Shepard, quoted in Michiko Kakutani, "Myths, Dreams, Realities—Sam Shepard's America," *New York Times*, 29 January 1984, sec. 2, 26.

30. Cited in Catherine Hughes, *American Playwrights 1945–75* (London: Pitman, 1976), 11.

31. Cited in Lewis Allan, *American Plays and Playwrights of the Contemporary Theatre* (New York: Crown Publishers, 1965), 35.

32. This event is documented in Michael Smith, "Theatre Journal," *Village Voice*, 2 December 1965, 19, 24.

33. Richard Shepard, "Theatre 1965 Offers Test for Writers," *New York Times*, 11 February 1965, sec. 1, p. 45.

34. Sam Shepard, *Chicago*, in *The Unseen Hand and Other Plays*, 47. Further citations indicated within the text.

35. Joseph Chaikin, quoted in Smith and Orzel, *Eight Plays*, 202.

36. Erlene Laney Hendrix, "Open Theatre," in Weldon B. Durham, ed., *American Theatre Companies 1931–1986* (Westport, CT: Greenwood Press, 1989), 418.

37. Cited in Oumano, *Sam Shepard*, 46.

38. Sam Shepard, *Icarus's Mother*, in *The Unseen Hand and Other Plays*, 76. Further citations indicated within the text.

39. Sam Shepard, *Red Cross*, in *The Unseen Hand and Other Plays*, 125. Further citations indicated within the text.

40. Shepard, quoted in Irene Oppenheim and Victor Fascio, "The Most Promising Playwright in America Today Is Sam Shepard," *Village Voice*, 27 October 1975, 9.

41. See Gay Gibson Cima, "Shifting Perspectives: Combining Shepard and Rauschenberg," *Theatre Journal* 38 (1986): 67.

42. Charles A. Reich, *The Greening of America* (New York: Bantam Books, 1970), 285.

43. Stanley Kauffmann, "Last Three Plays of '6 from La MaMa' Offered at the Martinique," *New York Times*, 13 April 1966, 36.

44. Edith Oliver, "The Theatre: Off Broadway," *New Yorker*, 11 May 1968, 91.

45. Shepard, quoted in Schroeder, *The New Underground Theatre*, 80.

46. Ross Wetzsteon, quoted in Allen, "The Man on the High Horse," 146.

47. Sam Shepard, *Fourteen Hundred Thousand*, in *The Unseen Hand and Other Plays*, 119.

48. David Reisman, *The Lonely Crowd* (New Haven, CT: Yale University Press, 1950), 21–22.

49. Sam Shepard, *4-H Club*, in *The Unseen Hand and Other Plays*, 100.

50. Cited in Shewey, *Sam Shepard*, 56.

51. Handman, quoted in Richard Schotter, ed., *The American Place Theatre: Plays* (New York: Dell, 1973), vii.

52. Sam Shepard, *La Turista*, in *Seven Plays* (New York: Bantam Books, 1981), 276.

53. Cited in David Madden, "The Theatre of Assault: Four Off-Off Broadway Plays," *Massachusetts Review* 8, no. 4 (1967): 713.

54. Shepard, quoted in Lewis Funke, "Singing the Rialto Blues," *New York Times*, 5 March 1967, sec. 2, p. 5.

55. Morgan, *The 60s Experience*, 176.

56. Banes, *Greenwich Village 1963*, 99.

Chapter 2

Shepard and the Culture Industry

As opposed to the fifties, which had given the country supermarkets, the Distant Early Warning (DEW) line, Disneyland, and the John Birch Society, the sixties brought the flowering of liberalism and social consciousness. Author of *Eros and Civilization* and a favored intellectual of the counterculture, Herbert Marcuse denounced the repressions of affluence and lauded the young for being "on the forefront of those who live and fight for Eros."[1] Much in the sixties would confirm this contention, as youthful idealism expressed itself in the Peace Corps, in student movements, in the Freedom Riders who furthered the cause of civil rights throughout the segregated South. The impulse toward a transformed society ignited as well an era of psychedelia. This was the period of free love, the electric Kool-aid acid test, and *Sergeant Pepper's Lonely Hearts Club Band*.

The Off-Off Broadway theatre also exhibited a youthful, revolutionary zeal. Its venues moreover gave platform to voices that had been submerged and repressed by mainstream culture. Such writers as Adrienne Kennedy and LeRoi Jones promoted depictions of the African American experience. Issues of gay identity were dramatized by a number of authors, including Doric Wilson and Robert Patrick. A nascent feminism was seen in the plays of Megan Terry and Maria Irene Fornés. The counterculture provided an open arena for the overlapping and interrelation of diverse populations, and its theatre fostered a nonhierarchical view of community. The movement's egalitarian mentality shows clearly in the words of Theatre Genesis playwright Murray Mednick, who proclaimed: "America should be run by the Chief of the Sioux. . . . Turn everybody loose. Save your napalm for Plutonium Steam Heat."[2]

The ascent of Shepard's career coincides with and is a by-product of Off-Off Broadway's remarkable rise to prominence. The success of this theatre, however, brought significant changes. If one assumes a Bakhtinian view, a dialectic always operates in public conversation, fueling a "never ending contest between heteroglossia and canonization."[3] The impulse toward novelty, subversion, and the expression of difference is crucial to the social process; yet, heteroglossic utterances often activate forces of conservation, evidenced in institutional controls that seek to regiment, legitimize, recast, or censor. By the late 1960s the experimental theatre would exhibit signs of a growing self-consciousness (some would say decadence). Its combustible sensibility began to calcify. In short, forces of canonization began to act upon the movement, and Off-Off Broadway found itself increasingly enmeshed in the entertainment business and the institutions of public culture.

This symbiotic interplay is well documented in the history of the Living Theatre.[4] Defining itself as an anarchist community, the group for years encountered run-ins with authorities, ranging from fire code violations to charges of tax evasion. In 1964 its founders Beck and Malina took flight and relocated the company in Europe. Nonetheless, when the Living Theatre returned to the United States in 1968 and toured with *Paradise Now*—one of the definitive pieces of sixties revolutionary theatre—the group enjoyed a new status and visibility. Incorporating drug use, nudity, and anticapitalist rhetoric, *Paradise Now* was performed at many prominent American universities, for the charge of $3,000 per show.[5] Ruby Cohn's observation, that the Living Theatre was "arrested, beaten . . . and sometimes subsidized,"[6] underscores the ironic and sometimes complicitous relation between the mainstream and the avant-garde, which often profited from the "system" its works decried. The Living Theatre remained activist in its orientation well into the 1980s; yet, even as the company was exploring new forms of guerrilla theatre and Third World performance, both its founders would act in Hollywood feature films. Beck even guest-starred on the flashy TV cop series *Miami Vice*.

Avant-garde artists have always grappled with the matter of sustaining, advancing, and funding what is essentially an anarchic, nonsystematic enterprise, and during the late sixties Shepard experienced both exhilaration and unease as his work drew increased attention. Although the dramatist had prohibited reviews of *La Turista*, Elizabeth Hardwick saw the production and wrote glowingly of the playwright in the *New York Review of Books*. Shepard was also at this time the recepient of numerous honors and awards. In 1966 he received a grant from the University of Minnesota; in the same year he was awarded, along with Megan Terry and John Guare, a fellowship from Yale University to explore relations between experimental writing and the TV/film industry. In 1967 the writer was honored with a prestigious Rockefeller Grant. Shepard, quite simply, faced the dubious prospect common to successful avant-garde artists—that of cultural respectability.

During his early years in New York, Shepard lived in impoverished conditions and held low-paying jobs in such establishments as the Hickory House restaurant, the Village Gate jazz club, and Marie's Crisis Café. With the monies he received from his various prizes he was able to write full time. Though he welcomed this change in situation, the artist faced a turning point in his career. According to Robert Coe, this moment signaled "the beginning of the end" of "Shepard's enchantment with Off-Off Broadway."[7] Thereafter the playwright would labor under rising expectations, increased apprehension, and an acute ambivalence toward fame. No longer just a vehicle for self-expression or ludic diversion, the theatre for Shepard became a job.

The funding Shepard received at this time points to the playwright's growing contact with legitimate cultural agencies. It also reflects the changes in arts patronage that were occurring more widely in American society. In response to the Soviet Union's Sputnik satellite, the United States took strong steps to ensure the country's technological competitiveness—and hence the success of the NASA space program. Likewise, the United States sought to cultivate a national art befitting its position as a world superpower. The 1960s consequently witnessed a boom in arts funding. Numerous private foundations (Mellon, Rockefeller, and Ford, for instance) contributed substantial sums to arts organizations. Between 1957 and 1975 the Ford Foundation donated hundreds of millions of dollars to performance groups, proving a primary patron of nonprofit and Off-Off Broadway theatre.[8] Importantly, in these years Congress pushed for federal subsidization, an effort that resulted in the National Endowment for the Arts. From an inaugural budget of $3 million in 1965, NEA funding had almost tripled by 1969.[9]

During the 1960s the increase in arts funding was only one indication of the federal government's changing role and the allocation of public resources. In his monumental work *The Other America*, Michael Harrington alerted mainstream America to the country's hidden pockets of poverty and decried that so many should suffer deprivation in a nation of abundant means.[10] Harrington's message found audience, and as social activism grew more commonplace in the early sixties the government began to respond in fiscal terms. Not only did the Kennedy administration pursue civil rights legislation; it pushed for increased funding in education, health care for the elderly, and the establishment of an Urban Affairs Department.[11]

This moment in U.S. history marks an influential turn in American political practice. Inspired by the interventionist, macromanagement model advanced by British economist John Maynard Keynes, which linked full employment and social well-being to government spending and market manipulation,[12] federal policymakers championed "growth" as a social panacea. This outlook informed Kennedy's New Economics and also shaped the policies of Lyndon Johnson, who continued the mandate for social renewal after Kennedy's assassination. Johnson launched a war on poverty and implemented sweeping social programs, ranging from Head-start to Medicare. Government funding was directed in a ubiquitous fash-ion, not only toward health and social problems but to highways, housing, agriculture, and, as mentioned, the arts. These efforts toward creating the Great Society signify a paradigmatic shift in American culture: the nation-state of the 1950s gave over to the welfare state of the 1960s.

Beginning with *Melodrama Play*, first produced at Café La MaMa on May 18, 1967, Shepard's works began to reflect these changes in American society. Viewed as the writer's response to his newfound celebrity, the play broadsides the cultural establishment and extends a sardonic com-mentary on how American society renders its artists products for mass consumption, a topic to which Shepard would return a number of times, in *The Tooth of Crime*, *Suicide in B-Flat*, and *True West*.

Melodrama Play tells the story of Duke Durgens, a rock and roll singer who has achieved instant stardom with his hit tune, "Prisoners, Get Up Out of Your Homemade Beds." Shepard parodies his own media hype when Duke explains: "By the people of my generation. I was admired and cherished because the song was true and good and reflected accurately the emotions, thoughts and feelings of our time and place."[13] A sociologist from Corning University, Dr. Daniel Damon, seeks an interview with the artist for research purposes; the professor hopes to ascertain how artists are personally affected by public acclaim. Duke dismisses the professor's suit and escapes the imposition of the academy; yet he cannot so easily extricate himself from the reaches of the entertainment industry.

An imminent concert in Phoenix, and the demand for a follow-up hit impels Floyd—Duke's mobster manager—to sequester his star. Drake—Duke's brother—and Cisco are enlisted for creative collaboration. When Duke discloses that his hit song was pirated, stolen from his own brother, Floyd declares that record sales, not authorship, are his concern. Duke is subjected to bullying, ridicule, and Floyd's truncheon-wielding henchman. These indignities reveal the artist's existence as one governed by industry mechanisms and the whimsy of the market. Throughout the piece, two large posters, one of Bob Dylan and one of Robert Goulet, hover above the stage. The eyes of both faces have been erased, suggesting that star-dom empties the artist of personal identity altogether.

Near the opening of *Melodrama Play* Dr. Damon inquires if Duke Dur-gens's success has brought him other media opportunities. This query, like much of the play, speaks to the changing circumstances of Shepard's ca-reer, for the playwright during these years pursued a number of ventures outside the theatre. He cowrote the screenplay for Robert Frank's *Me and My Brother*; he also contributed as screenwriter to *Maxagasm*, a piece executed on behalf of the Rolling Stones, and *The Bodyguard* (with Tony

Richardson), neither of which saw production.[14] The most influential project of this time, however, was his collaboration with Michelangelo Antonioni, the new wave European filmmaker who had recently garnered international acclaim with his modish hit, *Blow-Up*. Antonioni knew little about the dramatist, but when he sought a young American writer to script his upcoming film on the upheavals in American society, Shepard's counterculture credentials brought him the job. The playwright joined Antonioni in Rome, though the director's preconception of Shepard—as the young American firebrand—was subsequently proved inaccurate by the writer's aloofness and apolitical outlook. His writing was in fact rejected, considered too tame for Antonioni's tastes, and while his name is included in the film's credits, Shepard would disclaim his involvement in *Zabriskie Point*.

Melodrama Play merits attention as the first of Shepard's works to use rock music; the play's action is punctuated by songs, and a live band is demanded in the stage directions. From Elvis to the British Invasion to Creedence Clearwater Revival, rock and roll had proven the cachet of the youth culture, and we find that the playwright himself even achieved modest success as a rock-and-roller. During his early days in New York he frequently performed as a drummer, including a stint with a folk guitarist who called himself "the heavy metal kid."[15] The Holy Modal Rounders proved his most enduring alliance. The outfit took various incarnations, at one point spawning the Moray Eels, which performed the background music for *Forensic & the Navigators*. Described by Shepard as an "amphetamines band,"[16] the Holy Modal Rounders recorded little but gained a cult following. The band toured the West Coast and once opened for Pink Floyd at the Avalon Ballroom in San Francisco. Just as he had experienced aggravation with the film business, Shepard encountered friction in the recording industry. At one point he cut his hair, in defiance of the longhaired hippie stereotype, thus infuriating a record company executive who refused to put his picture on an album cover.

Shepard's dealings with universities, foundations, record companies, movie studios, and theatrical entrepreneurs inflamed his bureaucratic antipathies. This attitude appears with increasing prominence in his plays and reflects a general trend in American society toward a radical critique of American institutionalism. While the early sixties exhibited a desire to change society from within—through the organs of government and public policy, many in the late sixties sought to detach themselves from the system—to "turn on, tune in, and drop out." Many sought the system's overthrow altogether.

Liberal vision had raised the specter of a Leviathan-like government, with vast networks of codification, which grew ever larger and seemingly less effective. The ballooning of the federal bureaucracy was furthermore paralleled by restructuring in the private sector. Conglomeration proved the dominant practice, evidenced by more than four thousand corporate mergers in 1968 (a postwar peak). By this time, five hundred U.S. companies accounted for 64 percent of the country's industrial sales.[17] The close alliance of "big" government and "big" business elicited fears of an all-pervading establishment, characterized by one detractor as "a mindless juggernaut,"[18] which threatened to preempt diversity and local initiative.

Tensions on the domestic front were exacerbated by shifting international alignments. The bipolar world of the Cold War era, which had solidified American consensus, began to erode in the 1960s, a change which in part issued from the emergence of suppressed cultures and the rise of Third World self-determination (beginning after World War II with the decline of European colonialism).[19] This phenomenon was nowhere more apparent than in Vietnam, a country whose civil war would tragically affect America for many years to come.

While one can view the Vietnam War as a U.S. attempt to halt the spread of Communism, the conflict can also be seen as an effort by the United States to maintain Western dominance in a region once under French control. Vietnam thus became a focal point, a test case for the will of the American superpower and its desire to maintain political and economic hegemony in a changing geopolitical climate. It was ironically Kennedy, the Camelot president, who initiated U.S. entry into the Vietnam conflict, and Johnson, the "peace" candidate, who oversaw its escalation. That the party of liberalism should pursue what was perceived by many as a colonial war suggests the complicity between big government, the welfare apparatus, and an expansionist corporate economy. At its height, the war saw over half a million U.S. military personnel stationed in Vietnam. At home, the war brought widespread civil disobedience and deep suspicion toward the military and government alike. The Vietnam War marked a defining moment in twentieth-century U.S. history, triggering a struggle between authority and dissent that would rupture any semblance of an American consensus. It would also lead many to question the very value and viability of nationalist-based notions of cultural identity.

Shepard's following play, *Forensic & the Navigators*, was first performed at Theatre Genesis on December 29, 1967. The effort would initiate a series of works, culminating in *Operation Sidewinder*, in which the playwright's personal concern for the artist trapped in an overarching system would yield to a more topical investigation of political machinery and social division. While *Melodrama Play* makes oblique and casual reference to the period's protest mentality, *Forensic & the Navigators* draws wholesale from the rhetoric of counterculture radicalism.

Set in the hideout of Forensic and Emmet, two wanna-be revolutionaries, *Forensic & the Navigators* depicts the pair's incompetent plottings to overthrow a vaguely defined institution, where people "are really trapped for real."[20] Oolan, a former inmate, serves the men breakfast and reveals the hyprocrisy of the buffoonish radicals. When she brings Emmet a pancake he responds, "How many times I gotta' tell you I don't eat that buckwheat Aunt Jemima middle-class bullshit? I want Rice Krispies and nothing else" (p. 159). Oolan later emerges as the love interest when two exterminators, equipped with masks and hoses and dressed like California highway patrolmen, enter the revolutionaries' quarters. Yet, the anticipated rebel/authority confrontation fails to materialize. Before we discern any real resolution, unnamed forces bang at the hideout's door. Smoke fills the stage (and auditorium), and when the stage clears, all the characters have vanished.

The world of *Forensic & the Navigators* is that of a police state, informed by intrusion, obstruction, and surveillance. The play's opening song—"Oh Lord . . . We gonna be saved tonight" (p. 158)—plants the expectation of liberation, and the characters do escape into the mist. Still, the ambiguity of this ending leads one to wonder whether the revolutionaries gained release or were themselves simply exterminated. A thin, loosely constructed effort, the play takes swipes at the malignancy of institutionalism yet finally emerges as little more than a flimsy, hip parody of revolutionary posings.

Following his various projects in the film and music industry, Shepard authored *The Holy Ghostly* in 1969, a one-act whose anger counterpoints the flippancy of *Forensic & the Navigators*. Invoking the resentment and discontent common to America's youth, the work was toured by a La MaMa troupe and performed before university audiences both in America and Europe.

Heavily autobiographical in content, *The Holy Ghostly* depicts a father-son confrontation occasioned by Pop's call for his son, Ice, to leave New York and join him in the desert. Though the elder seeks the son's aid in rebuffing the spirits that assail him, Pop's treatment of Ice is derogatory. He impugns his son's manhood and dismisses his artistic success. Ice finally storms back: "Go fuck yourself, you old prick! I'm going to New York and you can stay here and jerk yourself off forever."[21] The clash of values seen in this interplay underscores the oft-noted generation gap of the period. It further dramatizes a fundamental power dynamic. When Ice addresses his father as "the oppressor's cherry" (p. 187), Pop is equated with political authority, and Ice's revolt is thus tantamount to insurrection.

At various times in *The Holy Ghostly*, an Indian spirit (dressed in a black blanket) and his wife the white witch appear onstage. The play admits a mystical order, and in its closing moments, Pop dances wildly in the campfire, shouting "BURN! BURN! BURN! BURN!" (p. 196). Stage directions call for flames to engulf the stage and the auditorium. This apocalyptic enactment may bring to mind the incendiary anger of the late sixties—the torching of the inner cities, the razing of ROTC buildings. Yet, the ending espouses no pragmatic political recourse, instead invoking a primitive, otherworldliness (which presages the climactic moments of *Operation Sidewinder*).

Hailed by the avant-garde as "the first prophet" of the American drama,[22] Shepard began to assume a greater sense of self-importance and approached his art with a new seriousness. In a 1969 interview he termed his early plays "facile" and voiced his commitment to a more studied approach to writing.[23] If one regards these early one-acts as intense, abbreviated energy bursts, venting the playfulness and paranoia of a youth striving to assert his personal will to power, Shepard's following plays take up a broader (often overstretched) canvas and a more ambitious aim. Expressing an interest in "mythic" characters, he would attempt a more public art, an art of epic proportion, fueled by topical politics, folklore, revolutionary slogan, and pop-culture imagery. In almost obligatory fashion, Shepard accepted his designation as the counterculture dramatist of the nation and in turn strove to capture the fulsome and fractured contemporary American moment.

As a teenager in the fifties, a time when comic books, drive-in movies, and TV Westerns were enjoying tremendous success, Shepard was inculcated in the popular media. It is therefore not surprising that mass culture references would dominate his work. Indeed, the media provided the subject and form for much avant-garde writing of the time. Jean-Claude van Itallie's acclaimed *American Hurrah* contains a sequence titled "TV." Megan Terry subtitled her *Viet Rock* a "folk war movie." Ronald Tavel's *The Gorilla Queen* transfigured the Saturday matinee jungle movie into high camp hijinx.

Like many of his peers, Shepard followed an antiaesthetic, seeking less a rarefied "artwork" than an art event of immediacy and relevance, infused with a hip sensibility. Described as an "urban folk art,"[24] these efforts drew less from the canon than the commonplace—the stuff of mass culture. In this order, Shakespeare gives pride of place to Sam Spade, Mick Jagger, and Mickey Mouse. Shepard's works of this period thus emerged as high-speed, cartoon-color pastiches. Characterized by the term *postmodern*, this sort of bricolage practice exhibited a bold interweaving of heterogenous texts and images; it furthermore indicated seismic rumblings that carried beyond the theatre or art world. Fredric Jameson has argued that this aesthetic decentering and its challenge to formal unity (and meaning) issued from the political and economic turmoil of the time.[25] In this view, Shepard's stylistics (and the postmodern emphasis on surface over depth) reflect the collapse of central authority and the subversion of established hierarchies. As the welfare state and its legitimacy were shaken by global realignment and internal domestic pressures, such postmodern performance expressed something of a guerrilla impulse, releasing the dispersive energy of cultural categories under siege.

One of Shepard's most fascinating and amusing efforts, *The Unseen*

Hand, first performed at the La MaMa Experimental Theatre Club on December 26, 1969, manifests this new complexity in the playwright's approach. Exhibiting a mixture of character types and an unstable narrative line, the work offers a rich excursion into the pop sensibility. Set on a California desert highway, *The Unseen Hand* opens with Blue Morphan, an old-time cowboy of the nineteenth century, camped along the roadside, living out of the rusted hull of a 1951 Chevrolet. Coke bottles and other consumer-culture detritus litter the ground. The roadside junk heap serves to counterpoint the speeches of the Kid, a local high schooler who appears on the scene after having been abused by teenagers from a rival school. In his stirring defense of small-town life, the Kid catalogs key components of the American experience, which range from drive-in movies, to bowling alleys, to the Junior Chamber of Commerce, to madras shorts. His speech recalls a 1950s America, a period marked by cohesion and centeredness. The hull of the Chevrolet conversely summons a fragmented order, where splintered shards of Americana reside in an undifferentiated desert night-world.

Shepard's recurrent concern with totalitarianism surfaces in the play's extraordinary visitation; Willie, a "space freak" from Nogoland, travels across two galaxies to enlist the Morphan brothers in a scheme to free his people from the repressive order of the High Commission. The overlords of Nogoland are described in nebulous terms, yet their influence is clear and immediate, demonstrated in a painful form of mind control. Willie, who has the black imprint of a hand burned into his scalp, goes into convulsions whenever he thinks "unsanctioned" thoughts. Blue's brothers, Cisco and Sycamore, are conjured up from the Wild West past and after some debate are convinced to join in Willie's revolutionary enterprise.

The high point of the play is reached when the Kid—believing himself the savior of the American way of life—holds Willie and the cowboys at gunpoint. The standoff is suddenly disrupted when Willie enters a trance state and breaks free of the "unseen hand." He discovers the power of self-liberation and embarks upon an ecstatic dance of celebration while Day-Glo Ping-Pong balls shower the stage.

The borderland locale of *The Unseen Hand* functions as a point of intersection, where several worlds and competing discourses collide. The nearby town of Azusa—"Everything from 'A' to 'Z' in the USA"[26]—reinforces the repository motif, and the play may been seen as an American compendium, replete with clichés of science fiction, movie Westerns, revolutionary activism, and Rotary club luncheons. It has been argued that Shepard's "postmodern technique" provides his audience "with a vision of multiplicity and choice,"[27] and indeed *The Unseen Hand* is a multivalent work, venting a heteroglossic impulse. Still, the postmodern credo—heteronomy without hierarchy—may not fully apply in this case. Shepard's vision of America will emerge as a crucial factor in the playwright's success, and one must understand how his work differs from the Stars and Stripes pop art that proliferated in the sixties. In the latter, patriotic iconography demonstrated a realignment, or leveling, in which such emblems were divested of sacrosanct status and posited alongside mundane or even obscene materials. Shepard's treatment of American imagery frequently takes a satiric bite; it also however retains traces of affection. When David DeRose writes that the Morphan Brothers represent an "authentic and potentially formidable force,"[28] we are alerted to the playwright's fondness for the cowboy icon and the connotations it holds in the American imagination. In this light, the work may not invite an arbitrary audience response (and may defy classification with the product art of Andy Warhol, or Peter Max's psychedelia). Rather, the play may implicitly confirm something of the Old West worldview. And in spite of Shepard's bricolage format and heteroglossic technique, one may question the extent to which *The Unseen Hand* ascribes to or even reproduces the rank and file ideology of the American heartland. This intriguing feature of Shepard's dramaturgy will become more central to his later plays and will contribute to his ironic status as America's avant-garde traditionalist.

Experimental visual artists of the early 1960s quickly found devotees in posh, upscale galleries: as early as 1962 the Sidney Janis Gallery showed works by Dine, Lichtenstein, and Oldenburg; in 1963 Pop Art was featured at the Guggenheim Museum.[29] Shepard's experience confirms this increasing legitimization of the avant-garde. In *Writing Sites*, Jon Stratton points out how marginal spaces are often regarded as sites of "surplus,"[30] holding mythical booty—from gold, to spices, to eternal youth. This insight illuminates the commercial theatre's relation to Off-Off Broadway and the latter's status as a borderland, ripe for plunder. In the late sixties Broadway experienced flagging attendance and skyrocketing production costs (a musical at this time could cost $500,000 to mount[31]). The mainstream theatre thus journeyed into the jungles of the avant-garde, and Shepard was soon exhibited before uptown audiences as something of a rare and exotic creature.

The experimental theatre in many instances made itself available for commodification. The practice of "moving up," that is, taking a successful show from an Off-Off Broadway space and producing it in a commercial theatre, was commonplace for many groups—from Café La MaMa to the Open Theatre to Caffe Cino.[32] Several of Shepard's early works were revived in "upgraded" venues; *Red Cross*, for example, was moved from the Judson Poets' Theatre to the Provincetown Playhouse. Even though some groups remained haphazard in their management, many became increasingly organized, especially sophisticated in obtaining grant and foundation support. While such theatres maintained nonprofit status, their annual production budgets could be substantial, ranging up to $250,000.[33] This trend toward bureaucratization resulted in an official federation—the Off-Off

Broadway Alliance—which by the mid-1970s would number nearly a hundred members.[34]

In short order counterculture theatre became big business. Originating at the Public Theatre, the hippie musical *Hair* went on to become a Broadway smash. The production's director, Tom O'Horgan, who had earlier staged *Melodrama Play* at Theatre Genesis, by this time commanded a six-figure salary.[35] One of the first gay-oriented plays to go mainstream, Mart Crowley's *The Boys in the Band* developed out of Edward Albee's playwriting workshop, then went on to Off-Broadway acclaim and great financial success. Regulars on the café theatre scene, John Guare and Lanford Wilson were now given opportunities on the Great White Way. An eclectic mix of plays—from *Scuba Duba*, to *Your Own Thing*, to *Futz*—received commercial stagings, indicating the New York theatre's new tolerance for unconventional works (providing they turned a profit at the box office).[36]

Nudity in performance moved mainstream, and sexual subject matter proved a big seller. Lennox Raphael's *Che!* simulated sex acts onstage between a revolutionary and the U.S. president; the show moved from Off-Off Broadway to a commercial run. Tom Eyen's *The Dirtiest Show in Town*, with its orgy scenes, enjoyed similar notoriety. Shepard would see his own work marketed in such an atmosphere: the last sequence of *The Rock Garden*, perhaps the most sexually explicit of his entire corpus, was incorporated in Kenneth Tynan's sexual review, *Oh, Calcutta!*. Valued for its salaciousness, this excerpt would prove the only Shepard material presented on the Broadway stage (until *Buried Child*'s revival in April of 1996).

Perhaps the most significant event in this chapter of Shepard's career was the Lincoln Center production of *Operation Sidewinder* (March, 1970). The experience proved a major step for Shepard's involvement in the cultural mainstream, for with this effort he left the friendly confines of Off-Off Broadway and ventured into an authorized space, a site of public culture. His work there encountered "the other America," that is, the audience of affluence and influence who would during intermission sip "five-dollar glasses of champagne."[37]

The Lincoln Center for the Performing Arts developed as a nonprofit enterprise (financed by foundation support and private donations) in the late 1950s and sought to establish a cultural arts complex that would house the nation's finest work in classical music, ballet, opera, and theatre. Drawing both encouragement and censure—many feared the complex would become a cultural supermarket—the project came into realization as construction was begun in 1959. Following the pattern of European national theatres, the Lincoln Center envisioned a resident company performing new and classic works of the American drama. Headed by Robert Whitehead and Elia Kazan, the Repertory Theatre of the Lincoln Center presented its first season in 1963–64 and moved into the newly built Vivian Beaumont Theatre in 1965. Problems, however, beleaguered the enterprise. The second season saw a precipitous drop in subscriptions,[38] and by 1967 the company was losing $750,000 annually.[39] Changes in leadership were all too frequent, and controversy abounded. Attacking the undertaking as "inadequate, pretentious, and self-serving," Richard Gilman spoke for many when he described the theatre as "a monument to the false and self-deluding."[40]

Reflective of its ambition as a showcase for national drama, the repertory theatre in 1970 essayed an all-American season. Shepard found his work shoulder to shoulder with that of canonical American dramatists William Saroyan and Tennessee Williams. *Operation Sidewinder* was enlisted in almost token fashion, a sampler of the contemporary scene, and Shepard was promoted as something of an underground novelty.

John Lahr, then literary manager of the Lincoln Center, has related how the playwright seemed out of place in the building and would roam the maroon-carpeted corridors in his cowboy boots and high-school windbreaker. According to Lahr, Shepard became "strappy" and stonewalled changes to his text. He would "sneak beers" into rehearsal under his shirt. Shepard was no habitué of uptown theatre and often denounced it as a "total bourgeois scene."[41] Nevertheless, the financial resources and technical arsenal of the Lincoln Center's Vivian Beaumont Theatre far surpassed the modest venues with which he had been associated (the average per-show budget for the 1970 season surpassed $120,000[42]). Despite whatever discomfiture this context may have caused the dramatist, he understood that the Vivian Beaumont could accommodate *Operation Sidewinder*'s massive scope and logistical demands, and indeed the production displayed much technological wizardry. Strobe lights, crystal globes, and spinning color wheels dazzled audiences; the play's true star was perhaps the sidewinder itself—a six-foot-long electronic snake.

The most sprawling of Shepard's works, with thirty-six characters and twelve scenes, *Operation Sidewinder* relies upon a computerized snake as the linchpin for its dramatic action and scenic continuity. Act One chiefly concerns the stratagems of the Young Man and the black revolutionaries, who have enlisted the mixed-breed Mickey Free to "dope" the reservoir at Fort George. Act Two shifts focus to the retrieval of the sidewinder, which has escaped from the laboratory of Dr. Vector—a Dr. Strangelove caricature—and is sought by both the military and the revolutionaries. The snake, however, ends up in the hands of a converted Mickey Free, who deploys the sidewinder in a Hopi ritual that draws the play to its mystifying conclusion.

Dedicated to 1968, a year that for many counterculture idealists "marked the end of hope,"[43] *Operation Sidewinder* surveys American culture in a condition of disarray. This year witnessed the assassinations of

Martin Luther King and Robert Kennedy, the Vietcong Tet Offensive, the protest of African American athletes at the Mexico City Olympics, the street violence attending the Democratic National Convention. While the early sixties had united people of various classes, religions, and racial backgrounds under the common banner of social renewal, the later years of the decade proved a fractious time. The civil rights movement, which had been championed as a cooperative enterprise (with white liberal support), took a more incendiary tone and separatist thrust. African American playwrights Ed Bullins, Douglas Turner Ward, and Amiri Baraka (formerly LeRoi Jones) advanced racial solidarity and vented the anger of many black Americans whose frustration had exploded in inner-city rioting, from Watts, to Newark, Detroit, and beyond. Universities, too, became the sites of discord—host to sit-ins, mass marches, and instances of sabotage. Many campus protestors moved to a more militant posture, seen in the formation of "the weathermen," who arose out of the SDS and advocated random acts of terrorism against the state.

In the late sixties new alliances rose in the swell of counterculture liberation: 1966 saw the founding of both the Black Panthers and the National Organization for Women (NOW). Native American discontent gave rise to the American Indian Movement (AIM), a radical group that gained national attention by seizing Alcatraz in 1969. While the decade's attitude of openness worked in salutary fashion to bring voice and power to many who had been marginalized, this time contributed to the crystallization of "subculture" identities and an acute sense of schism in American society. During these years the *e pluribus unum* vision of America experienced extreme distress, as the welfare state could not hold its center nor its claim upon the diversity of interests (or identities) in American culture.

Like *The Unseen Hand*, *Operation Sidewinder* cuts a wide swath across the American landscape and draws its material from topical events, pop media, and Native American myth. Documenting the multifarious energies tearing at the nation's unity, the play chiefly takes a satirical attitude toward its divisive characters. In one of the play's more comedic scenes, a carhop, serving fast food to black revolutionaries, breaks into clichéd dissident cant: "Armed struggle begins when the oppressed people pick up guns . . . I got a gun right in my house, man, and I'm ready to use it too."[44] Conversely, the hawkish Captain Bovine allows Shepard to mock the country's right wing and its "America, love it or leave it" mentality. Bovine laments the breakdown of law and order and attributes the disrespect of America's youth to "those bushy-haired creeps" who arrived from Britain in 1964 (p. 238). Shepard even offers elements of self-parody in his desultory rendering of the Young Man, who "shoots up" and goes into a drug-induced, dissociative blather: "I am depressed, deranged, decapitated, dehumanized, defoliated, demented and damned!" (p. 226).

Shepard's kaleidoscopic treatment of American culture takes a rather cartoonish dimension, with dazzling surfaces, caricatures, and haphazard plotting. The play nevertheless attempts to be more than a mere catalog of citations quoting the contemporary scene, and the rhetoric of *Operation Sidewinder* bears comparison to that of *Melodrama Play*. In its outlandish style and use of coincidence and mistaken identity, the latter work, as James Leverett correctly argues, takes the melodramatic form "as something to be 'played' with."[45] Nevertheless, the dramatist stresses in his preface that a production of *Melodrama Play* should not accentuate the satirical but should explore how the play "changes from the mechanism of melodrama to something more sincere" (p. 115). This point of advice implies that the work, for Shepard, is more than parody or simple send-up. The deconstruction of the melodramatic formula and its multitudinous pop-culture references in fact expose a conservative urge for grounding and coherence in the face of postmodern vertigo.

In Act Two, a lengthy passage is given to the Spider Lady, who recounts a creation myth concerning the Snake and Lizard clans. The gist of the story—that the "serpent spirit" was divided—points forward to a future moment of eschatological reunion. If we regard *Operation Sidewinder* as a study of division within the American community, the Hopi myth, for Shepard, promises unification: Mickey Free, upon hearing the words of the Spider Lady, renounces violence and travels to the mesa for a holy ritual; he intends to unite the two halves of the sidewinder (which he himself had severed in Act One).

The play closes with an esoteric display of cosmic convergence. Mickey Free, now dressed in Hopi garb and assisted by the Snake and Antelope priests, initiates a ritual involving dance, puppetry, and invocation (Shepard insisted on the ceremony's authenticity). After a banal discussion of Elvis movies, the Young Man and his companion, Honey, approach Mickey with the body of the computer-serpent. A group of Desert Tactical Troops soon arrive and attempt to reclaim the snake. Mickey Free joins the two halves of the sidewinder, igniting an explosive eruption of light and sound. The soldiers are stunned; they begin firing upon the celebrants but their bullets have no effect. A thick smoke—reminiscent of that in *Forensic & the Navigators*—fills the stage, and when it clears, Mickey Free, Honey, and the Young Man have vanished—that is, transcended.

Much of the sixties experimental theatre, including the efforts of the Open Theatre, the Living Theatre, and the Performance Group, sought to approximate the effects of "mystic religious experience"[46]; *Operation Sidewinder* follows in this vein but reveals itself as a rather schizophrenic effort. The play is made up, in large measure, of cultural criticism and political satire; the playwright maneuvers both his radicals and right wingers with bemused detachment. The work's irreverent voice (and delight in speed and sheen) nonetheless belies a spiritual concern. Like *The Holy Ghostly*, *Operation Sidewinder* posits a transcendent realm beyond the polyglot of the contemporary moment, and we thus discern Shepard's desire to find a center behind the swirling vortex of the American scene. Having taken no sides, the writer retreats from the immediacy of 1968, and instead of a politics of involvement he offers the play's cryptic, ecstatic conclusion as some vague expression of political, social, and metaphysical communion. In sum, *Operation Sidewinder* exposes its author as a would-be witch doctor of the avant-garde, presiding over a division-healing service of invocation—within the cushioned quarters and monied confines of the Lincoln Center.

On almost all accounts this production of *Operation Sidewinder* was regarded as a catastrophe. The critic Harold Clurman termed the play "dull" and its satire "banal."[47] Brendan Gill underscored the "tedium of the evening" and concluded that "once Mr. Shepard has exploited his POW!s and ZAP!s he is left with little but magical incantations to offer us, and they are not enough."[48] Audiences began laughing during the Hopi ritual, and of the fifty postperformance questionnaires that were returned, only two were positive.[49] Subscribers to the American play series canceled "in droves."[50]

In 1969 Lanford Wilson and John Guare received their first opportunities on Broadway. Like *Operation Sidewinder*, Wilson's *The Gingham Dog* and Guare's two one-acts *Home Fires* and *Cop-Out* fared poorly with critics and audiences. For all three Off-Off Broadway veterans, involvement in New York's uptown theatre left a bitter taste. After his failure with *The Gingham Dog*, Lanford Wilson confessed feeling that he "had to write the Great American Play," a burden that resulted in an "enormous decline" and a writer's block that lasted a year and a half.[51] Shepard's deflating experience at the Lincoln Center likewise prompted much self-reflection. It also propelled him back to the safe haven of Off-Off Broadway.[52]

Mad Dog Blues signals Shepard's outright break with political matters. It also begins one of his darkest periods as a writer. Recoiling from his experience with *Operation Sidewinder*, Shepard stepped back from the hip, high-tech, cosmic style and composed a series of highly introspective plays. In these personal explorations, the situation of the writer supplants social commentary as the playwright's subject of inquiry. These works may be understood as therapy pieces or personal expiations, and Shepard assumes a different stance, one that disavows his status as the generation's spokesman. In these plays, the playwright in effect licks his wounds and examines questions of self-doubt, personal stability, and the price one pays for artistic fame.

Presented on March 4, 1971, *Mad Dog Blues* returned Shepard to his "home" theatre, Theatre Genesis. He played drums in the three-piece rock group that accompanied the show.[53] The familiarity of the context proves illuminating as the play's lead characters, Kosmo and Yahoodi, search for grounding and connection. Yahoodi is fighting a drug addiction (as was Shepard at the time), and Kosmo emerges as the overwrought rock-and-roll star, exasperated with fame and longing for serenity. Discontent prompts both toward flight. Kosmo journeys to San Francisco, while Yahoodi flees to the jungle.

Subtitled an "adventure show," the play is often noted for its many colorful characters drawn from film and folklore. Kosmo and Yahoodi are accompanied on their journey by the likes of Marlene Dietrich, Mae West, Captain Kidd, and Paul Bunyan. Characterized as "saints in a cathedral of American popular culture,"[54] these figures convey a sense of simplicity and purity. *Mad Dog Blues* betrays a warmth and affection, and the nostalgic attitude of the play is underscored by the text's call for sound effects to be produced live on stage, according to the conventions of the "old-time" radio show.[55] In this work, which is less an effort at deconstruction than resuscitation, Shepard plumbs the image pool of America's collective memory, as though checking its heroes and icons for any flickering signs of life.

Despite the laugh lines, sight gags, and the wildly colorful pageantry of the piece, *Mad Dog Blues*' evocation of innocence and wonder cannot mask the bleaker aspects of the play. Loss is pervasive: Kosmo's musical heroes, such as Brian Jones and Otis Redding, have all met violent or untimely deaths; near the end of the second act, Yahoodi himself commits suicide. Yet, by appealing to the conventions of the "happy" ending, Kosmo summons his friend back to life. A sense of wish fulfillment pervades the play's conclusion, even when the treasure the characters have been seeking turns out to be a stash of bottle caps. In fact, the play's final sequence calls for all the characters—while singing the tune "Home"—to join hands and dance into the audience then out of the theatre and into the street. The unabashed optimism of the closing ends the work on an ironic note. The piece extends a dream-vision of unity, which, given the darker realities of Shepard's life at the time, exposes its chimerical nature, a possibility alluring yet unattainable.

Presented as a double bill, Shepard's next two plays, *Cowboy Mouth* and *Back Bog Beast Bait*, were also staged in a smaller venue, one with which the writer had previously experienced a comfortable relationship: the American Place Theatre. *Cowboy Mouth* reveals Shepard's weariness with the eschatological expanse of his previous works and continues his downward spiral into melancholia. While *Mad Dog Blues* exhibits a sense of the picaresque alongside its more brooding musings, *Cowboy Mouth* is strident, often grating, and reveals an edginess not seen since Shepard's early works. The piece is violent, laced with obscenities, obsessed with death, apotheosis, and the lure of a rock-and-roll suicide.

In 1969 Shepard had married the 19-year-old O-lan Johnson (who had played Oolan in *Forensic & the Navigators*). Their folk-rock wedding, held at St. Mark's Church, was the quintessential sixties event: poetry was read; music was performed; members of the Holy Modal Rounders greeted guests with purple "tabs" of LSD.[56] By 1971, though, the marriage was on the brink of failure. Although unwilling to divorce O-lan, Shepard carried on a tempestuous affair with the rock poet/singer Patti Smith. *Cowboy Mouth* draws from the couple's escapades at the Chelsea Hotel and dramatizes the playwright's ambivalent emotional state (his son Jesse Mojo had recently been born). The piece resulted from a collaboration, as legend has it, with Shepard and Smith alternately writing lines, pushing a typewriter back and forth across a table to one another. Slim's opening speech in the play—"What a ratpile heap of dogshit situation!"[57]—ably summarizes Shepard's confusion at the time and points to the many personal problems troubling the playwright.

In *Cowboy Mouth* we learn that the ravenlike Cavale has captured the cowboy Slim off the street and seeks his transformation into a rock deity. She tutors Slim on the lives of decadent French poets—Nerval, Villon, Baudelaire—and the death of Johnny Ace, the rock-and-roller, who played Russian Roulette onstage and blew out his brains before his adoring fans. In her bizarre pedagogy, Cavale espouses a neo-Hegelian view of history, one that claims the demise of Christianity and the imminence of a new savior, a "saint" with "a cowboy mouth . . . rocking to Bethlehem to be born" (p. 156).

When Cavale tells Slim that he has to be "a rock-and-roll Jesus" (p. 157), we understand the sacrificial obligation of the artist and the tyrannical power of the stage. Cavale explains that it is the duty of the rock-savior to assuage the community's collective desire, that "stuff in them that makes them wanna' see God's face" (pp. 156–57), and Slim thus recognizes that the artist is a slave to the dreams of others. He turns on Cavale, declaring his reluctance to attempt what Mick Jagger and Bob Dylan have failed—to be the rock Christ.

The entry of the Lobster Man however arouses Slim's competitive instincts, and the latter initiates a "style" test—a device Shepard would put to excellent use in *The Tooth of Crime*. Slim plays his electric guitar, Cavale sings, and the Lobster Man takes center stage. His shell begins to crack, and the rock-and-roll savior—dressed in black—emerges. Slim concedes superiority to the Lobster Man then surreptitiously exits the room. Cavale takes up the education of the new student, and shortly thereafter the rock-and-roll savior puts a pistol to his head and pulls the trigger. The weapon gives a "loud click as the hammer strikes an empty chamber" (p. 165).

A suicidal impulse also pervades the mindset of *Back Bog Beast Bait*, the work that marks the nadir of this depressive phase of Shepard's writing. More obscure and murky than any of his previous works, *Back Bog Beast Bait* is a dark trip into the Louisiana underworld. The locale is significant for it represents the underbelly of American culture, a remove from the conflagrant political scene Shepard had surveyed in *Operation Sidewinder*. The play is no polemic on the fractured state of the nation but a journey into enchantment and dementia. Several critics have attributed the darkness of the play to the writer's drug addiction, and indeed the work evokes both a strong sense of despondency and a fascination with the Lethe-like allure of the bayou.

Slim and Shadow arrive at the cabin of Maria, a Mexican woman terrorized by a demonic pig-beast, and offer their services as hired guns. They suggest the heroic order of the Western genre but exhibit less machismo than comic ineptitude. Slim is revealed as the top gun near the end of his reign, and in his broodings, we detect a high degree of performance anxiety and self-doubt. The malevolent tapir has killed Maria's husband, emasculated many others, and now threatens the viability of her unborn child. The beast thus emerges as a castratory threat, a feature that highlights Slim's insecurities and perhaps alerts us to the nagging sense of entrapment and failure plaguing the playwright himself.

Shadow leaves the cabin and returns with the Cajun temptress Gris Gris (played by O-lan), who offers golden mushrooms to all. Despite Slim's warnings, Shadow ingests the "beast bait" and soon enters a state of delirium. A vagrant preacher, who had been savaged by the beast and took shelter in the cabin, breaks into fevered, messianic execrations. The play comes to no plot resolution but concludes with widespread possession (and the surrender of consciousness). Foregoing any enigmatic reunion, *Back Bog Beast Bait* ends in disjunction. Even when the pig itself appears onstage it goes unnoticed, as each character remains locked in private torment and the throes of animalistic transformation.

The trio of plays performed in 1971 deals heavily in disappointment, and like many survivors of the 1960s, who saw the luminous qualities of the decade growing faint, Shepard at this point undertook much soul-searching. These years had not brought the "greening" of America, as Charles Reich had predicted,[58] but much darkness and travail. The vaunted efforts toward a transformed society had also released madness, as the Charles Manson murder spree testified. In 1970 rock icons Janis Joplin and Jimi Hendrix succumbed to drug overdoses; the nation learned of secret bombings in Cambodia. As if to certify the country's malaise, national guardsmen turned their rifles upon American citizens, killing student protestors on two separate occasions, at Kent State in Ohio and Jackson State in Mississippi. The country stumbled into the 1970s, worn, disunited, and morally fatigued.

While Shepard's early one-acts may be viewed as sniperlike gestures against the dictates of conformity, during the late 1960s the playwright found himself drawn into and given position within the established organs of the American culture industry. The freedom and exultation displayed throughout his one-acts gave over to a sense of self-importance and obligation as his work frequently strained toward statement-making commentary. Yet, despite the regularizing tendencies inherent in an artist's cultural legitimization, Shepard's drama retained a recalcitrance and could not be neatly packaged—hence, the debacle at the Lincoln Center. This sanctioning process in some measure explains the writer's consequent feelings of rejection and betrayal. In the hurly-burly of the late 1960s Shepard dared to ascend the pedestal the culture industry had provided yet found its heights inhospitable. Given his more public and vulnerable position, his work received greater scrutiny and was evaluated according to standards that ill-matched his aesthetic aims. Critics looking for the next Great American Playwright wrote without reserve of Shepard's inadequacies, in maturity, craft, and discipline. Typical of the pillorying Shepard endured, Clive Barnes joked that Shepard's plays were to the drama "what Kleenex was to the handkerchief."[59]

Career pressures, combined with his embattled marriage and an increasingly incapacitating drug habit, brought Shepard to a point of descent but also forced a reckoning. It is curious that when he and Smith performed the roles of Slim and Cavale in the American Place Theatre production of *Cowboy Mouth* (April 29, 1971) Shepard was stricken by an acute apprehension not unlike that experienced by the character; the playwright abandoned the show after opening night and bolted to New England.[60] In face of the personal and professional strains besetting him, he would in the fall of 1971 take similar recourse. If evasion is the foundation of resistance, then Shepard acted the rebel's part and exiled himself from the American theatre. The writer heralded as the rising playwright of the nation responded by running—he moved his family to London. In a strangely self-revealing manner, the elder gunslinger's lines in *Back Bog Beast Bait* portend this move and speak to the playwright's pressing need for respite and recovery: "I'll take a little vacation! . . . No harm in a little rest . . . Sure. A nice long rest. Get my nerves back. (He howls)."[61]

NOTES

1. Herbert Marcuse, "Political Preface 1966," in *Eros and Civilization* (Boston: Beacon Press, 1974), xxv.

2. Murray Mednick, quoted in Robert J. Schroeder, ed., *The New Underground Theatre* (New York: Bantam Books, 1968), 102.

3. Katerina Clark and Michael Holquist, *Mikhail Bakhtin* (Cambridge, MA: Harvard University Press, 1984), 14.

4. For an overview of the company's history see Ulrica Bell-Perkins, "The Living Theater," in Weldon B. Durham, ed., *American Theatre Companies, 1931–1986* (Westport, CT: Greenwood Press, 1989), 333–38.

5. Cited in John Lahr, *Up Against the Fourth Wall* (New York: Grove Press, 1970), 107.

6. Ruby Cohn, *New American Dramatists 1960–1990* (New York: St. Martin's Press, 1991), 86.

7. Robert Coe, "Saga of Sam Shepard," *New York Times Magazine*, 23 November 1980, 120.

8. Cited in Virginia White, *Grants for the Arts* (New York: Plenum Press, 1980), 157.

9. Ibid., 60.

10. See Michael Harrington, *The Other America* (Baltimore: Penguin Books, 1963).

11. Cited in James Gilbert, *Another Chance: Postwar America, 1945–1985* (Chicago: Dorsey Press, 1986), 206. Though Kennedy advocated these measures, the realization of many of these programs did not occur until the Johnson administration.

12. Keynesian theory is discussed in Joel Krieger, *Reagan, Thatcher, and the Politics of Decline* (New York: Oxford University Press, 1986), 110–22.

13. Sam Shepard, *Melodrama Play*, in *Fool for Love and Other Plays* (New York: Bantam Books, 1984), 134. Further citations indicated within the text.

14. Cited in Lynda Hart, *Sam Shepard's Metaphorical Stages* (Westport, CT: Greenwood Press, 1987), 131.

15. Information on Shepard's adventure in rock music is found in Don Shewey, *Sam Shepard* (New York: Dell, 1985), 61–64.

16. Shepard, quoted in Coe, "Saga of Sam Shepard," 120.

17. Cited in Gilbert, *Another Chance*, 187.

18. Charles A. Reich, *The Greening of America* (New York: Bantam Books, 1970), 17.

19. This phenomenon is discussed in Crawford Young, "The Dialectics of Cultural Pluralism," in Crawford Young, ed., *The Rising Tide of Cultural Pluralism* (Madison: University of Wisconsin Press, 1991), 3–21.

20. Sam Shepard, *Forensic & the Navigators*, in *The Unseen Hand and Other Plays* (New York: Bantam Books, 1986), 159. Further citations indicated within the text.

21. Sam Shepard, *The Holy Ghostly*, in *The Unseen Hand and Other Plays*, 180. Further citations indicated within the text.

22. Cited in John Glore, "The Canonization of Mojo Rootface: Sam Shepard Live at the Pantheon," *Theatre* 12, no. 3 (1981): 53.

23. Shepard, quoted in Mel Gussow, "Sam Shepard: Writer on the Way Up," *New York Times*, 12 November 1969, 42.

24. Sally Banes, *Greenwich Village 1963* (Durham, NC: Duke University Press, 1993), 94.

25. Fredric Jameson examines the cultural contexts of postmodernism in "Periodizing the 60s," in Sohnya Sayres et al., eds., *The Sixties Without Apology* (Minneapolis: University of Minnesota Press, 1984), 194–200.

26. Sam Shepard, *The Unseen Hand*, in *The Unseen Hand and Other Plays*, 5.

27. Rodney Simard observes this as a general feature of Shepard's writing in "American Gothic: Sam Shepard's Family Trilogy," *Theatre Annual* 41 (1986): 35.

28. David J. DeRose, *Sam Shepard* (New York: Twayne, 1992), 46.

29. Banes, *Greenwich Village*, 58.

30. Jon Stratton, *Writing Sites* (Ann Arbor: University of Michigan Press, 1990), 16.

31. Cited in Howard Greenberger, *The Off-Broadway Experience* (Englewood Cliffs, NJ: Prentice-Hall, 1971), 20.

32. Ibid., 21.

33. Cited in Donald C. Farber, *From Option to Opening* (New York: Drama Book Specialists, 1977), 123.

34. Cited in Mindy N. Levine, *New York's Other Theatre: A Guide to Off Off Broadway* (New York: Avon Books, 1981), xvi.

35. Cited in Lahr, *Up Against the Fourth Wall*, 105.

36. The commercial theatre's embrace of the avant-garde (and its sexual liberation) is recounted in Greenberger, *The Off-Broadway Experience*, 20.

37. John Lahr, *Automatic Vaudeville* (New York: Alfred A. Knopf, 1984), 42. Shepard's behavior during the production of *Operation Sidewinder* is recounted by Lahr in pages 42–45.

38. Cited in Ralph G. Martin, *Lincoln Center for the Performing Arts* (Englewood Cliffs, NJ: Prentice-Hall, 1971), 91.

39. Cited in Robert E. Gard, Marston Balch, and Pauline B. Temkin, *Theater in America* (Madison, WI: Dembar Educational Research Services, Inc., 1968), 29.

40. Richard Gilman, *Common and Uncommon Masks* (New York: Random House, 1971), 152.

41. Shepard, quoted in Gussow, "Writer on the Way Up," 43.

42. Cited in Weldon B. Durham, "The Repertory Theatre of Lincoln Center," *American Theatre Companies, 1931–1986*, 453.

43. Charles Kaiser, *1968 in America* (New York: Weidenfeld & Nicolson, 1988), xii.

44. Sam Shepard, *Operation Sidewinder*, in *The Unseen Hand and Other Plays*, 218. Further citations indicated within the text.

45. James Leverett, "Old Forms Enter the New American Theater: Shepard, Foreman, Kirby, and Ludlam," in Daniel Gerould, ed., *Melodrama* (New York: New York Literary Forum, 1980), 68.

46. Mimi Kramer, "In Search of the Good Shepard," *New Criterion* 2, no. 2 (1983): 57.

47. Harold Clurman, review of *Operation Sidewinder*, *Nation*, 30 March 1970, 381.

48. Brendan Gill, "The Theatre: Getting on with the Story," *New Yorker*, 21 March 1970, 115.

49. Cited in Lahr, *Automatic Vaudeville*, 43.

50. Shepard, quoted in Coe, "Saga of Sam Shepard," 12.

51. Lanford Wilson, quoted in Esther Harriott, *American Voices* (London: McFarland, 1988), 77.

52. Following soon after *Operation Sidewinder*, Shepard had a double bill of his plays (*The Unseen Hand* and *Forensic & the Navigators*) produced commercially Off-Broadway in April of 1970. Generating little critical attention or box office success, this project too proved disenchanting for Shepard. He retreated to Café La MaMa where *Shaved Splits*, one of the writer's least-praised efforts, was given a four-night run in July of 1970. *Shaved Splits* begins and ends in fantasy. The play

opens with a pampered housewife—reading from a pornographic novel—whose insulated world is invaded by Geez, a revolutionary seeking sanctuary. The work presents an easy dismissal of political questions (along with a vague appeal to music's regenerative capacity) and may be viewed as a gestural act of withdrawal on Shepard's part.

53. Cited in Arthur Sainer, "Shepard's Collision Course: Stung in the Land of Honey," *Village Voice*, 11 March 1971, 53.

54. George Stambolian, "Sam Shepard's *Mad Dog Blues*: A Trip through Popular Culture," *Journal of Popular Culture* 7, no. 4 (1974): 780.

55. Sam Shepard, *Mad Dog Blues*, in *The Unseen Hand and Other Plays*, 257. Further citations indicated within the text.

56. Shewey, *Sam Shepard*, 76.

57. Sam Shepard, *Cowboy Mouth*, in *Fool for Love and Other Plays*, 147. Further references cited in text.

58. Reich, *The Greening of America*, 2.

59. Clive Barnes, "Theatre: A Sam Shepard Double Bill," *New York Times*, 2 April 1970, 43.

60. Cited in Ellen Oumano, *Sam Shepard: The Life and Work of an American Dreamer* (New York: St. Martin's Press, 1986), 90.

61. Sam Shepard, *Back Bog Beast Bait*, in *The Unseen Hand and Other Plays*, 332.

Chapter 3

A Yankee at the Royal Court

Despite the fact that he emerged as the leading playwright of the 1960s counterculture, Shepard has on numerous occasions derided the supposed glory of the decade and its touted liberation. He has spoken of his days in the Lower East Side not in terms of celebration but desperation, characterizing the experience as "a kind of survival act."[1] A dismissive attitude can also be seen in his regard for the New York theatre. The scene had become oppressive for the playwright; he was uncomfortable with his status as the man of the moment, an emblem of the hip and trendy, whose plays had become chic events attended by such celebrities as Andy Warhol, Abbie Hoffman, and Robert Redford.[2] Artistic and personal problems triggered a crisis point, and Shepard—like the country itself—entered a period of retrenchment. In the fall of 1971 he took his family to London.

The writer in exile is a common feature of many national literatures, and Shepard keeps the esteemed company of Jack London, Ernest Hemingway, and F. Scott Fitzgerald as American authors who accomplished some of their most important work abroad. Shepard's contemporary, John Guare likewise took flight to England after his two one-acts *Home Fires* and *Cop-Out* failed on Broadway. Just as Guare's time in England had salubrious effect on his writing—he returned to New York with *The House of Blue Leaves*, the play that would establish his reputation and popular success—Shepard's London experience would mark a fertile and transitional period in his own career, one that contributed greatly to his maturation as a playwright and poet of the American experience.

Shepard had gone to England hoping to join a rock band; while this aspiration went unfulfilled, what he did find was a theatrical environment that encouraged and accelerated his development as a dramatist. American critic Robert Brustein, while serving as a reviewer for the London *Observer*, wrote glowingly of the city's theatre at the time and expressed his continued surprise at how play-going was enjoyed by Londoners of all classes and backgrounds. Brustein confirmed that London theatre was flourishing while New York theatre "was buckling at the knees."[3]

London in the 1970s indeed offered a highly variegated and often ambitious range of performance. Its West End theatre, which operated much in the manner of Broadway commercialism, numbered over forty houses.[4] Not just escapist in its fare, the West End produced and found profit in the works of numerous serious writers, including Stoppard, Pinter, Bolt, and Shaffer. Londoners as well enjoyed the work of two major state-supported theatres. With Peter Hall at its helm the Royal Shakespeare Company (RSC) had emerged in the sixties as an adventurous enterprise, controversial in both its aesthetics and politics, and gained itself worldwide acclaim. This time also saw the realization of the National Theatre, a state repertory company first headed by Laurence Olivier, which moved from the Old Vic to its South Bank facility in 1976. Beyond the city's commercial and institutional theatres, London experienced an explosion of experimental theatre that became known as "the fringe." Promoting an iconoclastic art in unconventional sites—basements, pubs, community centers—this movement came to the fore in the late sixties and engendered a score of new projects, including the Portable Theatre, Incubus, the Wherehouse Company, and the Pip Simmons Group. By 1972 over half of the new plays presented in England were staged by London's fringe companies.[5]

The London theatre in short boasted a rich and celebrated heritage—as the cradle of English-language drama—and a contemporary climate that drew widespread public support and fostered a sweeping array of dramatic fare, from the classics of William Shakespeare to the experiments of Heathcote Williams. If one views Shepard as an embattled (and somewhat embittered) writer staggering out of the tumult of the sixties, his stay in England may be regarded as a period of convalescence that provided him with the opportunity to stabilize his personal life and reconsider the nature of his writing.

One principal consequence of this London exile was the playwright's reassessment of dramatic art itself—its forms, conventions, and legacies. Although he admitted some familiarity with Williams and O'Neill, Shepard's literary heroes were almost exclusively from the avant-garde, such as American Beat writers Kerouac, Corso, and Ferlinghetti. Shepard recalls *Waiting for Godot* as one of the few plays he read in high school, and without question the absurdist sensibility of Samuel Beckett informed his early one-acts. Nevertheless, he would remark that Beckett had no more influence on his work than did Buddy Holly or Little Richard.[6] One may surmise that this cavalier and often disdainful view of traditional aesthetic forms (and intellectualism per se) stemmed in part from Shepard's modest educational background. He once contended that his arrogance prevented him from reading,[7] though he later admitted that fear more than pride kept him from the study of literature. During his London years, Shepard addressed his want of literary sophistication and began reading many of the "great" Western plays. He gave particular emphasis to Greek drama and in essence assumed the posture of a student.[8]

This time consequently gave the playwright a greater regard for craft and a new sense of workmanship. His experience in the London theatre proved an alternative to his days in the quixotic and often unruly arena of Off-Off Broadway. He in fact would speak disparagingly of the impulsive and irregular playing associated with café theatre and complained of "people throwing themselves against the walls in the name of freedom of expression."[9] Shepard came to appreciate the approach of British actors and found them "better equipped"[10] than their American counterparts. This insistence on the work and technique of theatre was reinforced by his acquaintanceship with Peter Brook, the visionary RSC director whose advice led Shepard to understand more fully the labor and intensive attention demanded by "great" art. The playwright recognized the instructive value of these influences and would credit the English theatre with remedying the loose habits he had developed in Greenwich Village.[11]

Above all, Shepard's London experience precipitated a cultural awakening for the playwright. In 1951 African American novelist James Baldwin—writing in Paris—conveyed some surprise at how the experience of being abroad had made him feel so acutely "American."[12] Twenty years later, Shepard would make much the same assertion, as his immersion in the unfamiliar customs of British life clarified his own sense of identity and person. In an interview the playwright announced that he was "rhythmically" an American, his "talk," his "walk, everything was American."[13] Given this sharpened awareness of cultural differences, his works in this period manifest a keen fascination with national heritage and the codes and myths that helped shape his distinctly American sensibility.

The United States has long intrigued the British, who regard the vastness and violence of America with both curiosity and distaste. Coincident with Shepard's stay in London, a restaurant in the Chelsea district capitalized on the lurid appeal of American culture. Serving hamburgers and milkshakes, the establishment named itself "The Great American Disaster" and wallpapered its interior with newspaper headlines announcing sensational incidents of twentieth-century American life.[14] (The restaurant had as its slogan: A great place [the United States] for hamburgers, but who would want to live there?) This fascination has oftentimes spilled over into the theatre, for Londoners have frequently displayed a support for American playwrights, even when their works found little approval in their home country. As recently as 1993 Arthur Miller's work, *The Last Yankee*, which received a lukewarm reception in New York, played to strong public and critical applause at the Duke of York's Theatre. In a similar manner,

Shepard's "Americanness" endeared his writing to the London theatre community, who relished with some prurience his checkered world of gangsters, saddle tramps, and rock-star wanna-bes.[15]

On a pragmatic level, Shepard's origins expedited his entry into London's fringe theatre, since many of the movement's key figures—Jim Haynes, Ed Berman, and Nancy Meckler—were American expatriates themselves (Haynes had arranged the 1967 Café La MaMa tour). Most prominent of the Americans in exile however was Charles Marowitz, who had arrived in London in 1956.[16] In his early years Marowitz taught American acting technique—"the method"—though he later rejected illusionistic theatre and established an alliance with Peter Brook, who employed Marowitz as assistant director for his stunning, Brechtian staging of *King Lear* (1962). Marowitz also joined Brook in the famous RSC "theatre of cruelty" workshop at the London Academy of Music and Dramatic Art, where Artaudian techniques were investigated in a rigorous laboratory format (this project came to fruition in Brook's 1964 landmark *Marat/Sade*). Committed to experimental work, in 1968 Marowitz appropriated a basement space on Tottenham Court Road and launched the Open Space Theatre, a company that in its first five years would produce over fifty world premieres,[17] including Marowitz's own *Hamlet*, the highly controversial and much discussed collage construction that reduced Shakespeare's play to a forty-minute performance piece.

While Marowitz had conversed with Shepard and had assisted him in finding an apartment for his family, the director was surprised when the playwright invited him to read his newly written script, *The Tooth of Crime*. La MaMa's European tours had brought Shepard's work to London, and the Open Space had itself staged *Red Cross*. Still, Marowitz had resisted, as he described it, the "Shepard hard-sell which had been emanating from the states."[18] Marowitz understood that his acquaintance's status in the American avant-garde would advance the Open Space's reputation as a prominent player in the London fringe. The director also recognized the risk of the undertaking; the theatre's financial state was at best precarious, and Marowitz surmised that *The Tooth of Crime* would mean little to an English audience. Marowitz nevertheless discerned the rare opportunity the play afforded: "[I] knew it was the most 'American' work that had come my way in a long time."[19]

Set in a dramatic realm that fuses rock culture and science fiction, *The Tooth of Crime* is dominated by one imposing piece of scenery, a nefarious looking black chair, which serves as an ominous emblem of the powers, pleasures, and pitfalls of rock stardom. The play's action depicts the cosmic "show down" between Hoss, the gifted "killer" who has labored to the top of the rock-gangster confederation, and Crow, the upstart rocker who pursues a renegade path to fame and glory. Living in a futuristic sort of Graceland, with movies, sauna, drugs, and women at his command, Hoss discovers himself immured within his celebrity. Terming himself "a trained slave,"[20] he recognizes his status as a cog-in-the-entertainment-machine and complains: "I'm a fucking industry. I even affect the stocks and bonds" (p. 225). Though *The Tooth of Crime* reiterates themes seen earlier in *Melodrama Play* and *Mad Dog Blues*, the work goes beyond Shepard's recurrent indictment of the artist's commodification and explores the complex matter of tradition and the individual talent.

The Tooth of Crime reveals Shepard at something of an aesthetic crossroads, and in the stances of the play's adversaries competing models of artistic production are set at odds. Hoss remarks that he was a lawbreaker before he became legitimate, and his career—much like that of Shepard himself—exhibits the artist's move from the avant-garde to the mainstream. Nonetheless, Hoss espouses a respect for aesthetic authority and recognizes that mastery comes from discipline and labor. He confesses as a youth he would have sold his "leathers" to have had "a crack at a good teacher" (p. 216). The Starman reminds Hoss: "You don't wanna be a fly-by-night mug in the crowd. You want something durable, something lasting" (p. 206), and Hoss, the rocker-killer, ironically stands as a defender of the canon. He believes that without a code, the rock-gangster performance is simply a crime—"No art involved. No technique, finesse. No sense of mastery" (p. 216).

Hoss's status as the top gun makes him the target of the mercurial Crow, the Gypsy Marker who lives by the mask, disregarding the conventions of rock-gangster warfare. Crow represents the threat of novelty and iconoclasm and is categorized by Hoss, who renounces the modish and the ephemeral, as one of many assorted "flash heads" (p. 213). Hoss, though, understands that an underground movement is taking form and that today's hit may become tomorrow's cliché. The confrontation between the two may be viewed as an expression of the avant-garde/canonical dialectic, and the Manichean nature of this struggle is displayed most graphically in the ensuing gladiator-style competition, in which guns, fists, and "shivs" are dismissed—performance itself becomes the weapon of choice.

Under the auspices of "the referee," Hoss and Crow each work to subdue the other through verbal assault and injurious gesture. Crow assumes an initial edge by launching a fusillade of fabricated accusations that slander Hoss's past and vilify his manhood; Hoss recovers and gains advantage by celebrating his performative origins. Recalling a litany of blues heroes, including Little Brother Montgomery, King Oliver, Ma Rainey, and Chuck Berry, he in essence gives Crow a history lesson—the history of rock and roll. Though shaken, Crow deflects the attack, spurns the past, and responds with nonchalance—"Very retrograde" (p. 237). Crow settles into a slithering, metamorphosing strut—getting "the image in line" (p. 240) as he calls it, and mounts his final charge, unleashing a wild invective that gains him a T.K.O. victory in the match.

Like Crow, the play wants to be flashy and at times disruptive. Shepard acknowledged the play's Brechtian influence, evident in the prominent musical sequences and unexpected presentational ploys (in one instance of alienation the minor characters appear as cheerleaders and bare their buttocks to the audience). Despite the play's verbal novelty and theatrical stunts, *The Tooth of Crime* is the most well-wrought and classically shaped of any of Shepard's efforts to this point, generally recognized as his first "finally balanced, entirely fulfilling masterwork."[21] In its agonistic encounter between Hoss and Crow, the old rocker versus the punk-outsider, the play for some critics recalled Shakespearean tragedy. The drama no doubt evokes a sense of tragic fatality as Starman and Galactic Jack caution Hoss and foreshadow his tumble from grace. Noting the classical aspect of the work, John Barber, in the *Daily Telegraph*, wrote that the story told in *The Tooth of Crime* was "as old as theatre itself."[22]

In *The Tooth of Crime* one sees a new sense of traditionalism in Shepard's writing. The playwright recognized much of himself in Crow, the iconoclast from the underground; yet, at this point Shepard had passed beyond his aesthetic apprenticeship and had begun to consider the value of craft, virtuosity, and established form. Leonard Wilcox has written most insightfully about the conflicting aesthetic stances of the play and argues that Crow represents a postmodern attitude, one fascinated with surfaces, style, and shifting, ever-combining images. Hoss, on the other hand, recalls a modernist temperament, one that values coherence, unity, and aesthetic standards.[23] Unlike the brashly irregular works of his early career, *The Tooth of Crime* exhibits a more stately demeanor and suggests Shepard's turn to the canonical. Confirming this perception, critic Michael Billington expressed disappointment that the drama did not break "new ground"; he termed it a "deeply old-fashioned work" and quipped that the play would "go straight to the heart of all theatrical conservatives."[24]

Marowitz was correct to discern the unique Americanness of the work, for the traditionalism of *The Tooth of Crime* has not only stylistic but nationalistic implications. This is obvious in the language of the piece, which is a dazzling amalgamation of American speech idioms drawn from sports vernacular, hoodlum slang, and musician jargon. In addition to the play's unmistakable American sound, *The Tooth of Crime* borrows wholesale from the distinctly American orders of late-night DJ's, dual-cam roadsters, and teen-gang rumbles. Although victory goes to Crow, it is perhaps the figure of Hoss himself that most effectively conveys the rudiments of an American character.

While the work may admit the ruthless inevitability of an image-driven future, Shepard portrays Hoss with great sympathy, especially in the handling of the elder rocker's suicide. Vanquished and demoralized, Hoss laments: "I'm pulled and pushed around from one image to another. Nothin' takes a solid form ... Where do I stand! Where the fuck do I stand!" (p. 243). In exchange for Hoss's turf, Crow agrees to update Hoss with a stylistic makeover. Hoss finally revolts under Crow's tutelage, rejects the lure of surface, and asserts the primacy of his own identity: "IT AIN'T ME!!" (p. 247). Hoss withdraws a pistol, puts the barrel in his mouth, and pulls the trigger, joining the ranks of James Dean, Duane Allman, and Jackson Pollock (heroes of Hoss and also of Shepard).

Hoss's denouncement of Crow should not be read as a slavish defense of convention for its own sake (or by extension Shepard's endorsement of American institutionalism). Hoss pays homage to the Keepers, the enigmatic rule makers and guardians of the charts, yet he contends that the system itself is not inviolable; genius can exist outside the game. What Hoss affirms is a commitment to art, to the mastery of craft. This appeal to integrity suggests an internal value system, and one notes the echo of David Reisman's important contrast between the inner and outer directed American.[25] The latter is a contemporary creature of corporate America whose self is fashioned according to group approbation and the ephemeral images of the media. The inner-directed American represents a pretechnological age and is characterized by self-motivation and internalized mores. This is the frontiersman, a type long cherished in American mythology, and Hoss's appeal to a code endows him with an odd nobility, even in defeat, and more importantly validates him as the genuine article—American individualism personified.

The confrontation between Hoss and Crow consequently becomes not simply a contest of aesthetics but a battle between time frames and cultural identities. Crow is an urbanite, all style and sheen, engendered by the multimedia images of mass communications. Hoss refers to Crow as a "master adapter" (p. 249). Hoss, to the contrary, voices an allegiance to the past—he is born of the blacktop and the blues—and when he chides his adversary, "You could use a little cow flop on yer shoes, boy" (p. 239), we note his connection with the land and his agrarian sensibility. Moreover, Hoss proves the American rocker, Crow the Brit (Hoss was performed by American playwright Michael Weller). Crow is described as a Keith Richards lookalike—foreign and exotic—with a swastika earring.

Despite the fact that the Open Space production of *The Tooth of Crime* did not win unanimous praise, it served for Shepard, a newcomer to London, as an effective calling card. However, a downside followed, evidenced in the strained relations between Marowitz and the playwright. Both strong-willed individuals, the two had gone head-to-head over interpretive matters (Shepard believed Marowitz's emphasis on spectacle and artifice detracted from the play's language and story). The animosity between the playwright and director inflated to such a degree that Shepard publicly avowed that he would never again allow the Open Space to produce one of his plays. The writer threatened a lawsuit and published an open letter venting his grievances. He criticized Marowitz for irregular attendance at rehearsals and for utilizing the same "high pressure tactics as the West End or Broadway."[26]

In the wake of his imbroglio with Marowitz, Shepard had a second dubious experience with *The Tooth of Crime*, this involving another idiosyncratic director—Richard Schechner. *The Tooth of Crime* received its American debut at Princeton's McCarter Theatre in November of 1972. Shortly thereafter, Shepard gave approval for the play to be presented in New York by Schechner's Performance Group, a company at the forefront of the American avant-garde. Both a theatre scholar and practitioner, Schechner had achieved notoriety by redefining the parameters of performance studies. A founding editor of the *Tulane Drama Review*, Schechner not only pursued theoretic work in ritual and spatial dynamics but tested his hypotheses in laboratory productions. As with Euripides' play *The Bacchae*, which Schechner transfigured into his notorious *Dionysus in 69*, Shepard's text served as something of a pretext, and *The Tooth of Crime* was fashioned into a piece of environmental theatre.

The Schechner production of *The Tooth of Crime* gave emphasis to the actor/audience interplay and the spatial dispersion of the play's action. The scenic design, which included numerous rails, pylons, and scaffoldings, encouraged an ambulatory experience in which both actors and audience members circulated throughout the theatre. Quite simply, Schechner's interest lay in the *mise en scène*, and Shepard's language was regarded as only one element of the performance event. Spalding Gray, who would later achieve acclaim for his autobiographical monologues (*Swimming to Cambodia* and others), won wide favor for his portrayal of the doomed Hoss. Though many reviewers lavished praise upon the production, Shepard withheld approval. Critic Irving Wardle aptly discerned the production as one working at cross purposes and noted that the Performance Group "unscrambled" the "precise literary shape" of Shepard's play according to its own "anti-literary bias."[27] Wardle praised Schechner's ensemble as the best American group he had seen since the Open Theatre but opined that their efforts had simply been directed to "the wrong play."

Shepard's experiences with the Open Space and the Performance Group indicate the writer's increased impatience with experimental performance companies, especially when his plays were used to advance an aesthetic agenda other than his own. Just as he had chafed under the impositions of New York's uptown theatre, the playwright at this point in his career felt some frustration with the avant-garde. He had been coopted by companies on both sides of the Atlantic and his plays treated as fodder for a director-centered order of performance. Though he had participated in collective contexts, most notably with Chaikin's Open Theatre, Shepard began to exhibit an increased protectiveness of his plays. Assuming a more conservative stance, Shepard became more text-centered in his approach and expressed a desire to "limit" the interpretations of his work (especially those he viewed as "lame" and "off the wall"). Lamenting that the oft-noted pop art features of his plays frequently encouraged directors "to go bananas,"[28] he asserted the playwright's pride of place and the preeminent status of the word.

Such litigious experiences no doubt contributed to Shepard's interest in the Royal Court, whose reputation as a writer's theatre was "unequaled by any other professional theatre operation in Great Britain."[29] Under the artistic direction of George Devine, the English Stage Company launched its first season at the Royal Court in 1956; its third production, John Osborne's *Look Back in Anger*, would stun the London theatre and recon-figure the course of the British drama for years to come. Osborne's work sounded a clarion call for young writers, and the Royal Court would put a remarkable host of British dramatists on the international map, including among others, John Arden, Ann Jellicoe, David Storey, Edward Bond, and Christopher Hampton. As a noncommercial theatre, the Royal Court often gave platform to a committed, fiery brand of drama born of working-class origins. The company's support of its writers and their right to free expression led to a monumental confrontation with the Lord Chamberlain in 1968 and the ultimate overthrow of England's censorship codes.

Outside of its main stage season, the Royal Court had essayed a number of formats to further its commitment to the playwright. In its first year of operation, the company launched its "Sunday night productions without decor" as a way of showcasing new scripts on a weekly basis. 1958 saw the initiation of the Writer's Group, which would include Arnold Wesker, Wole Soyinka, Edward Bond, and David Cregan. Nearly a decade later, this same impetus would lead to the opening of an experimental theatre space, the Theatre Upstairs, which served the Royal Court's younger generation of writers and their fringe sensibility.

Even before his arrival in London, Shepard's reputation held currency with the group. Director Nicholas Wright had mounted a staged reading of *Red Cross* in 1968.[30] In 1969 *La Turista* was selected as the second offering in the Theatre Upstairs's inaugural 1969 season, a choice that highlights the American writer's perceived status as a trend-setting young dramatist. Directed by Roger Hendricks-Simon, an Open Space veteran, the show exhibited the scenery of John Napier, who would later achieve fame as designer for such blockbuster hits as *Les Misérables*, *Miss Saigon*, and *Sunset Boulevard*. The production curiously emphasized the Ameri-canness of the play. American actors were employed, and the piece was promoted as a "poetic and theatrical image of an undeniable, here-and-now, uniquely American madness."[31]

Tony Richardson, who had staged John Osborne's first plays and had served as Devine's principal associate from the company's inception, had met Shepard some years before and facilitated his involvement with the company.[32] As a fiercely independent theatre with a passionate commitment to original work, the Royal Court well matched Shepard's temperament and outlook. The playwright also felt at ease with the directors he encountered, especially the Australian Jim Sharman, who approached Shepard with the idea of reviving *The Unseen Hand* in the Theatre Upstairs. Both foreign born, the two shared a rocker spirit, an outback sensibility, and their compatibility quelled Shepard's concern that his work might be pirated for ulterior aims. Sharman's deft and energetic direction contributed to the successful production of *The Unseen Hand* (March, 1973), which made a splash in London theatre circles and was recalled years later as a triumph for the city's alternative theatre.

According to Martin Esslin, the Royal Court served as a "home" for Shepard,[33] and the playwright's liaison with the theatre provided him the opportunity to work with first-rate young talent of the British stage. The company also proved willing to nurture, even indulge, his artistic license. He was commissioned by the Neville Blond Fund to write a new play for the Royal Court, and upon the script's completion, the company obliged Shepard's request that he be allowed to direct the work's premiere production, this despite the fact that he had never directed before. His next production at the Royal Court, *Geography of a Horse Dreamer*, thus displayed the artist in the dual role of playwright/director; it also manifested his latest avocational obsession—greyhound racing.

When Shepard and his family arrived in London they first settled in the Shepherd's Bush district, a working-class neighborhood known for its White City Stadium, the site of the 1908 Olympic trials. The structure had been converted to a greyhound track, and the playwright thus found easy access to the dog races. This new interest recalled for Shepard his youthful experience in California working at the Santa Anita horse track. It also provided him much enjoyment, and he took great delight in the excitement, color, and broad appeal of the event—a point that discloses something important about Shepard's vision (and pleasure) of the performative moment as a phenomenon born of competitive fury, celebrating sinew and speed.

Shepard's fondness for greyhound racing would lead him to purchase his own dog, which he named Keywall Spectre.[34] More than an investment, the dog lived with the family in their later Hampstead flat. Upon its demise Shepard eulogized the animal, praising its beauty and killer instinct, in a feature for *Time Out*,[35] the London publication that had proven the most adamant backer of the playwright's work.

As a precursor to *Geography of a Horse Dreamer*, Shepard wrote a short piece, *Blue Bitch*, for presentation on BBC's "Open House" series. The play involves an American couple—Cody and Dixie—residing in England, who attempt to negotiate the sale of their greyhound bitch. A cockney milkman is enjoined for assistance, and after a period of racetrack conversation the milkman transforms into a growling doglike beast.[36] The play achieves no real resolution but succeeds in conveying a communicative breakdown and the clash between British and American cultures, an issue the playwright would explore more fully in his next play.

In a season that included Athol Fugard's *Sizwe Banzi Is Dead* and Ann Jellicoe's *Jelliplays* (two plays for children), *Geography of a Horse Dreamer* offered the Royal Court patron a taste of the American popular imagination found in gangster movies, TV Westerns, and detective pulp fiction. First performed in the Theatre Upstairs on February 21, 1974, *Geography of a Horse Dreamer* displayed the work of two performers who would gain international recognition in film. Bob Hoskins, later star of *The Long Good Friday*, *Mona Lisa*, and *Who Framed Roger Rabbit?*, played the role of Santee. Cody, the work's cowboy-artist-hero, was performed by Stephen Rea, the actor celebrated for his sympathetic portrayal of an IRA defector in *The Crying Game*.

The plot of the piece pits Cody, a Wyoming sheep rancher who can "dream" the outcome of horse races, against a mercenary group of lowlifes seeking to profit from his extraordinary powers. Kidnapped and kept under constant surveillance, Cody has begun to lose his prophetic accuracy, and Act One depicts two of the gangsters, Santee and Beaujo, in a down-and-out British hotel, guarding Cody and lamenting his fall from grace. Near the end of the act, Cody recovers his gift, though greyhounds have supplanted horses in his dreams; the play's second act finds the entourage in more lavish surroundings, indicating Cody's success at forecasting winners at the dog track. In a surprising turn of events, Fingers, the supposed leader of the gang, becomes guilt-ridden by Cody's incarceration and determines to give the dreamer his freedom. His ominous companion (the Doctor, a Sydney Greenstreet look-alike) interdicts this plan, however, and threatens a lethal surgical procedure, one that would transplant Cody's neckbone—the locus of Cody's powers—into Beaujo. Cody's brothers, Jason and Jasper, draw the play to an abrupt ending when they burst into the room with shotguns and six-guns blasting and rescue Cody, declaring they will return the dreamer to his home.

In his depiction of Cody, Shepard's concern with the artist's subjection to the marketplace gives way to rumination upon the creative impulse itself. His first efforts in playwriting have always been described by the playwright in terms of spontaneity and intuition; he once compared himself to one who "whittled" and "all of a sudden discovered he could make sculpture."[37] In *Geography of a Horse Dreamer* this rhapsodic mode of creation is given analogue in the phenomenon of dreaming, the sign of Cody's gift. Yet, recalling his early dreams, Cody states, "It was accidental. It just sort of came to me outa' the blue . . . At first it's all instinct. Now it's work."[38] A writer in midcareer, Shepard had come to recognize the fickleness of inspiration, and Cody's complaint may suggest the author's maturing and sometimes uneasy relationship with his own muse. As

Beaujo notes, the "touch" can prove elusive, and the play's tacit acknowledgement that impulse alone may at times not suffice indicates Shepard's growth as a writer and increased self-consciousness of his aesthetic craft.

With an eclectic mix of character types, surprise plot twists, and unmotivated behavioral turns, *Geography of a Horse Dreamer* still exhibits the wildly spontaneous side of Shepard's artistry. The piece functions as a postmodern parody of American cinema whose patchwork language consists of cowpoke talk, racetrack slang, and underworld lingo. Despite the irregularity and whimsy of the work, *Geography of a Horse Dreamer* is in many ways a very conventional play. It harkens back to a popular American stage comedy of the 1930s, *Three Men on a Horse*, which also involved horseracing, gangsters, and prognostication. The piece has a discernible conflict and what one London critic called "old-fashioned plot development."[39] Given the traditional features of the play, London audiences found it more comprehensible than Shepard's other works. Writing in *The Financial Times* (no ally of the avant-garde), B. A. Young praised this turn in the dramatist's career: "The less experimental Mr. Shepard becomes—and I found some of his earlier plays hard to penetrate—the better I like him."[40]

Geography of a Horse Dreamer is very much a play of yearning, of a quest for substance and solidity. If one correlates dreaming with art making, the aesthetic enterprise is here shown to be intimately linked to place. Cody's dreams are bound to locale—Cody dreams American dreams. His ability to forecast horseraces is originally tied to his Wyoming home and its bucolic environs. Having been abducted and divorced from the wellspring of his powers, Cody must labor to manufacture an "internal environment." To coax the restoration of his dreams, his handlers force-feed him Americana, playing American record albums *ad nauseum*. The themes of tradition, geography, and identity coalesce in the play, suggesting that poetic art owes more to "grounding" than flight of fancy.

In Act Two, Fingers delivers a lengthy monologue detailing his visit to Wyoming:

> I remember thinking this is the West! This is really The West! . . . So vast and lonely. Just the brisk cold night blowing in through the hotel window. And outside, the blue peaks of the Big Horn mountains. The moon shining on their snowy caps. The prairie stretching out and out like a great ocean. I felt that God was with me then. The earth held me in its arms. (p. 301)

While the passage deals heavily in hyperbole and satire, its importance should not be underestimated. Fingers's recitation directs attention to a key element in *Geography of a Horse Dreamer*, the invocation of the American West. Like Cody, Shepard himself has drawn his inspiration from the Western experience, and his time in London served to accentuate his regard for geography and the sensibility of place. With some justification one may argue that in casting a glance back across the Atlantic, Shepard envisaged not the America of the conflagrant sixties but the country of a century past.

Writing that "the idea of the nation is inseparable from its narration,"[41] Geoffrey Bennington discusses how national identity is often conveyed through stories of origins, founding fathers, and heroes. While the settlement of the West involves a specific historical period in U.S. history, the images and outlooks of the West have extended beyond the conditions of this era and have taken form in myth and legend. Quite simply, the "story" of the frontier—and its implicit value system—has emerged as a dominant one in the narration of the nation. It has taken the status of a foundational moment—an origin—in the creation of an American identity. Shepard's deployment of Western motifs, even as he reconstitutes its iconography, consequently links the playwright with a deep-rooted notion of Americanness and imbues his work with a resonance that echoes long-held notions of the national character. This aspect of Shepard's writing assumes even greater prominence in his later plays, whose surreal expressions of American family life would catapult the playwright to his preeminence in the U.S. theatre.

If *Geography of a Horse Dreamer* wears its patriotism on its sleeve, it is because Cody not only faces the loss of his gift but the loss of his cultural identity. He complains that the foreign cities of his captivity have "poisoned" his dreams, and when he begins speaking in an Irish accent, one notes the full extent of his assimilation to the British Isles. As Jasper and Jason break into the room and liberate their brother, Shepard quotes the Saturday afternoon matinee and the cavalry's carefully timed, heroic arrivals. Though the effect is comic, the *deus ex machina* moment is as much patriotic as parodic. These characters are no "dime-store" cowboys but "men"—standing "about six foot five" (p. 306)—who rescue Cody from the Brits and their effete, bejeweled ringleader. The "happy," even chauvinistic, ending tagged onto the play is not without ironies: Cody blathers in a dissociative state as the brothers lead him from the room, his recovery remaining an open question. Still, the play closes with a distinctly American flourish: the lights fade to the Southern Louisiana music of Clifton Chenier.

Shepard's visibility in the city's theatre grew steadily over the course of his London residency. In March of 1974 his one-act *Little Ocean* was performed in a late-night format at the Hampstead Theatre Club. Given the writer's interest in American manhood, *Little Ocean* stands as an anomaly in his career. A free-wheeling affair described as a "45 minute fantasia,"[42] the play depicts three female characters extemporizing on subjects that range from childbirth to Cuban cigars. Directed by Stephen Rea, the production included O-lan in its cast and was something of a lark for the playwright. The writer's increased recognition and the proliferation of the Shepard camp also led to various revivals. *Cowboy Mouth* was staged by the Tricycle Theatre Company, a fringe group founded by Kenneth Chubb (who would prove a strong and persistent advocate of the playwright's work). Outside of his growing exposure in the London fringe, Shepard received wide attention when the Royal Court decided to produce *The Tooth of Crime*, even though the play had premiered in London less than two years earlier.

The Tooth of Crime was the first of Shepard's plays to be given full production in the Royal Court's four-hundred-seat main stage house. Publicity materials highlighted "the fight" between Hoss and Crow and advertised the play as "the Three Round Entertainment Bout of the Century."[43] The Royal Court sought again to match Shepard's work with Jim Sharman, who had so adroitly staged *The Unseen Hand* in the Theatre Upstairs. Having directed the London production of *Jesus Christ Superstar*, Sharman had become something of a hot item, and his recent Royal Court staging of *The Rocky Horror Show* (starring Tim Curry) had proven a great success. *The Tooth of Crime* followed easily on the heels of the campy, youth culture send-up of Hollywood horror flicks. Sharman, in fact, employed the same design team, and Richard O'Brien, the author of *The Rocky Horror Show*, who had played Willie in *The Unseen Hand*, was cast as Crow. Seen as something of an encore to the rock/sex antics of *Rocky Horror's* Dr. Frank N. Furter, the Royal Court production of *The Tooth of Crime* was universally deemed superior to that of the Open Space Theatre, and the attention it generated lifted the playwright to the peak of his London acclaim.

Even though these years in England brought Shepard much personal enjoyment and professional recognition, the plays of this period exhibit a strong awareness of change and loss. Shepard felt a keen sense of cultural displacement throughout his stay, and this period for the artist was not just reflective but also retrospective. It is not surprising that his works from this period should exhibit strains of disappointment and nostalgia, for the early seventies witnessed much disenchantment in American culture. With a populace wearied by the many upheavals of the sixties, the early years of the decade saw the dissipation of revolutionary fervor and a reactionary shift in national mood. The two-term presidency of Richard Nixon—a consummate 1950s politician—in large measure resulted from the electorate's communal wish for the idealized security of a bygone day. The country indeed experienced a wave of 50s *redux*: *Grease* proved a Broadway hit, the group Sha Na Na enjoyed immense popularity, and a number of TV shows (including "Laverne and Shirley" and "Happy Days") portrayed American life in a simpler, more innocent time, one in which "people were proud to be Americans."[44]

Though Shepard's London plays by and large avoid sentimentality, their appeal to the past, while not facile or without ironic dimension, does reveal the dramatist's concern with a heritage lost. His work abroad seems less enthralled with the rush of heteroglossia, less urgent in its need to shock or disrupt. In a Bakhtinian sense, these plays reveal a centripetal pull, evident in the playwright's increased attention to canonical forms. This is also apparent in his sharpened sense of nation and the American self. In sum, Shepard at this time took a conservative turn and investigated images and instances of cohesion in American culture—a shared sense of story and site—even while he recognized their imminent decline or disappearance altogether.

While *The Tooth of Crime* was in rehearsal, Shepard saw The Who in concert and wrote a review of the event for *Time Out*. In this piece he emphasized the primal bond he felt when thousands of spectators joined together in singing "The Pinball Wizard"; no theatrical performance, Shepard argued, could elicit that electric moment of mass solidarity. His confession of a "weird cynicism"[45] concluded the article, an admission that may on one hand simply reflect his growing homesickness for the States. The declaration may however betray a more profound apprehension, one that bears upon the limits of American culture and the very possibility of community itself.

The last play written in his London residency, *Action*, returned the playwright to the unconventional stylistics of the European absurdist theatre. Just as it appeared that Shepard's work might be moving toward an increased degree of narrative lucidity, he composed an antidrama of dislocated and circuitous enactments. In essence, *Action* portrays a world without teleology, a world where Aristotelian "action" is conspicuously absent. Though the work seems an about-face from *The Tooth of Crime*, Shepard's overture to classical drama, the play retains, perhaps in even more conspicuous fashion, a yearning for shared belief. *Action* in essence follows a strategy of *via negativa*—its denial of coherent structure and accessible meaning aggravates the very desire for such.

The scholar Kenneth Burke some time ago encouraged a form of criticism that views literature as "equipment for living,"[46] and in light of Shepard's growing restiveness regarding his remove from American soil, *Action* may be seen as an aesthetic gesture of longing. Just as Cody expresses his need for landmarks, the characters in *Action* are all afflicted by a hunger for contexts and connections. Shepard's own anxiety is betrayed by the fact that he returned to the United States even before the play's opening at the Royal Court in September of 1974.

Though the piece gives attention to the fascinating innner lives of its characters, the chief concern of the work is not with individual psyches but with the spaces "between" the characters. *Action* is about dialogue— that is, the contexts and structures that allow for social intercourse. Set in the aftermath of a vaguely defined crisis, *Action* depicts the benighted existence of two men and two women sharing the cramped confines of a remote cabin. Dominated by "a plain board table with four wooden chairs"[47] the spartan living quarters afford Shepard a laboratory for the inspection of communal behavior, as his characters live in wintry isolation, divorced from outward society, beset by hunger, paranoia, and dwindling expectations.

Like the order of Beckett's *Endgame*, this realm seems on the verge of extinction (lights fade during the course of the show), a condition which emphasizes the inhabitants' various attempts at outreach. A number of "actions" or performative exercises are highlighted in the course of the piece. The character Shooter "plays" at being a circus bear. Lupe dances a soft-shoe shuffle. Such behaviors evoke a heightened degree of self-consciousness and anxiety. After completing her dance, Lupe remarks: "It was like somebody was watching me. Judging me . . . Chalking up points . . . And then it turned into murder" (p. 174). Performative gestures function alternately as acts of personal assertion and tentative efforts toward contact. For these individuals, who vacillate between myopic self-regard and obsessive attention to the other, communication itself seems in jeopardy of expiring.

Shepard's central point of investigation surfaces when the characters discuss the meaning of "community." Unable to define the word, Lupe stammers: "A sense of—A sense um— . . . Something uh—" (p. 183). The ineffable nature of the term points to the greater difficulty of maintaining relationships in actuality. One finds that the problematic status of community issues in large measure from the characters' loss of a shared culture, specifically an American culture. The world of the play has been called "a post American limbo,"[48] and in this austere and colorless no-man's-land America is evoked only through memory and disemboweled ritual. One of the few scenic pieces of the play is that of a Christmas tree, which together with the group's minimalistic turkey dinner serves to present an emptied image of holiday celebration. The recession of cultural identity moreover informs Lupe's query, "Remember the days of mass entertainment?" (p. 182). With fondness, Jeep speaks of Judy Garland, Gene Kelly, and Fred Astaire. Early in the play Jeep recalls a room he once occupied, which held a number of highly charged American images, including pictures of "an antelope on a yellow prairie" and the Golden Gate Bridge. (p. 170). These iconic images—from the prairie, to the ocean white with foam—exist as disparate impressions in Jeep's memory yet retain a mythic resonance, evoking a sense of past fullness *vis-à-vis* the vitiated present.

During the course of the play the audience witnesses many bizarre occurrences. Lupe chews ravenously upon her arm; Shooter crawls on hands and knees with a stuffed chair riding his back. Such stunts engaged the particular skills of the production's director, Nancy Meckler, an American native who had cultivated a highly physical performance style in her years leading Café La MaMa/Wherehouse workshops in London. Meckler's staging capitalized upon the seething energy of the piece and accentuated the quirky theatrics for which the writer's plays are famous. In *Action*, however, Shepard's idiosyncratic stage business works somewhat differently from that of his earlier pieces. The bits here serve less to assert a performed, phenomenal presence than to reveal a contextual absence. This perhaps is most clear in the emasculated behaviors of Jeep and Shooter, who seem unable to complete any significant undertaking.

Like the beleaguered Hoss, who witnesses the erosion of his social order, Jeep and Shooter long for certitude in a world where the grounds for action have become problematic. In *West of Everything* Jane Tompkins underscores the assuredness and the earnestness with which the cowboy approaches his work; indeed, for Tompkins, the allure of the Western genre derives from the unitary experience of its hero, whose thought, desire, and deed are one. By living in "the fully saturated moment,"[49] the cowboy in essence knows purposeful action. By contrast the nebulous world of Jeep and Shooter lacks straightforward and identifiable obstacles (no cattle drives or warfaring "Injuns") and standards by which one's efforts might be gauged. We note how the two, when not paralyzed by self-preoccupations, vainly attempt gestures of assertion. Jeep repeatedly vents his frustration by smashing dinner-table chairs; he launches a verbal assault upon Lupe after her dance sequence. Shooter lectures on how to clean a fish.

This realm's lack of fixed structures has a particularly corrosive effect on the pair's sense of manhood, and the two thus labor to recuperate a Western machismo. Early in the play, Jeep recalls a picture of himself posed with a gun. The two also follow a butch dress code: they wear lumberjack shirts and heavy work boots; their heads are shaved. At one point, the frontier experience is invoked in reverie. Shooter details a string of exhilarating outdoor images: "My head imagines forests! Chain saws! Hammers and nails in my ears!" (p. 184). This imaginative outburst is ironically counterpointed by Shooter's immobility and his promise never to rise from his armchair. As the men chafe, brood, and flail, the women cook, sweep, and hang clothes to dry; the tenuous masculinity of Jeep and Shooter seems to demand Lupe and Liza consignment to rigid sex-role performance.[50]

Near the conclusion of *Action* Jeep relates his one-time imprisonment in a juvenile detention center and expresses how the experience changed his point of reference. He tells of discovering "Something bigger. Bigger than family. Bigger than school. Bigger than the 4-H Club. Bigger than Little League Baseball" (p. 189). This passage raises an Orwellian image of modern society, where no detail escapes bureaucratic control. The play's close finds Jeep gripped by a state of panic, and the ending of *Action* thus issues an indictment against institutionalism and the repressions it breeds. This moment may on some level express Shepard's wary regard of centralized authority and its particular manifestation in the American welfare state. Yet, in *Action* the dislocated, abstracted existence of the characters (outside of all system) begs the question: Where do Americans turn for values and community?

In his tempestuous New York days Shepard had purchased a farm in Nova Scotia and had more than once considered applying for Canadian citizenship.[51] It is hard to imagine that any place in Canada could have proven as galvanizing a force in his development as did the city of London. There the playwright gained increased appreciation for the master skills of the theatre and its traditions. England also provided Shepard a fertile vantage point for consideration of his homeland.

In view of its failing institutions and despondent national spirit, Shepard recoiled from the American post-sixties scene and its condition of drift. It is revealing that *The Tooth of Crime*, *Geography of a Horse Dreamer*, and *Action* are not set in the present-day United States. It is also telling that each play conveys the sense of a past fullness that has been surrendered. In *Action* Jeep relates that his room once held a picture of Walt Whitman (wearing an overcoat); Whitman is later described as a writer "who expected something from America" (p. 179). Jeep's allusion is noteworthy, for Shepard himself has always held strong convictions about the nature of his country. The nationalistic evocations of these plays thus invite speculation regarding the playwright's vision of America. What are the constituents of this conception? How, for Shepard, do mythologies of the past bear upon the politics of the present? In what parts do his dramas mix satire and sentimentality? Regardless of how one chooses to address such questions, there can be little doubt that Sam Shepard's time as an American in exile contributed in an indispensible way to the identity of Sam Shepard, the Great American Playwright.

NOTES

1. Shepard, quoted in Samuel G. Freedman, "Sam Shepard's Mythic Vision of the Family," *New York Times*, 1 December 1985, sec. 2, p. 20.

2. Cited in Don Shewey, *Sam Shepard* (New York: Dell, 1985), 75.

3. Robert Brustein, *The Culture Watch* (New York: Alfred A. Knopf, 1975), 51.

4. Cited in Peter Roberts, *Theatre in Britain* (London: Pitman Publishing, 1973), 12.

5. Cited in John Elsom, *Post-War British Theatre* (London: Routledge & Kegan Paul, 1979), 147.

6. Shepard, cited in Stephen Fay, "The Silent Type," *Vogue*, 4 February 1985, 216.

7. Shepard discusses his education in Jonathan Cott, "The Rolling Stone Interview: Sam Shepard," *Rolling Stone*, 18 December 1986, 170.

8. Shepard's knowledge of dramatic literature and his reading of classical texts is covered in Henry Schvey, "The Master and His Double: Eugene O'Neill and Sam Shepard," *Journal of Dramatic Theory and Criticism* 5, no. 2 (1991): 49–60.

9. Shepard, quoted in Michael White, "Underground Landscapes," *Manchester Guardian*, 20 February 1974, 8.

10. Ibid.

11. W. J. Weatherby, "Rile 'Em, Cowboy," *Guardian*, 4 June 1991, 7.

12. James Baldwin, "The Discovery of What It Means to Be an American," *New York Times Book Review*, 25 January 1959, 14.

13. Interview recounted in Michiko Kakutani, "Myths, Dreams, Realities—Sam Shepard's America," *New York Times,* 29 January 1984, sec. 2, p. 26.

14. Brustein, *The Culture Watch*, 63.

15. The British fascination with Shepard is discussed in Steven Putzel, "An American Cowboy on the English Fringe," *Modern Drama* 36, no. 1 (1993): 131–46.

16. Charles Marowitz recounts his London experience in *Burnt Bridges* (London: Hodder & Stoughton, 1990).

17. Cited in Roberts, *Theatre in Britain*, 147.

18. Charles Marowitz, "Sam Shepard: Sophisticate Abroad," *Village Voice*, 7 September 1972, 59.

19. Ibid.

20. Sam Shepard, *The Tooth of Crime*, in *Seven Plays* (New York: Bantam Books, 1981), 225. Further citations indicated within the text.

21. John Glore, "The Canonization of Mojo Rootface: Sam Shepard Live at the Pantheon," *Theatre* 12, no. 3 (1981): 55.

22. John Barber, "Pop-Singer Drama Strains Too Much," *Daily Telegraph*, 18 July 1972, n.p.

23. See Leonard Wilcox, "Modernism vs. Postmodernism: Shepard's *The Tooth of Crime* and the Discourse of Popular Culture," *Modern Drama* 30, no. 4 (1987): 560–73.

24. Michael Billington, review of *The Tooth of Crime*, *Guardian*, 6 June 1974, n.p.

25. See David Reisman, *The Lonely Crowd* (New Haven, CT: Yale University Press, 1950), 29–32.

26. Shepard, quoted in Kenneth Chubb, "Fruitful Difficulties of Directing Shepard," *Theatre Quarterly* 15, no. 4 (1974): 22.

27. Irving Wardle, review of *The Tooth of Crime*, *London Times*, 4 September 1974, sec. C, p. 9.

28. Shepard, quoted in Amy Lippman, "Interview: A Conversation with Sam Shepard," *Harvard Advocate* 117, no. 1 (1983): 3.

29. Bill Harbin, in Bill Harbin and Gresdna Doty, eds., *Inside the Royal Court Theatre, 1956–1981* (Baton Rouge: Louisiana State University Press, 1990), 1. Harbin's introduction provides an excellent survey on the history and evolution of the Royal Court.

30. Nicholas Wright, "Shepard's Asphalt Jungle," *The Irish Times*, 29 April 1981, n.p.

31. Ronald Hastings, "Plays and Players," *Daily Telegraph*, 15 March 1969, n.p.

32. Cited in Fay, "The Silent Type," 19.

33. Martin Esslin, quoted in Harbin and Doty, *Inside the Royal Court Theatre*, 76.

34. Cited in Kenneth Chubb, "Sam Shepard's London," *Canadian Theatre Review* 10 (1976): 121.

35. Cited in Chris Peachment, "American Hero," *Time Out*, 23–29 August 1984, 15.

36. Plot summary given in Patrick J. Fennell, "Shepard's Lost Sheep," in Kimball King, ed., *Sam Shepard: A Casebook* (New York: Garland, 1989), 8–9.

37. Shepard, quoted in Fay, "The Silent Type," 213.

38. Sam Shepard, *Geography of a Horse Dreamer*, in *Fool for Love and Other Plays* (New York: Bantam Books, 1984), 285. Further citations indicated within the text.

39. Irving Wardle, "Review: *Geography of a Horse Dreamer*," *London Times*, 22 February 1974, n.p.

40. B. A. Young, "Theatre Upstairs: *Geography of a Horse Dreamer*," *Financial Times*, 22 February 1974, n.p.

41. Geoffrey Bennington, "Postal Politics and the Institution of the Nation," in Homi K. Bhaba, ed., *Nation and Narration* (New York: Routledge, 1990), 132.

42. Irving Wardle, "Little Ocean," *London Times*, 27 March 1974, 11.

43. Promotional materials for *The Tooth of Crime* found in the Royal Court files of the Covent Garden Theatre Museum.

44. J. Ronald Oakley, *God's Country: America in the Fifties* (New York: Dembner Books, 1986), 434. Oakley examines the wave of fifties nostalgia in pages 428–29.

45. Sam Shepard, "News Blues," *Time Out*, 31 May 1974, 7.

46. Kenneth Burke, *The Philosophy of Literary Form* (Berkeley: University of California Press, 1974), 292–304.

47. Sam Shepard, *Action*, in *Fool for Love and Other Plays*, 169. Further citations are indicated within the text.

48. Michael Coveney, "Action," *Plays and Players*, November 1974, 29.

49. Jane Tompkins, *West of Everything* (New York: Oxford University Press, 1992), 14.

50. This feature of the play is insightfully discussed in David Savran, "Sam Shepard's Conceptual Prison: *Action* and the Unseen Hand," *Theatre Journal* 36, no. 1 (1984): 57–73.

51. Cited in Shewey, *Sam Shepard*, 85.

Chapter 4

The Return of the Native

It has been argued that the era known as the sixties in America ended somewhere around 1972–74.[1] If we accept this periodization, then Shepard returned from England to find the United States entering a new era. By this time the country was experiencing an ignominious conclusion to the Vietnam War, the Watergate scandal (and resultant resignation of an American president), and a demoralized national economy—by 1975, the country would experience its highest jobless rate since 1941.[2] These approximate events hastened the demise of counterculture utopianism; they also signify the decline of the paradigms that had fashioned national consciousness following World War II. The nation-state, which had reached ascendance in 1950s America and had dominated postwar international relations, mushroomed in the next decade into a vast military/government/industrial complex whose inadequacies were exposed by civil unrest, racial violence, and an unsuccessful colonial war. It was clear by the early 1970s that the Great Society was unattainable and that the liberalism of the sixties had run its course.

As well intentioned as welfare-state policy may have been, at its core it assumed an assimilationist understanding of American culture—*let us help others to be like us*—and held an unspoken faith in middle-class values and comforts. Moreover, as Joel Krieger has suggested, the welfare state, seen stripped of its cloak of idealism, operated on the principle of appeasement.[3] To sustain an expanding and often exploitive national economy, the government increased and institutionalized entitlements, mitigating threats to national consensus by placating those most marginalized (for example, the poor, the elderly, and the racially oppressed).

As the fiscal pressures and philosophical challenges of the post-Vietnam era began to weaken the institutions and ideologies of the welfare state, notions of common purpose and national attachment came under revision.

The dispersive impulse toward subgroup identity that had begun in the sixties came to full realization at this time, and we note a shift in cultural perspective from the broad to the particular. While Michael Novak proclaimed the 1970s "the decade of the ethnics,"[4] these years exhibited the wider diversification of group consciousness and identifications based in not only ethnicity but also race, religion, class, gender, and sexual orientation. *Roe v. Wade* in 1973, for instance, and the push for an equal rights amendment indicated the rising profile of American women (and their power as a voting bloc). Following the Stonewall riots of 1969, the gay and lesbian community became increasingly politicized and brought issues of homosexuality into mainstream conversation. Werner Sollors has written that this period marks the demise of "assimilationist hope,"[5] and the decade thus witnessed the contestation and critique of American identity, along with an unprecedented interest in exploring and celebrating one's individual origins and existence outside of national definition.

When one considers that Shepard could have settled virtually anywhere in the United States, it is telling that the playwright bypassed the major urban media centers of New York and Los Angeles and opted for the San Francisco Bay Area. His desire to get back to his roots had informed his departure from London, and indeed returning to the West Coast provided him greater contact with his family (his mother, sisters, and in-laws lived in California). His return also allowed him to reconnect with the state itself: its topography, outdoor lifestyle, and Western sensibility.

Due to the financial strain attending his relocation, the playwright took employment as a construction worker and moved in with his in-laws in Marin County, just north of San Francisco.[6] Once established, he settled his family in a suburban tract house in Corte Madera and soon leased a small ranch, the Flying Y. He labored to upgrade the property, repairing its domicile and mending fences, and soon began to pursue his dream of raising Appaloosa horses. His new California life gave him opportunity to live out a cowboy regimen; he relished the physical demands of the Flying Y and even began participating in local rodeo events. Shepard once declared, "If I'm at home anywhere it's in the West,"[7] and his plays of this period consequently take an inward turn, expressing a preoccupation with origins, identity, and regional roots.

While Lanford Wilson had by this time experienced a Broadway success in *Hot l Baltimore* and had seen the work spawn a TV sitcom, Shepard almost by choice sought a position of obscurity. The playwright consciously avoided the high-pressure contexts of U.S. commercial entertainment and saw San Francisco as fertile territory for his personal aesthetic enterprise (which included the hope of starting a company). In *Angel City* and *True West*, Shepard deploys Northern California as a foil to the mercenary world of Hollywood, and indeed the Bay Area for many years had provided a climate supportive of experimental performance, evident most notably in the work of the San Francisco Actor's Workshop and the San Francisco Mime Troupe. Furthermore, home of Ferlinghetti's City Lights Books, the city had been the West Coast mecca of the Beat writers, Shepard's aesthetic forebears, and the playwright's station in San Francisco thus marked his return to a seminal source of his avant-garde sensibility.

Bob Dylan's imminent concert tour of the Northeast—what became known as the Rolling Thunder Review—unexpectedly drew Shepard to New York shortly after he had gained oversight of the Flying Y. This surprise invitation had come upon the recommendation of the director Jacques Levy, who had known the playwright from their Off-Off Broadway days and with whom Dylan had cowritten "The Ballad of Rubin Carter." Shepard was brought aboard as the scriptwriter for an anticipated film project, which due to the anarchic nature of the tour never materialized. Though the film was abandoned, he throughout the journey maintained a collage-style diary that would later be published as the *Rolling Thunder Logbook* (1977), a work characterized by one reviewer as a "particularly interesting addition to a particularly uninteresting literary genre, the rock-tour-as-mythic-quest-narrative."[8]

Running throughout the fall of 1975, the Rolling Thunder Review followed a helter-skelter, carnivalesque trek through New England and may be seen as a last-gasp expression of the counterculture mindset. The tour evinced an activist spirit, as the effort aimed to publicize the plight of Rubin "Hurricane" Carter, a boxer imprisoned upon a questionable murder charge. Hyped as a "return to the sixties,"[9] the project also spurred a reunion of folk-rock and literary figures including, among others, Joni Mitchell, Roger McGuinn, Joan Baez, and Allen Ginsberg.

Shepard's logbook reveals both an astonishment with and cynicism toward the business and promotional aspects of the enterprise. He reports the amenities lavished upon the entourage (Valiums delivered to hotel rooms) and often conveys contempt toward the managers, handlers, groupies, and "parasites" besetting the tour. The logbook takes some delight in the unpredictable antics of the musicians themselves; Shepard, for example, writes of guitarist T. Bone Burnett driving golf balls on the lawn of the Biltmore mansion. However, the focus of the playwright's journal is above all Dylan himself, who with boot heel grinding to the beat ignited his concert audience with a mesmerizing, charismatic performance Shepard likened to an Arapaho rain dance.

Despite Shepard's high regard for the musician, he found Dylan impenetrable, and no great friendship resulted between the two. The logbook often reflects upon the self-cultivated mystery of Dylan's identity, an impression fostered by the singer's almost spectral visage and inclination to perform in whiteface. Shepard credits Dylan with having "made a vagabond minstrel in his own skin" (p. 28), and gremlin-like images of the rock-poet are evoked as Shepard tells of Dylan smiling impishly at the wheel, piloting his green and white camper along the back roads of New England and the city streets of Manhattan.

Perhaps Shepard saw reflected in Dylan's countenance his own tendency toward self-mythologizing, since the two had much in common. Like the playwright, Dylan (born Robert Zimmerman) arrived in New York in the early sixties and immediately assumed a new name. Dylan also rode a counterculture wave to popularity and would garner numerous accolades and honors (he received an honorary doctorate from Princeton in 1970[10]). Dylan prompted Shepard to reflect upon the mercurial nature of the artist, a matter that would dominate his ensuing plays, and the logbook reveals not only the playwright's reconsideration of the sixties (and their fallout) but an obsession with self and the dynamics of identity—the struggle between personal grounding and artistic self-creation.

As an artist then in his thirties, Shepard at times invests his diary with a sobriety that indicates his age and station in life. While the sojourn's full-throttle pace provided an amusing pageant of liminality, it did not elicit a maudlin affection for psychedelia and folk-rock radicalism. Regarded as a strained attempt to replicate some lost sense of sixties *communitas*, the adventure served to seal off and distance Shepard from his counterculture associations. By the time of the tour's farewell concert at Madison Square Garden, Shepard was hungry for California—the mountains, horses, "his woman" (p. 135)—and eager for work in the Bay Area theatre.

Shepard's calculated disregard of New York by no means fated the playwright to oblivion. By the time he had settled in Marin County, theatre in the United States had experienced a profound shift of focus and organization. The early 1970s saw the Broadway district blighted by porn shops, drug trafficking, and prostitution; the theatrical life of the Great White Way similarly languished.[11] Between 1970 and 1974, seventeen shows did not survive past opening night; during this time Broadway's annual gross income dropped 18 percent. Successful productions of this period chiefly included revivals (such as *No, No, Nanette*), Neil Simon comedies, and a number of British imports.[12] Broadway limped into the new decade financially distressed—without compelling aesthetic or moral vision—and could hardly claim itself the fountainhead of the American theatre.

It has been argued that in 1970s America "the inadequacy of solutions dictated from above" forced individuals "to invent solutions from below,"[13] and indeed one notes at this time a local approach to social renewal. In these years the magazine *Mother Earth News* gained its readership by sharing information on how to grow organic vegetables, how to build teepees—in short, how to live outside America's corporate consumer society. This impulse to retreat from the America of big business and big government also spawned a multitude of grass-roots collectives and cooperatives, groups unified by issues that ranged from antinuclear protest to creative nonviolence training. In *Seeds of the Seventies*, Arthur Stein writes that the decade was marked by a "movement toward human-scaled institutions,"[14] and one may contend that the desire to localize and humanize also informed the American theatre, which found its lifeblood in an invigorating burst of regional activity.

The regional (also called "resident" or "repertory") theatre reached its zenith in the seventies,[15] yet its origins go back at least as far as America's "little theatre" movement and the early decades of the century. Modeled after the European art theatres, groups such as the Provincetown Players, Washington Square Players, and the Theatre Guild refused to succumb to the commercial theatre's entrepreneurial methods. Despite its noble ambitions, the little theatre movement remained essentially an amateur enterprise, and while a number of important community theatres had earlier appeared outside of New York—for example, the Cleveland Playhouse, the Pittsburgh Theatre, and the Barter Theatre in Virginia—the regional theatre that emerged in the late forties envisioned itself as a "serious" or "art" theatre that was also professional in status. The birth of this phenomenon is credited to Margo Jones, who in 1947 founded the Theatre 47 in Dallas, the prototypical regional theatre that proved an important ally to such writers as William Inge and Tennessee Williams. Jones's efforts inspired Nina Vance, who founded the Alley Theatre in Houston. Two other important regional theatres soon emerged—the Arena Theatre, founded in Washington, D.C., by Zelda Fichandler (1950), and the San Fransico Actor's Workshop, led by Jules Irving and Herbert Blau (1952). Throughout the fifties and into the sixties the momentum of this movement accelerated, and in 1966 *Variety* reported that for the first time more professional actors were working in the regions than in New York.[16] A host of theatres opened in cities across the country—among them Seattle, Memphis, Baltimore, and Milwaukee—and by the end of the decade, the number of equity resident houses in the United States had surpassed forty.[17]

One should not underestimate the regional theatre's debt to corporate and federal funding: between 1962 and 1965 the Ford Foundation made contributions exceeding $10 million,[18] and in 1966 awarded an unprecedented sum of $60 million to regional theatres.[19] Nor should one overlook the opportunism of city leaders promoting theatre as a means to upgrade their community's cultural and economic standing; business and civic leaders in Minneapolis raised a $2 million building fund in order to draw the internationally renowned Tyrone Guthrie. Nonetheless, regional theatre attempted to resist the outlook that had dominated the centralized American theatre. This order of performance challenged the ascendancy of the New York stage and pursued organizational structures and policies contrary to the protocol of commercial theatre. The regional theatre did not seek the onetime box-office smash but envisioned itself as an institution that would continue operation regardless of season-to-season vagaries. Though conceived as nonprofit organizations, such theatres maintained high production standards by supporting a resident company of professional actors. Not preoccupied with the production of entertainment commodities, regional theatres enhanced their community roots by offering educational and recreational programs, demonstrating their missions as service organizations less interested in economic gain than the social good.

Over the years a number of resident theatres emerged with university affiliations (Yale, Michigan, Stanford, and others); this points to another significant facet of the decentralized American theatre, that of educational theatre. The first four-year theatre curriculum was not offered until 1914 (at Carnegie Mellon University in Pittsburgh), and even though a handful of programs—at New York University, the University of Iowa, Cornell, and Yale—soon followed, the study of theatre struggled to attain respectablity as a discipline and was more often than not relegated to English literature programs.[20] The growth in the student population of the 1960s and increased funding levels brought a rise in educational theatre activity. It has been estimated that over two thousand theatres were built during the decade, the majority of them on college and university campuses.[21] By 1967, over 75 percent of U.S. colleges and universities offered courses in theatre, and 50 percent offered majors.[22] While only a handful of universities have enjoyed an affiliate resident company, many theatre departments boast first-rate physical facilities and highly skilled, professional faculty. The multitude of American professional actors, directors, and designers who have gained training and experience in the university theatre indicates the importance of educational theatre, and a number of noted writers, including David Rabe, Christopher Durang, and Wendy Wasserstein, inaugurated their careers in a university context.

The 1970s revealed the American theatre as a decentralized theatre whose myriad energies found expression on the stages of regional, university, and community theatres. Original work at this time gained new prominence as many theatres sought to discover and nurture new voices. The career of Marsha Norman, author of *Getting Out* and *'night, Mother*, was, for example, launched by the Actors Theatre of Louisville, an outfit that in 1977 initiated a new play festival that has since become an annual theatre event of national importance. The regional theatre also promoted work by minority artists, and in 1972 the Theatre Communications Group (TCG, the informational network of regional theatre) expanded services to assist emergent ethnic theatres.[23] Whereas regional theatre had traditionally been viewed as a tributary system that circulated New York–tested fare, in the 1970s it was the commercial theatre that turned its attention to the vibrant and diversified work of the regions.

If one sees Broadway as a component of an overly bureaucratized (and fossilized) status quo America, its decline reflects the decentralization at work throughout American culture. During these years regional theatre proliferated at an astonishing rate, and by the late 1970s over 175 permanent nonprofit theatres were operating across the country, drawing an annual audience of over twelve million.[24] Seen against the backdrop of a nation whose overarching structures (and identities) were yielding to emergent energies and alliances born on the local level, Joseph Zeigler's observation that the regional theatre followed a centrifugal impulse proves especially noteworthy,[25] suggesting that this theatre has in an important way given play to the heteroglossic voices of American culture. While the institutionalization of the regional theatre has been charged with homogenizing fare and artistic practices (a phenomenon to be addressed in Shepard's rise as a dramatist of the American family), it can be asserted with some justification that this order of theatre proved a liberalizing influence, opening the stage to new ideas, new voices, and new audiences. Sara O'Connor (a former TCG president), looking back upon the events of the 70s, celebrated the regional theatre as a "national treasure":

> *One* national theatre company, or even a few companies, cannot serve adequately as the model we need if we are to reflect the American experience. We *have* a national theatre—a multiple and diverse one. . . . In a democratic society, a national theatre is theatre for all the people.[26]

This organizational shift in the American theatre affected Sam Shepard's career in a crucial way. Just as Shepard profited from the Off-Off Broadway scene of the sixties, in the following decade the playwright enjoyed a felicitous relationship with the regional (and university) theatre, whose institutional organization and noncommercial aims well suited his adventuresome drama. In view of Shepard's later prominence in the regional market (and that New York critic Ross Wetzsteon had declared him "the most important living American playwright"[27]), it is surprising that San Francisco's highly respected American Conservatory Theatre (ACT) rebuffed the playwright's initial inquiries. Undaunted, Shepard approached one of the Bay Area's smaller performance groups, the Magic Theatre, and there found a company that would prove to be his "theatrical homestead"[28] for years to come.

Founded by John Lion in the late 1960s, the Magic Theatre had first been based in Berkeley and had passed its infancy in that chaotic and exhilarating period defined by student movements on the University of California campus. Initially housed in a second-story space (with bleacher seats) above The Rose and Thistle Pub,[29] the company later moved into an alternative arts complex on the former military base, Fort Mason. Located virtually at the foot of the Golden Gate Bridge, the Magic Theatre began production in an unpretentious "long yellow building" with two performance spaces, described in plain terms as "a pair of big block rooms."[30] Utilizing professional actors under an equity waiver agreement, the spartan enterprise operated in the mid-seventies with an annual budget that ran at $90,000 (that of the ACT approached $4 million).[31]

The Magic Theatre had established a reputation for its imaginative staging practices and dedication to new American work; John Lion welcomed the acclaimed avant-garde playwright, and at the Magic Shepard found something of a creative incubator. Recalling Jeep's reference to the Golden Gate Bridge in *Action*, one senses the iconic allure the Magic's locale must have held for the playwright; Shepard would recall how as a child he saw Fort Mason in passing when his family set sail for his father's military assignment in Guam.[32] It seems fitting that he return to the site and achieve his artistic maturity as an American writer under the watch of the Golden Gate, a structure resonant in both his communal (national) and familial memory.

The playwright's combative experiences with several noted directors steeled his resolve to protect his work, and at the Magic he staged many of his plays himself. Under his own direction, Shepard revived *Action* and the short monologue *Killer's Head* (the two pieces had just recently been produced at New York's American Place Theatre by Shepard's longtime acquaintance, Wynn Handman; *Killer's Head* featured the young actor Richard Gere). Shepard's close involvement with the mounting of his plays became a pattern, and the writer developed continuous working relationships with a number of artists. The theatre provided the writer something of a safe haven, and Shepard used the Magic to try out several of the plays that would establish his reputation, including *Angel City*, *Buried Child*, and *Fool for Love*.

These years in Northern California (and their relative stability) may be credited with tempering the playwright's talent and bringing a new determination to his work. As Felicia Londre describes it, Shepard at this time "put himself through training to discipline his form,"[33] and the playwright thus seems less a young turk driven by an adolescent compulsion to subvert than a secure and seasoned artist testing the borders and possibilities of his medium.

While his residency in England had brought an infusion of classicism to his work, California reawakened Shepard's instincts for challenge and experimentation. In contrast to the conservative impulse evident in his London plays, his efforts at the Magic exhibit a wayward, eruptive energy, propelled by a curiosity for new forms and modes of expression. This work also manifests a keen fascination with the voices of the mind, the inchoate nature of the ego, and the imagistic activity of preconscious/subconscious states. This orientation is portended in the meandering, stream-of-consciousness technique explored in *Killer's Head*, where a felon shares his thoughts and mental images in the moments preceding his execution.

With the Magic Theatre as his institutional base, Shepard received a $15,000 Rockefeller Grant. This funding afforded him the chance to pursue investigative stage work. He gathered a group of actors and musicians in a laboratory environment and oversaw exercises aimed at exploring the interplay of music and language. Catherine Stone, a local musician and jazz composer, who had been instructing Shepard in music theory and jazz structure, assisted in this project and helped design a number of techniques that sensitized the performers to sound, rhythm, and music's emotional affect.[34] These laboratory sessions culminated in the *Inacoma* project (premiered on March 18, 1977), an unconventional play for voices inspired by the real-life story of Karen Ann Quinlan, whose coma experience had incited a national debate on euthanasia. No polemic on medical ethics, the collage-like piece took up the challenge of conveying the interior world of a comatose patient through musical pieces and recitation.

Shepard's fascination with an "impaired" or alternate mode of consciousness (and the possibility of conveying its nature on stage) calls to mind the oeuvre of the American avant-garde figure Robert Wilson, whose clinical work with autistic children inspired his dreamlike theatre of nonsequential stage pictures. One may indeed argue that much of seventies experimental performance evinced an autistic impulse, that is, a tendency toward the abstract and highly private. Termed the "theatre of images,"[35] this type of performance was advanced by a number of influential figures, including Richard Foreman and Lee Breuer, who composed surreal image scores devoid of linear development or narrative cogency. This phenomenon signals a shift in the orientation of the American avant-garde. The sixties experimental ensembles often stressed the public and communal nature of performance; their works conveyed a strong sense of fervor and "heat." The theatre of Wilson, Breuer, and Foreman conversely appears aloof and introspective—it is a "cool" art, in keeping with the sensibility of the decade, a time characterized as "an era of serious exploration into the far reaches of inner space."[36] Shepard's affiliation with the Magic Theatre offered the playwright a laboratory for his own rather solipsistic exercise in formalism (though more aural than visual), and his resulting efforts are inwardly directed, preoccupied with subjective realms and the perceptual life of the artist.

Shepard's study in musical theory and his experimentation in a fluid form of performance technique had a great impact on his next major plays. This investigation provided the playwright a set of conceptual and stylistic tools that helped regulate his wildly fertile imagination. From as far back as his Open Theatre days, Shepard had never written characters that could be considered well-constructed or internally consistent. It is thus telling how in his introduction to *Angel City*, the playwright explains this feature of his dramaturgy in jazz terminology. Underscoring the protean nature of his characters, he encourages the actors in his play "to consider a fractured whole with bits and pieces of character flying off the central theme."[37] While Shepard's theatre had always valued the spontaneous and the aleatory, often to the point of paroxysm or hallucinatory overload, he at this point sought in his work a sort of controlled anarchy, a virtuoso display of improvisatory skills comparable to those evident in the solo excursions of the accomplished jazz musician. Though Shepard began to eschew blatant surrealism in his later plays, his commitment to a jazz-style characterization remained firm, and even within the realistic confines of his American family dramas his characters often seem to fluctuate, to erupt, and to follow the reflexive urgings of their author's psyche.

Over the next few years Shepard wrote three new works—*Angel City*, *Suicide in B-Flat*, and *Seduced*. These plays deal with what had become an obsessive theme for the playwright, the identity and ontology of the artist. Utilizing a fluid jazz structure, these highly imagistic works address issues of community and social regimentation, yet their chief focus is upon the inward experience of the creator and his existential dilemma.

Given Shepard's eventual success as a film personality, *Angel City* holds many ironies and veiled prophesies. The work vents the writer's antipathy toward the film industry, a hostility expressed in the character Tympani's invective: "They'll swallow you whole and spit you out as a tax deduction" (p. 73). *Angel City* nonetheless exposes the author's childhood fondness for the movies, and though he at this time was enjoying a degree of creative freedom (and personal stability) as a Magic Theatre playwright, the work betrays a nagging fascination—born equally of disgust and desire—with L.A.'s siren call.

The playwright's self-preoccupation is manifest in the play's central figure, Rabbit, a character described by one critic as a "pure artist of almost religious dimensions."[38] Rabbit has been summoned from "up north" by movie executives Lanx and Wheeler to save a foundering film project. Shepard includes a number of self-referential details. Like the playwright, Rabbit refuses to travel by air—he travels to L.A. by horse and buckboard. Rabbit also makes a point of announcing his hipster credentials; echoing Shepard's own biography, Rabbit traces his origins to "the deepest cracks of the underground" (p. 68). Rabbit arrives at the studio dragging magic bundles behind him, signifying that he is not just a script doctor but an artist with shamanistic powers. It is curious that Shepard cast the young, lithe and lanky actor Ebbe Roe Smith in this role. Critics have commented upon the actor's strong physical resemblance to the playwright, and one notes the uncanny phenomenon of a Shepard look-alike performing the part of the author's alter ego (he would later play Wesley, another Shepard doppelgänger, in the Public Theatre production of *Curse of the Starving Class*).[39]

Wheeler has determined that only a disaster picture will save his career and ameliorate the plaguelike infection that is ravaging the local populace (and his own body). Wheeler's movie requires no conventional catastrophe; in the executive's view, it demands something "unearthly," and Rabbit is asked to conjure "an actual miracle" (p. 68). Wheeler's call for an art product that can penetrate "every layer of their dark subconscious" (p. 71) gives Shepard opportunity to dramatize a jam session in which Rabbit, Miss Scoons the secretary, and the drummer Tympani attempt to invoke the most horrifying of all fears. In something of an improvisational situation (much like Shepard's own performance workshops at the Magic), the trio explores words, rhythm patterns, and percussive effects and generate a mesmerizing energy that brings Rabbit to a revelation—that the fear of death is the greatest of all fears.

Elements in the play also evidence Shepard's reflection upon his Western origins. Near the piece's beginning Miss Scoons speaks of the East as a place of refinement and envisions a cushioned Bostonian retirement: "You have a golden retriever at your feet, *The New York Times Review of Books* in your lap, an after-dinner mint in your mouth" (p. 82). This image of urbanity suggests an order of intellectualism and erudition. Each of Rabbit's magic bundles is accorded a geographical position with a particular meaning and property, and the bundle of the West marks the "Looks-Within" place, an assignation that clarifies Shepard's metaphoric geography; that is, the West, in contrast to the Eastern establishment, is oriented toward personal insight and intuition. Wheeler follows with his own definition of the West: "It's a place of discovery. Things are uncovered here. Gold! Oceans! LOOK INSIDE OF ME!" (p. 103). Wheeler's self-involvement is a manifestation, albeit a perverse one, of a Western ethos that esteems self-reliance and private belief. Though this outlook can engender megalomania, the West and its introspective turn hold a privileged position in Rabbit's magic and stand as a telling feature of Shepard's regionalism.

Throughout *Angel City* the studio bureaucracy is presented as an apparatus of domination, subjecting the artist and his inner life to an industrial mode of mass production. A more subtle type of subjection however is conveyed in *Angel City*'s dialogic understanding of the cinematic form itself. Regarding the screen as the point of contact between the public and the private, the play explores the relation between communal consciousness and individual thought (an element that will be explored again in *Suicide in B-Flat*). On more than one occasion, the order "wet your lips" is dictated to a character, who summarily obliges. This command and its ready response signify the degree to which movie conventions infiltrate private behavior. In essence, the screen is seen as the medium through which the communal other is introjected into the individual mind. Shepard recognizes this as a dangerous thing and dramatizes how movies threaten not only to invade the personal sphere but to eradicate original thought altogether. This point is made when Tympani, in a state of some dissociation, looks to the audience and entreats: "What dya' say we just lose ourselves in the miracle of film? We nestle down . . . with a big box of buttered popcorn . . . and we just chew ourselves straight into oblivion" (p. 97).

Wheeler grows increasingly reptilian through the piece as his skin turns green and his fingernails lengthen. In morality-play fashion, Wheeler serves an allegorical purpose. He becomes the physical embodiment of the film industry (and its corrosion) and confesses as much: "I HAVE A MILLION MOVIES! AND DO YOU KNOW WHERE THEY ARE! THEY'RE IN MY BLOOD!" (p. 100). Wheeler's transformation is indicative of the dark ending of the play and its inadmission of any redemptive aspects. After Wheeler presents his scenario—a cosmic samurai battle—Rabbit assumes a position of command and dismisses the pitch. Wheeler is reduced, stripped of power, and the play concludes with an unexpected role reversal as Rabbit becomes the driven monster-mogul and Wheeler his prey. One sees that Rabbit has been infected by the medium and that his private poetic vision has been preempted by the totalizing mentality of the movie machine. *Angel City* concludes with no sense of escape or appeasement, and the play's final image is one of revulsion—green slime oozes from Rabbit's magic bundle out onto the stage floor.

Reflective of the playwright's interest in music theory and jazz structure, Shepard's next play, *Suicide in B-Flat*, depicts the personal crisis of an avant-garde musician. Often baffling and at times downright illogical, the work assumes an expansive, improvisatory form and follows what one critic called "its own inner orchestration."[40] Like *Angel City*, the play employs hallucinatory states, arbitrary character turns, frenetic monologues, and pop-culture allusions. The piece's surrealistic hijinks are linked by a narrative line that echoes Raymond Chandler's detective stories. The play's opening image, dominated by the chalk outline of a body on the stage floor, alerts the audience to the mystery element of the piece and immediately establishes *Suicide in B-Flat*'s crucial dramatic question: What has befallen Niles, the eccentric genius composer?

The rather bumbling gumshoes Louis and Pablo have arrived to investigate Niles's enigmatic murder/suicide/disappearance and soon encounter two musicians—Petrone and Laureen—who declare that they have come to meet with the composer. The detectives undertake an off-the-wall interrogation, which serves less to elucidate the facts of the case than to schematize the oppositional worlds of the public servant (in this case, police detectives) and the artist. Louis and Pablo grow increasingly perturbed as the musicians speak of their creative enterprise; Louis succumbs to a strange possession and exclaims: "Everything's crazy! . . . All this free-form stuff is disturbing to my inner depths . . . I'm a Republican by

nature!"[41] Conversely, the sensibility of the musicians is stridently unconventional. Petrone fingers the keys of his saxophone and claims to play a
silent form of music. He explains that "Dogs can't even hear it" (p. 204).
Petrone further relates that before his disappearance Niles had been attempting to create a form of visual music, an endeavor that in some measure parallels Shepard's own pursuit of a fluid, lyrical theatrical form.
Laureen's comment, "This music has no room for politics" (p. 207), highlights the asocial inclination of the artist and advances the view that art
exists in a purely formal state, beyond the material conditions of cultural
process.

It is Niles who serves as the dramatic fulcrum for *Suicide in B-Flat*. At
one juncture he tells of his childhood experiences overseas in Southeast
Asia—the incident appears almost verbatim in Shepard's semiautobio-
graphical piece *Motel Chronicles*. Niles in short gives utterance to
Shepard's ruminations upon the artist's condition, and in the dilemma of
the genius composer Shepard plays out many of his own conflicted stances
regarding art, asceticism, and communal attachment.

When Niles first appears onstage with his accomplice Paulette, we
quickly understand that the two inhabit an alternative dimension and are
thus invisible to the other characters of the play. Although the metaphysics
of this dynamic remain unexplained, Paulette and Niles have covenanted
to remove the encumbrances that inhibit Niles's creativity. Quite simply,
Niles desires the utmost liberation (to sever his dialogic relation with community) and thus seeks the extermination of the Other. This ridding is
effected by a sort of ritual murder in which Niles costumes himself as
various personae who are subsequently dispatched by Paulette. At one
point, Niles dresses as a cowboy and digresses upon the heroism of Pecos
Bill; Pablo summarily tumbles over with an arrow in his back. This be-
wildering process aims at liberating Niles from the "voices" that besiege
him, suggesting the artist's entry into a purely aesthetic realm, unimpeded
by any former identity or communal imposition.

The pivotal point of *Suicide in B-Flat*, which may be considered Niles's
conversion, follows close upon a reverie sequence in which Petrone tells
of his first encounter with Niles and how the composer's "magic" and
"music" brought new enthusiasm to his life. Now visible to the others,
Niles responds to Petrone's disclosure with derision: "you think that just
by coming in contact with me that your asslicking life will be saved from
hopelessness" (p. 226). However, as the upstage lights reveal Louis, Pablo,
and Laureen together in tableau, Niles, despite his contemptuousness, is
forced to face his community and is brought to a moment of decision.
Petrone announces that they are "ready to play" (p. 229), and in his im-
portunate posture Niles detects the encroachment of the Other. Paulette
orders Niles to stay away, warning that he will be devoured. Niles does

not flee but confronts the group and poses a searing litany of questions bearing upon the self and its social relation:

> Are you inside me or outside me? Am I inside you? Am I inside you right now? Am I buzzing away at your membranes? Your brain waves? Driving you berserk? Creating explosions? Destroying your ancient patterns? Or am I just like you? Just exactly like you? So exactly like you that we're exactly the same. So exactly that we're not even apart. Not even separate. Not even two things but just one. Only one. Indivisible. (p. 229)

Perhaps as clearly as any passage in Shepard's writing, this excerpt addresses the dialogic relation between the artist, the art expression, and community. Niles's monologue delivers the insight that the "group" somehow inheres within the mind of the artist, and Niles in essence arrives at the Bakhtinian notion that consciousness exists on the border between self and Other. In this light, there is "no isolated act of consciousness. Every thought is connected to other thoughts and, what is more, to the thoughts of others."[42] The self cannot therefore achieve any blissful state of autonomy, for the reach of community touches the most introspective and incorrigible movements of the mind. The nature of language and consciousness is public (this point is scenically asserted in Niles's group of attending admirers), and the composer's journey into a purely private aesthetic realm is thus misguided, if not delusional.

Pablo and Louis snap their handcuffs around Niles's wrists, and the stage image of the three manacled together serves as a striking visual commentary upon the play's conclusion. Although Niles moves to protest, he halts, allows a moment of silence, then admits that someone "should pay" for the life of the unknown man that was taken in Niles's initial attempt at escape. In short, the artist accepts his social obligation, a turn described by one critic as a step "both fatal and joyous," and at close the composer joins rank—Niles "comes back to the real world."[43]

In *Suicide in B-Flat*, we see Shepard's (perhaps reluctant) dismissal of the artist as a free-spirited, asocial cybernaut. The play's ending suggests commitment, not escape, and the play thus presents the artist as one inseparably connected to community, to the multitude both within and without. In this work Shepard acknowledges the communal burden of the writer, and, given his later designation as America's preeminent dramatist, *Suicide in B-Flat* prefigures not only the writer's turn to a more socially oriented drama but his future service as playwright of the nation.

Outside of San Francisco, Shepard's plays during these years were featured in a number of the country's most prestigious resident theatres. These productions indicate the broadening of the writer's reputation and underscore the regional theatre's eagerness to promote new American work. The first resident theatre to enjoy a university affiliation, Princeton's McCarter Theatre had staged the American premiere of *The Tooth of Crime* in 1972. In 1976, facing a budget shortfall, the McCarter undertook an aggressive marketing campaign; touting *Angel City* as the crown jewel of its season, the theatre not only maintained solvency but generated a record number of season subscriptions. Though protest by African American students had derailed *Operation Sidewinder*'s production in the company's 1968–69 season, *Suicide in B-Flat* (1976) brought Shepard's work into another prominent venue—the Yale Repertory Theatre. Founded by then dean of the School of Drama Robert Brustein, the theatre served the university's renowned conservatory training program and gained national reputation for its innovative and often controversial work. The last of Shepard's major studies of the artistic persona, *Seduced* (1978), was premiered by the Trinity Square Repertory, the Providence, Rhode Island company that had for over two decades flourished under the able leadership of Adrian Hall. Commended as "one of the excellent and enterprising groups that have made the regional theatre the site of most of the best work now being done on U.S. stages,"[44] Trinity Rep would remain a faithful backer of Shepard's art and would regularly schedule each new Shepard play in its season, including *Buried Child, Fool for Love, True West,* and *A Lie of the Mind.*[45]

Like *Angel City* and *Suicide in B-Flat, Seduced* too follows a dreamlike, meandering structure. Harold Clurman would in fact liken Shepard to a "hopped-up jazz musician,"[46] and while the play often seems a strange and somewhat bizarre series of "riff" sequences, the work is given focus by the actions and desires of the play's principal character, Henry Hackamore, a hermit-like aeronautics entrepreneur modeled after Howard Hughes. The term "hackamore" refers to a rope device used to break horses,[47] and the appellation is thus used by Shepard in ironic fashion to signify the lead character's paradoxical status; he has mounted and mastered the world of commerce, yet his bouts of delusion and compulsion to withdrawal have rendered him broken, a sullen and isolated misanthrope. Set in a Third World, south-of-the-border remove, Hackamore's sparsely furnished domicile is distinguished by a set of velour drapes, an effective image of the recluse's partitioned existence and distance from the world beyond.

Hackamore harbors a malevolent side, a trait actor Rip Torn emphasized with a "crackling nasality and ugly power."[48] Shepard nonetheless ascribes an aesthetic sensibility to the character evident in his active imagination and visionary tendencies. When he is massaged by his attendant Raul, Hackamore gives articulate description to the imagery that arises in his mind. Hackamore's preoccupation with his own mental esoterica, however, is symptomatic of the profoundly egocentric outlook that has posited him at the edge of civilization. Henry is a fantasist, a version of the artist who seeks the farthest outposts of the imagination, and in his compulsive use of Kleenex tissues, which he blankets across his body, we see his abhorrence of contact, his denial of the world of social transaction.

The play's dramatic tension quickens when Hackamore summons two sultry and seductive women from his past. Appearing onstage as memory figures, Luna and Miami are called before Hackamore's inspection to "play out" scenes from former days. The women's presence grants Hackamore a sort of voyeuristic gratification, yet their conversation deepens the recluse's yearning for the life he has missed. Henry attempts to orchestrate a moment of cohesion and tells the women, "We have to be in communion."[49] This effort fails however, signifying that the emotional cocoon that Hackamore has spun for himself will not be compromised.

It is significant that, after reaching no rapprochement with the ghost-lovers from his past, Hackamore expresses his wish to return to America. He is brought his World War I flying gear, which he dons in anticipation of a nighttime flight across the border—with Las Vegas as his destination. After a life of aesthetic remove, Henry desires reintegration and argues that a "man's got a right to die in his homeland" (p. 270). This plan is thwarted, however, when Raul discloses that for many years he has been controlling the hermit's financial affairs and demands that Henry sign over all of his holdings. At this juncture, Hackamore approaches a bereft, Lear-like state and admits that he has been "seduced," that his life has been the chasing of a mirage. Recognizing his damned condition, Henry becomes infused with a Mephistophelian energy. He assumes his chair as though it were a cockpit and embarks upon one final nefarious flight. Raul fires his gun repeatedly at Hackamore, but the bullets have no effect. Hackamore pronounces himself the "nightmare of the nation" (p. 275) and rises up in menacing triumph, a phoenixlike figure before whom the mesmerized Raul must bow in supplication.

Seduced's final moments remind one of *La Turista*'s remarkable conclusion, where Kent barrels headlong through the motel wall. Both endings give vent to an energy that defies communal constraint and seeks imaginative expanse. Although Henry has desired connection both with his past and his homeland, he finally spurns all entrapments and becomes the pilot/ poet par excellence, one who launches outward into the lone spaces of personal fantasy. The recluse thus emerges as the centrifugal impulse incarnate. While Niles of *Suicide in B-Flat* accepts his manacles and joins the communal order, Hackamore stands emboldened and untethered, yet alone—a wild, winged force rising up against a blood-red sky.

By 1978 Shepard was committed to writing American domestic drama, and *Seduced* represents a point of closure in the playwright's imaginative life. The play may be understood as Shepard's swan song, his final full-scale dramatization of the aesthetic impulse and personality. Hackamore's furious self-assertion may be seen as a sort of fist waving, the playwright's

own willful, final indulgence in a fantastic outpouring, for even as *Seduced*
was being staged Shepard was taking upon himself the encumbrances of
a more conventional form, turning from the ego preoccupation of the self-
as-artist to the more global concern of the self-in-family.

Shepard's rise to prominence as a national playwright would be fueled
by a series of "major" works, from *Curse of the Starving Class* to *A Lie
of the Mind*. Still, it is important to note that he maintained his enthusiasm
for laboratory and workshop contexts. As his artistic fame increased, Shepard continued to foster small-scale experimental projects and to explore
new approaches to stage presentation. We in fact observe oppositional
impulses in his later career, concomitant desires to experiment on the
periphery of established theatre and to author well-shaped masterworks
for the American stage.

The *Inacoma* ensemble had in part been styled on Joseph Chaikin's
Open Theatre workshops, and it is fitting that Shepard would work with
Chaikin himself on a number of miniaturist performance pieces. Described
as "a collage of echoes from the dead,"[50] *Tongues*, the first of the pair's
collaborations, explored consciousness at the brink of expiration. Running
just over half an hour in length, this play for voices was presented at the
Magic Theatre in June of 1978.[51] Chaikin recited the piece's verbal text
(facing the audience); with his back to Chaikin's, Shepard played various
percussion instruments and executed a series of abstract manual gestures.
The two shortly thereafter collaborated on *Savage/Love*, a collection of
lyrical utterances expressing the manifold nature of love and its many
paradoxes. This work was presented on a double bill with *Tongues* at the
Public Theatre in New York (directed by Robert Woodruff) in November
of 1979.

After Chaikin had suffered a near-fatal stroke during heart surgery in
1984, he was coaxed by Shepard to join in another voice-play creation,
this despite the fact that the stroke had caused an impairment in his
speech. Almost as an exercise in rehabilitation, the two composed *The
War in Heaven: Angel's Monologue*, a rich and evocative poetic piece spoken from the vantage point of an angel in contact with earthly life. Having
struggled to overcome his disability, Chaikin recited the text himself when
the work was performed at the Public Theatre (Shepard provided musical
accompaniment). Hailed as a most poignant event, *War in Heaven* brought
Chaikin applause for his courageous return to the stage and prompted
widespread tribute for his lifelong commitment to a visionary American
theatre.

Outside of the Chaikin voice-play collaborations, Shepard on numerous
occasions participated in the work of the Overture Theatre, a music ensemble that included Catherine Stone, O-lan Johnson Shepard, and performers from the *Inacoma* cast. He contributed to the music-word creation
Superstitions and later joined five other percussionists in an experimental

musical performance piece entitled "Drum Wars."[52] As something of a lark, he also accepted choreographer Daniel Nagrin's invitation to compose a libretto for his dancework *Jacaranda*, a piece that subsequently received a New York staging. In addition to this eclectic list of credits in experimental performance, Shepard has participated in various workshops and playwriting labs, including the Bay Area Playwrights Festival and the Padua Hills Writers Conference in Los Angeles. Such endeavors testify to the playwright's commitment to experimentation and his delight in novelty. One also notes an irrepressibility in his imaginative disposition, a compulsion to always reach, to push outward toward unexplored combinations and formations of aesthetic structure and subjective perception.

Defining American society as a culture of narcissism, an appellation that would prove a catchphrase for future discussion of the seventies, Christopher Lasch argued that these years marked the "apotheosis of individualism,"[53] evident in an ethos of immediate gratification, a preoccupation with self, and, importantly, in artworks that focused upon the artist's "inner state of mind."[54] Concurring with this contention, Samuel Leiter has noted that the experimental theatre of this time generated an art of withdrawal, reflecting a solipsistic "addiction to visual and aural aesthetics."[55] Though *Angel City*, *Suicide in B-Flat*, and *Seduced* on one level bear out Lasch's thesis—the playwright's work has sporadically drawn censure for its "gratuitously hip narcissism"[56]—Shepard's fascination with formalism and the interiority of consciousness did not lead the playwright to complete self-absorption. These pieces are not insular or opaque, and one might say that Shepard has always kept one eye on the nation. Even in his highly subjective piece *Inacoma*, the inner voice of the comatose patient is juxtaposed with the "authority" voices of the father, doctor, and nurse. One may conclude that even in Shepard's most idiosyncratic efforts, there resides a consciousness of the collective (the movie audiences of *Angel City*, the groupies in *Suicide in B-Flat*). Amid the jazz, the fantasists, and all the masks of his introverted artist-heroes, the presence of community has remained a constant in Shepard's dramas, acting often as the playwright's imaginative loadstone.

Given Shepard's concern with the individual and communal relations, notions of national attachment and the idea of America itself have played an integral role in the playwright's dramatic vision. As Robert Coe has observed, "America has always run deep beneath his [Shepard's] unruly pop mythologizing,"[57] and certainly the writer's aesthetic self-explorations acknowledge the influence of the "homeland" and the debt that self-definition owes to group belonging. One should bear in mind, however, that the changes facing the United States in the 1970s problematized matters of national identification. In the estimation of Christopher Lasch, the period's rampant narcissism was the symptom of a more profound disorder, the sign of a wholesale cultural unraveling. For Lasch, citizens were losing touch with the country's institutions, public rituals, and sense of historical continuity. Echoing this motif of cultural collapse, Shepard would himself declare that in the seventies "one could hear the sound of America cracking open and crashing into the sea."[58] It is telling that the *Rolling Thunder Logbook* depicts a number of national shrines as tawdry tourist sites, emptied of significance and gravity. We read of a chanting Allen Ginsberg squatting among the wax figures of Native Americans at a Plymouth Rock museum. Evoking only bemusement in the playwright, such incidents speak to the diminished authority of civic symbols and the numbing of patriotic sentiment.

While social critics such as Lasch describe the seventies chiefly in negative terms, the atomization of American consciousness allowed for renegotiation, reformation, and a different understanding of identity. American history itself came under rethinking and revision. Certainly this time presented an opening for many of those citizens who had been before marginalized, who had never been allowed voice or visibility. Changes in the American theatre confirm this point. The 1960s witnessed a number of enterprises that contested the organization of commercial theatre (and its dominant cultural views). Both founded in 1967, the Negro Ensemble Company and the New Lafayette Theatre proved to be catalysts for African American playwriting and performance. Also in these years the work of the Puerto Rican Traveling Theatre and Luis Valdez's El Teatro Campesino drew attention to issues affecting the country's Hispanic population. In the 1970s the activity and acclaim of minority performance groups accelerated. One notes Hanay Geiogamah's Native American Theatre Ensemble, the Asian-American Theatre Workshop in San Francisco, and New York's Pan American Repertory. A host of feminist-oriented theatres also appeared at this time, the Women's Project and At the Foot of the Mountain among them.[59] Shepard applauded these developments in decentralization and argued that the American theatre would grow stronger and increasingly diverse as people became "more and more aware of the places they're from."[60] It is clear from this comment that Shepard recognizes the increased valuation of local identification in the decade. Yet his words are also unintentionally ironic, for, as determinants of ethnicity, race, and gender rose to focus, Shepard's sense of his own roots and cultural identity consolidated his status as an all-American male.

It is curious that in 1976 Shepard penned a work in celebration of the nation's bicentennial (though it was not produced until late in the year). Originally commissioned by the San Francisco Opera, *The Sad Lament of Pecos Bill* was staged at the Bay Area Playwrights Festival under the direction of Robert Woodruff. This occasional piece portrays Pecos Bill with majesty and might; the work, however, mourns the mythic figure as the last of his breed, and the extinction of the hero can be read on one level as an analogue to the decline of America and the loss of national might in the post-Vietnam era.

Shepard's appeal to such symbology at a time when the nation's sense of itself (and its past) faced extreme challenge prompts one to consider possible reasons for his imminent success and stardom. As many writers at this time investigated their roots from perspectives that often relegated national heritage to a secondary status, we see Shepard's own roots-conscious theatre operating in a different manner. When Clive Barnes compares the playwright to other prominent dramatists of the seventies and writes that Shepard's "roots . . . are more deeply embedded in the bedrock of our environment and our national mythology,"[61] we understand how Shepard's drama has so often been ascribed nationalistic implications. This begs a justifiable question: As opposed to the work of Ntozake Shange, author of *For Colored Girls Who Have Considered Suicide When the Rainbow Is Enuf*, or even that of Marsha Norman (*Getting Out; Third and Oak; 'night, Mother*), why have Shepard's plays registered on a national scale? That his regionalism in some manner recovers a traditional understanding of America (and its conception of belonging) invites both scrutiny and evaluation. Like Whitman before him, Shepard sings of himself—why is his heard as an American tune?

NOTES

1. Fredric Jameson, "Periodizing the 60s," in Sohnya Sayres et al., eds., *The 60s Without Apology* (Minneapolis: University of Minnesota Press, 1984), 183.

2. Cited in William E. Leuchtenburg, *A Troubled Feast: American Society Since 1945* (Boston: Little, Brown, 1979), 273.

3. Joel Krieger, *Reagan, Thatcher, and the Politics of Decline* (New York: Oxford University Press, 1986), 24.

4. Michael Novak, *The Rise of the Unmeltable Ethnics* (New York: Macmillan, 1971), 70.

5. Werner Sollors, *Beyond Ethnicity* (Oxford: Oxford University Press, 1986), 20.

6. Cited in Martin Tucker, *Sam Shepard* (New York: Continuum, 1992), 106.

7. Shepard, quoted in Michiko Kakutani, "Myths, Dreams, Realities—Sam Shepard's America," *New York Times*, 29 January 1984, sec. 2, p. 1.

8. Robert Palmer, "A Rock Tour Recalled," *New York Times*, 17 September 1977, 21.

9. Sam Shepard, *Rolling Thunder Logbook* (New York: Viking Press, 1977), 10. Further citations indicated within the text.

10. Cited in Leuchtenburg, *A Troubled Feast*, 233.

11. Samuel L. Leiter, *Ten Seasons: New York Theatre in the Seventies* (Westport, CT: Greenwood Press, 1986), 1. Leiter describes the Times Square area of this time as a "putrid mess."

12. Statistics and cited plays found in ibid., 3–4.

13. Christopher Lasch, *The Culture of Narcissism* (New York: W. W. Norton, 1978), xv.

14. Arthur Stein, *Seeds of the Seventies* (Hanover, NH: University Press of New England, 1985), 3.

15. For a historical survey of regional theatre, see Joseph Wesley Zeigler, *Regional Theatre: The Revolutionary Stage* (Minneapolis: University of Minnesota Press, 1973), and Julius Novick, *Beyond Broadway: The Quest for Permanent Theatres* (New York: Hill and Wang, 1968).

16. Cited in Zeigler, *Regional Theatre*, 1.

17. Cited in Stephen Langley, *Theatre Management in America* (New York: Drama Book Publishers, 1980), 135.

18. Cited in Zeigler, *Regional Theatre*, 5.

19. Cited in Judith A. Katz, *The Business of Show Business* (New York: Barnes & Noble, 1981), 14.

20. For a historical survey of educational theatre, see Langley, *Theatre Management in America*, 163–67.

21. Ibid., 14.

22. Ibid., 167.

23. Zeigler, *Regional Theatre*, 236.

24. Langley, *Theatre Management in America*, 135.

25. Zeigler, *Regional Theatre*, viii.

26. Sara O'Connor, "Foreword: On Being American," *Theatre Profiles* 5 (1982): xiii.

27. Ross Wetzsteon, quoted in Michael White, "Underground Landscapes," *Manchester Guardian*, 20 February 1974, 8.

28. Robert Coe, "Saga of Sam Shepard," *New York Times Magazine*, 23 November 1980, 56.

29. Description in Irene Oppenheim and Victor Fascio, "The Most Promising Playwright in America Today Is Sam Shepard," *Village Voice*, 27 October 1975, 9.

30. Michael ver Meulen, "Sam Shepard: Yes, Yes, Yes," *Esquire*, February 1980, 79.

31. Cited in *Theatre Profiles* 2 (1975): 19, 109.

32. Recalled by Shepard in ver Meulen, "Sam Shepard," 80.

33. Felicia Londre, "Sam Shepard Works Out: The Masculization of America," *Studies in American Drama* 2 (1987): 20.

34. This project and Stone's influence are related in David J. DeRose, *Sam Shepard* (New York: Twayne, 1992), 75–79.

35. For analysis of this movement, see Bonnie Marranca, *The Theatre of Images* (New York: Drama Book Specialists, 1977).

36. Stein, *Seeds of the Seventies*, 70.

37. Sam Shepard, *Angel City*, in *Fool for Love and Other Plays* (New York: Bantam Books, 1984), 62. Further citations are indicated within the text.

38. Patrick J. Fennell, review of *Angel City*, *Educational Theatre Journal* 29, no. 1 (1977): 113.

39. Smith has been described as "the perfect Sam Shepard actor/alter ego," given his "matchstick" body and "Southwest drawl." See Terry Curtis Fox, "Family Plot," *Village Voice*, 13 March 1978, 77.

40. Mel Gussow, "Shepard's *Suicide in B-Flat* Presented by Yale Repertory," *New York Times*, 25 October 1976, 42.

41. Sam Shepard, *Suicide in B-Flat*, in *Fool for Love and Other Plays*, 213. Further citations indicated within the text.

42. Katerina Clark and Michael Holquist, *Mikhail Bakhtin* (Cambridge, MA: Harvard University Press, 1984), 77.

43. Michael Feingold, "Kleist and Shepard Flirt with Death," *Village Voice*, 15 November 1976, 113.

44. Jack Kroll, "Crazy Henry," *Newsweek*, 8 May 1978, 94.

45. Background information on these theatres can be found in Weldon B. Durham, ed., *American Theatre Companies, 1931–1986* (Westport, CT: Greenwood Press, 1989). See McCarter Theatre Company, 354–62; Yale Repertory Theatre, 533–48; and Trinity Square Repertory Company, 507–17.

46. Harold Clurman, review of *Seduced*, *Nation*, 24 February 1979, 221.

47. Term defined in Vivian M. Patraka and Mark Siegel, *Sam Shepard* (Boise, ID: Boise State University Press, 1985), 27.

48. Rip Torn performed the role of Hackamore in the American Place Theatre's revival of *Seduced*. This production was directed by former Living Theatre playwright Jack Gelber, whose play *The Connection* took Off-Broadway by storm in the late fifties.

49. Sam Shepard, *Seduced*, in *Fool for Love and Other Plays*, 260. Further citations indicated within the text.

50. Mel Gussow, "Intimate Monologues That Speak to the Mind and Heart," *New York Times*, 9 December 1979, sec. B, p. 36.

51. The production is described in William Kleb, "Shepard and Chaikin Speaking in *Tongues*," *Theater* 10, no. 1 (1978): 66–69.

52. These experimental pieces are discussed in DeRose, *Sam Shepard*, 77.

53. Lasch, *The Culture of Narcissism*, 66.

54. Ibid., xiv.

55. Leiter, *Ten Seasons*, 70.

56. Thomas Allen Greenfield, *Work and the Work Ethic in American Drama* (Columbia, MO: University of Missouri Press, 1982), 164.

57. Coe, "Saga of Sam Shepard," 160.

58. Shepard, quoted in Christopher Bigsby, "Sam Shepard: Word and Image," in Marc Chenetier, ed., *Critical Angles: European Views of Contemporary American Literature* (Carbondale, IL: Southern Illinois University Press, 1986).

59. For information on minority theatre see Don B. Wilmeth and Tice L. Miller, "Introduction," *Cambridge Guide to American Theatre* (New York: Cambridge University Press, 1993), 17; C.W.E. Bigsby, *Modern American Drama, 1945–1990* (New York: Cambridge University Press, 1992), 254–341; and Maxine Schwartz Seller, ed., *Ethnic Theatre in the United States* (Westport, CT: Greenwood Press, 1983).

60. Shepard, quoted in John Dark, "The *True West* Interviews," *West Coast Plays* 9 (1981): 58.

61. Clive Barnes, "The Theater: Sam Shepard's *The Tooth of Crime*," *New York Times*, 12 November 1942, sec. 4, p. 77.

Chapter 5

Playwright, Patriot, and Prophet

By 1976 Sam Shepard had if nothing else proved his durability as an American playwright. By this time, he had been a practicing dramatist for over a dozen years and had composed more than thirty plays. While scores of artists gained notoriety in the theatrical foment of the sixties (then faded), Shepard refused to disappear. Like the many protean characters that people his plays, he adapted, re-created himself, and managed to survive the changeable climate of the American theatre. In 1976 the playwright was honored with an award from Brandeis University for mid-career achievement; yet, despite his prolific output, considerable accolades, and voluminous press clippings, he had at this point not entered that select ring of luminaries inhabited by the likes of Eugene O'Neill, Tennessee Williams, and Arthur Miller.[1] He in fact could barely make a living as a writer. This would all change in a short span of time. Beginning with *Curse of the Starving Class* (1977), Shepard would compose a series of major plays that would assure him a place among America's most revered dramatists. No longer the East Village *enfant terrible*, the exiled writer abroad, or the jazz fusion aesthete, Shepard reached his maturation as the country's Woody Guthrie playwright, whose song seemed to emanate from the American soil itself.

This rise in Shepard's fortune is directly linked to a new orientation in his writing, one that would distance the playwright from the more aggressive theatrical innovators of the time. In *Contemporary American Theatre*, Bruce King chronicles how the minimalist experimentation of the mid-seventies in ensuing years blossomed into a diverse range of stage practices, from the deconstructionist efforts of the Wooster Group, to the new vaudeville of the Flying Karamazov Brothers, to the performance art of Karen Finley, Meredith Monk, and Laurie Anderson.[2] Signaling the high phase of postmodernism, such work proved self-reflexive and intertextual in orientation, and was geared to a sophisticated, erudite audience. It is thus telling that Shepard at this time embraced the most traditional of American dramatic forms, the family play.

Shepard's development interestingly parallels the work of other writers in his generation who grew beyond their Off-Off Broadway origins. Throughout the seventies, from *The House of Blue Leaves* to *Landscape of the Body* to *Bosoms and Neglect*, John Guare focused his considerable dramatic skills on the American family. Lanford Wilson's career illustrates a similar turn. Like Shepard, Wilson gave up the episodic, collage style of his early works and composed a series of realistic plays set in the American heartland. Dramatizing the history of the Talley family, Wilson looked to the world of his childhood home—Lebanon, Missouri—and consequently reaped both Broadway success and a Pulitzer Prize.

In explaining the evolution of his art, Shepard acknowledged how he had "been writing for ten years in an experimental maze—poking around, fishing in the dark." He confessed: "I needed an aim in the work versus just the instinctive stuff . . . [that] led me to the family."[3] This comment suggests that his turn to familial relations not only provided subject matter for his work but a new mode of formal organization, one more stable and centered, less given to the impulsiveness (and indulgences) of his improvisatory writing. This stylistic shift by no means dissipated the volatile power of his work; rather the conventions of the family play served to check and guide the playwright's singular imaginative energy. If we uphold Shepard's family plays as the master achievements of his writing career, we see the prodigious, often raw dynamism of his jazz pieces honed and tempered, channeled within the box-set interiors of the American domestic drama (and its modified realism).

Writing domestic drama has emerged as a requisite exercise for our country's playwrights, and Shepard joins the long line of dramatists—Clifford Odets, Eugene O'Neill, Arthur Miller, Tennessee Williams, William Inge, Lillian Hellman, Lorraine Hansberry, and Edward Albee, to name a few—who have worked that most fertile and hallowed field.[4] Though Shepard would admit a resentment toward the American dramatic tradition (for making him feel "ensnared"[5]), he nonetheless took on the strictures of the form, expanded them, and produced a dramatic universe both feral and familiar. Importantly, such work did not limit its appeal to a coterie of hipsters, intellectuals, or iconoclasts. Mainstream audiences experienced a recognizable world in these dramas, despite their often perplexing events, and Shepard's audience base began to broaden. Jack Kroll has written that the playwright "tamed himself" so that he might "speak to us rather than dazzle or shock us,"[6] and indeed these family plays, though intensely personal and filled with autobiographical detail, are informed by a communal aspect, a desire to converse more openly with a wider American public.

In a 1976 interview Arthur Miller emphasized that despite the upheavals of recent U.S. history the family was "still the central matrix of the entire civilization."[7] Miller's comment implies that the family can act as something of a cultural touchstone, a reliable indicator of national mood and vitality. Though there is nothing of the sociologist in Shepard, and while his domestic plays never undertake any Shavian polemic, a sense of timeliness issues from these works. Notwithstanding his comment that the American social scene "totally bores" him,[8] the images and emotions generated by his idiosyncratic domestic dramas struck a deep chord in theatre audiences and tapped the profound disquietude afflicting the country in the later years of the 1970s.

If the popularity of movie genres is an accurate gauge of public mood, then the decade of the seventies was a time clouded by paranoia and a sense of imminent catastrophe. One of the most profitable movie trends in these years was that of the conspiracy thriller—exemplified by such hits as *The Parallax View*, *Three Days of the Condor*, and *All the President's Men*—which vented a post-Nixon suspicion of authority (and its faceless institutional agencies). A second type of blockbuster capitalized upon the instability of the times and mined the fear of upheaval; hence, the big-budget disaster movies—the *Airport* series, *The Poseidon Adventure*, *The Towering Inferno*, *Earthquake*, and others.[9] Seen against the indelible images of exhilaration and outrage that mark our collective memory of the sixties, the seventies are often recalled in pallid terms, as an anticlimactic period of paralysis and introspection. However, it may be argued that the American landscape changed most radically not during the sixties per se but in the decade's aftermath, when the nation was forced to recalculate its future and reallocate its resources.

From the end of World War II until the early 1970s, no other country in the world enjoyed the economic vitality that the United States took for granted; from 1960 to 1970, middle-class income rose a remarkable 35 percent.[10] Such prosperity shaped the national outlook and spurred a psychology of abundance (the avant-garde is often an expression of cultural luxury). The most resounding blow to U.S. confidence in the post–World War II era therefore may have been neither the John F. Kennedy assassination nor the military's graceless exit from Vietnam but the oil shortage of 1973, an event that gave birth to widespread discontent and a host of key words (depletion, exhaustion) that would come to define this time in U.S. history.

With the OPEC embargo of 1973 the country was brought to a bracing awareness of its economic vulnerability and the tenuousness of American global influence. Between 1973 and 1978, the price of oil rose from $3 to $28 a barrel,[11] and the U.S. economy, which had been driven for years to world prominence by the ready supply of cheap fuel, fell into the throes of a severe recession.

In his influential work *The Lean Years*, Richard Barnet explained that the country had strained its capacities and had entered an age of scarcity.[12] A variety of economic indicators support this conclusion. In the ten years following 1973, the median U.S. household income dropped by 6 percent[13]; the nation's 1975 GNP experienced its sharpest decline since the depression. Inflation, high unemployment, and increased competition from foreign industry contributed to a deep apprehension in the American workplace. The country was forced to acknowledge its limits, and many questioned if the nation could lay claim to the promises of the American dream any longer.

Without the engine of an expanding economy, welfare-state policy could not sustain itself. In backlash fashion, many dismissed the federal government as indifferent and ineffective, a sentiment exacerbated by the abuses of the Watergate affair. Apathy bred resentment, and in 1976 the country experienced its lowest voter turnout in thirty years.[14] In California, citizens undertook something of a taxpayer's revolt and passed Proposition 13 (which capped property tax values). The country's crisis of confidence was addressed in 1979 by Jimmy Carter when he characterized the state of the union as a condition of "malaise." Carter's willingness to acknowledge this downcast national mood speaks to its severity, and near the end of his administration he authorized the President's Commission for a National Agenda for the Eighties. The resulting report documented the attitudinal changes of the seventies—for example, the percentage of Americans who believed "next year" would be better than the last fell from 57 percent in 1972 to 33 percent in 1979[15]—and concluded that hard choices would have to be made regarding the future role of government in an era of diminishing means.

From the outset of his career, Shepard had borne the carping of critics who asked, "When is he going to stop playing around and give us a really MAJOR NEW AMERICAN PLAY?"[16] Beginning with *Curse of the Starving Class*, the writer would counter this frequent caviling. If his early pieces at the Magic may be considered rifflike jazz improvisations, Shepard's family plays are symphonic in effect. Moreover, these works in an uncanny way spoke to the cultural moment, for *Curse of the Starving Class*, *Buried Child*, and *True West* are all, at core, dramas of decline.

A strong autobiographical impulse runs throughout Shepard's playwriting career, seen in the self-allusions and details of family history in such works as *The Rock Garden*, *The Holy Ghostly*, *The Unseen Hand*, and *Angel City*. This interest in his origins informs *Curse of the Starving Class*, whose concern with family ties takes a more expanded scope than in any previous work. In this play Shepard looks back to his teenage years on his family's Duarte farm, and through the character Wesley the playwright conveys many of the confusions he experienced as the young Steve Rogers. Autobiographical references fill the play, and the work expresses the profound sense of want—as much emotional as financial—that aggrieved the Rogers family. The play is by no means a literal transcription; rather the writer uses his past experiences as an ingredient in the creative mix, suffusing fact with fantasy, engendering a high octane art product that supersedes the personal and approaches the mythic.

The plot of *Curse of the Starving Class* is a standard one. Faintly echoing Chekhov's *The Cherry Orchard*, the play concerns the imminent sale of family property. This melodramatic narrative line—will the farm be lost?—reveals Wesley's household as one teetering on the point of collapse, since the farm functions throughout the work as the family's basis of cohesion. This predicament is not so much the result of external forces, though *Curse of the Starving Class* does have its villainous characters, as the internal disarray of the family itself. In the play's first two acts, Wesley's parents, Weston and Ella, both scheme behind each other's back to sell the property. The fact that the two work at cross purposes signals the dysfunction at the heart of the household. The alchoholic Weston is prone to periods of abandonment; Ella, cut from the same cloth as the dotty mother figures in *Buried Child* and *True West*, lives in a state of distraction and pursues a dalliance with Taylor, her "lawyer friend." Parental absence and inattention threaten to undo the family, and a sense of fracture is evident at the very outset of the play, made tangible in the door frame Weston has smashed in his drunken, late-night arrival. Wesley, importantly, serves as the conservator of the farm and argues against its sale; it is he who gathers the broken bits of the kitchen door and repairs its splintered frame.

The theme of starvation pervades the work, represented in a most memorable and significant scenic piece, the family's refrigerator, which seems constantly in want of the basic staples needed for the family's survival. In *Curse of the Starving Class* the family situation is one of blight and deprivation—a House of Atreus in the land of the artichoke. It is telling that Shepard counterpoints the impoverishment of the family to the wider prosperity of California. The play is set during the state's postwar boom, and Weston feels the pressures of a growing consumer economy; he complains that "everyone wants you to buy things. Buy refrigerators. Buy cars, houses, lots, invest."[17] Wesley's sister, Emma, tells of the neighbors' new heated swimming pool, and Ella likewise expresses class envy, evident in her desire for social status and upward mobility—what her daughter refers to as "esteem." For both Weston and Ella, the sale of the farm carries the promise of affluence; in short, they feel as though they have been cheated by the American dream and seek redress.

The melodramatic plotting of the play seems at times perfunctory; it is virtually dispensed with in the third act. The narrative acts instead as a base from which Shepard launches a succession of riveting stage moments, sequences that vacillate between the farcical and the tragic, in which the playwright displays his masterful sense of the bizarre.

"If they're [critics] expecting me to be Eugene O'Neill," Shepard once remarked, "they may be disappointed."[18] Although *Curse of the Starving Class* takes up many of the themes found in *Long Day's Journey into Night* (family attachment, betrayal, alcoholism, and poverty), Shepard has approached the American family play with daring and originality, imprinting the form with his signature avant-garde devices: the trance monologue, arbitrary character transformations, and surrealistic stage images. The dramatist imbues the "red-checkered kitchen curtain" world of the play with a lyrical and grotesque dimension, and the play frequently perplexes and often astonishes. In Act One, we watch Emma prepare charts for a 4-H Club presentation; Wesley enters the kitchen and summarily urinates upon her work. In the third act a naked Wesley carries his lamb out to the yard for slaughter; he returns in the mud- and vomit-stained clothes of his father. As one critic has noted, Shepard's plays "once took place at the frontiers of madness: now madness does a slow dance through the farmhouse door."[19]

Near the end of the play the farcical element subsides, and the work conjures a profound sense of poetic fatality. References to blood, bone, and disease are peppered throughout the text: Emma and Ella discuss menstruation; Wesley relates that his lamb has "Maggots clear up into the small intestine" (p. 187). Such imagery is cumulative in effect and highlights the play's thematic thrust. *Curse of the Starving Class* is in chief concerned with the inherited ills passed through the generations; the play consequently evokes a strong sense of blood determinism. This is dramatized in the crux of the piece when Wesley and his father experience a mystical interchange. At the beginning of the third act, Weston undergoes an unmotivated conversion and exhibits an unexpected sobriety. Wesley in turn assumes the disorderly aspects of his father. With his father's blood coursing through his veins, Wesley succumbs to familial poison and perpetuates the cyclical curse that afflicts the household.

As is frequently the case in Shepard's writing, the conclusion of *Curse of the Starving Class* offers no resolution. The matter of the farm's sale is largely ignored. Weston again disappears; Emma runs away from home. The dispersal of the family is attended by an offstage explosion as Weston's gangster creditors come and blow up his Packard. Against the backdrop of disintegration, however, Ella and Weston remain together in tableau. Ella recounts a bizarre anecdote concerning an eagle and cat locked in mortal combat, plummeting together to the earth. The impact of the story, along with the visual image of the mother and son in tandem, suggests an agonistic, almost Strindbergian view of family life, one that sees pain and struggle as inescapable facts of nature.

In *Curse of the Starving Class* Shepard makes no direct ideological comment upon American society. Nonetheless his evocation of mythic profundity resonated with the theatre audiences of the late 1970s. The motif of determinism, of helplessness born of familial curse, spoke to the grow-ing sense of impotence felt throughout American culture. Given the work's concern with starvation, the play no doubt exhibits a psychology of scarcity. Yet it is the work's sense of innocence lost that perhaps most appealed to the American sensibility of the time. Wesley's character con-veys a genuine affection for the land and a deep-rooted identification with his country; in the early moments of *Curse of the Starving Class*, Wesley delivers a lengthy monologue—described by one critic as a "Whitmanian soliloquy"[20]—in which he recounts lying in bed, waiting for the return of his father: "I could smell the avocado blossoms. I could hear the coyotes. I could hear stock cars squealing down the street. I could feel myself in my bed in my room in this house in this town in this state in this country. I could feel this country close like it was part of my bones" (p. 137).

During the course of the play, Wesley experiences the encroachment of forces that undermine this empathetic relation with his home. His slaugh-ter of the lamb in fact symbolizes the death of his childhood world and the loss of presuburban purity. Shepard outlines no program for social or economic revival; still, his play is imbued with imagery and emotion that ascribe a beneficent quality to the land (and to the past). *Curse of the Starving Class* has been characterized as a "paean to agrarian values,"[21] and its sense of a world surrendered found sympathy in the mindset of the time, when change appeared as an ever-present threat, sorely shaking the country's collective faith.

Though the Public Theatre's Joseph Papp controlled the rights to *Curse of the Starving Class*, the work was released for production in London at the Royal Court. Shepard's shift in form and subject matter drew curious critical responses. Reviewers were astonished by the play's conventional orientation. With no references to "rock culture"[22] or the "hipster fringe,"[23] the play confounded many reviewers and was noted as the writer's least characteristic play. Benedict Nightingale discerned a new depth and poignancy in Shepard's work, writing that *Curse of the Starving Class* lacked the "obscurity" of his other efforts and approached "some-thing suitably lofty and emblematic."[24] Charles Marowitz recognized the canonical aspect of the play and observed its surprising likeness to the traditional American drama of William Saroyan.[25]

Shepard's next domestic drama, *Buried Child*, would, like *Curse of the Starving Class*, exhibit compelling motifs of decline. Otis Geurnsey, Jr., a detractor of the play, in a backhanded way confirmed the timeliness of the piece when he characterized the work as "a dismal . . . exploitation of our malaise."[26] A gothic portrayal of corruption in the American breadbasket, *Buried Child* would register with critics and audiences alike and stand as a landmark work in the writer's career, earning Shepard his union card as a Great American Playwright—the Pulitzer Prize.

Often compared to Ibsen's *Ghosts*, Albee's *Who's Afraid of Virginia*

Woolf?, and Pinter's *The Homecoming*, *Buried Child* is at its core a play of reunion. Shepard's quasi-autobiographical writing, *Motel Chronicles*, recounts a cross-country trip in which Shepard stopped to visit the Illinois home of his grandparents; *Buried Child* draws from this experience, and the character Vince, a musician who wishes to show his girlfriend Shelly "his heritage"[27] and ancestral home site, functions as an alter ego for the writer. The central dramatic question of the play concerns whether or not Vince will be remembered (and embraced) by his relatives, and the ambivalence Shepard felt toward his past is perhaps expressed in the confounding reception Vince receives when he enters the farmhouse, stands before his father and grandfather, and goes unrecognized.

Buried Child is no heartland idyll, and Vince's dismissive treatment by his relatives is only one in a series of bizarre happenings that subvert expectations of small-town wholesomeness; as his companion Shelly (who comes from fast-paced Los Angeles) soon learns, this is not the realm of "turkey dinners and apple pie and all that kinda stuff" (p. 91). Rather, a decrepitude resides at the core of this household, conveyed most graphically in the figure of Dodge, the semiinvalid grandfather who lords over his threadbare couch and dilapidated farmhouse. His condition is made clear when his wife, Halie, rails: "You sit here day and night, festering away! Decomposing! Smelling up the house with your putrid body!" (p. 76). The play creates the impression of a world winding down, and, given the prominence of "depletion" in the work, it is telling that Shepard's first attempt to dramatize this material resulted in an unfinished script, curiously titled *The Last American Gas Station*.[28]

Halie's conversation frequently refers back to a halcyon time, one of sunshine and bougainvillea, and she ruminates upon her former liaison with a horse breeder. Halie's mention of this involvement ascribes a potency to the past, which contrasts sharply with the enervated state of the present. *Buried Child* in short presents an emasculated image of the American heartland. Wearing a baseball cap and enveloped in a blanket (his crown and mantle), Dodge is the parody of patriarchial authority, and the play witnesses an enigmatic, ritualistic power struggle as Dodge's offspring vie for the position of tribal figurehead. This brute competition accounts for what may be the most arresting moment of the piece, the conclusion of Act One, when Bradley slips into the living room and shears his father's scalp with a pair of electric clippers.

The lethargy and lassitude of the household prompt Halie to question: "What's happened to the men in this family!" (p. 124), and a conspicuous lack of strong-willed, commanding male figures pervades the play. Insinuations of Halie's infidelity contribute to this impression as does the impaired condition of Dodge's sons: though Tilden was once an All-America football player, he has become a transient, "burned out and displaced" (p. 69); Bradley, the most obvious representative of lost virility, having amputated his own leg with a chainsaw, is reduced to a whining mama's boy when his prosthesis is pirated. The debilitation of these characters is contrasted with the manliness of the deceased son, Ansel, whom Halie and her friend Father Dewis plan to commemorate with a memorial statue—a "big, tall statue with a basketball in one hand and a rifle in the other" (p. 73).

Audience fascination derives from the layers of mystery that shroud the history of Dodge's household. Much of the power of the play issues from Shepard's strategic withholding of information, and we thus often regard most unusual and disturbing enactments—as when Bradley forces his fingers into Shelly's mouth—without contextual understanding. The arrival of Vince and Shelly functions as the play's dramatic catalyst. Their presence aggravates the sullen relations of the household (chiefly between Tilden and Dodge) and triggers the disclosure of the horrible secret that lies at the root of the family's plagued condition. Though never stated without ambiguity, one becomes aware that Tilden—Vince's father—has had an incestuous relationship with his mother, Halie, producing an offspring that Dodge later killed and buried. This narrative element gives the play a strange depth and resonance, intimating in an almost Attic fashion that famine and blight have been brought upon the kingdom.

The backyard itself—site of the child's burial—functions as counterpoint to Dodge's desiccated household and contributes heavily to the mythic overtones of the play. We learn that the backyard garden, fallow for decades, has suddenly yielded a bumper crop of vegetables; at various times Tilden brings corn and carrots before his father to verify the yard's mysterious fecundity. The presence of these vegetables onstage brings an inordinate degree of audience fascination, and they assume an uncanny amount of power. The backyard also acts as an agent of providential retribution. This site unleashes the progress of a natural force that threatens to invade and preempt the family household, reasserting a moral equilibrium in face of incest and infanticide.

In *Buried Child* the turning point of the drama actually occurs offstage. Vince has left the farmhouse under the pretext of getting liquor for Dodge, yet he determines to flee the family and thus drives westward long into the night. In a mesmerizing monologue whose poetry echoes the blood and bone imagery of *Curse of the Starving Class*, Vince recounts a moment of epiphanic insight when he recognizes his inescapable identification with all the progenitors who have preceded him:

I could see myself in the windshield. My face. My eyes. I studied my face. Studied everything about it. As though I was looking at another man. As though I could see his whole race behind him. Like a mummy's face. I saw him alive and dead at the same time . . . And then his face changed. His face became my father's face. Same eyes.

Same bones ... And his father's face changed to his Grandfather's
face. And it went on like that ... I followed my family clear into
Iowa ... Straight into the Corn Belt and further. Straight back as far
as they'd take me. (p. 130)

This revelation prompts Vince's return and informs his status as an
avenging angel, the male destined to restore the fallen household. Knifing
his way through the back-porch screen, he drunkenly enters the living
room and in mock messianic fashion asserts his blood claim. At this moment, Shelly, who has been showering Dodge with maternal ministrations,
gives up on her relationship with Vince and exits. Conversely, for the first
time in the play Dodge declares Vince to be his grandson and proceeds
to dictate his last will and testament, naming Vince as his heir. Dodge
expires, and Vince summarily takes his grandfather's position on the
couch. With the conclusion of this generational power cycle, Tilden brings
the corpse of the buried child into the room. Vince's rent in the screen
has in a figurative sense made way for the homecoming of the buried child,
whose mummified corpse indicates the full revelation of familial guilt and
corruption.

The final image of *Buried Child* challenges the viewer, for it allows no
closure or easy understanding of what has preceded. As the buried child
appears in Tilden's arms, Halie regards the yard from her upstairs window
and notes its profusion of vegetables. An Easter-like moment ensues, and
Halie reports: "It's like a paradise out there" (p. 131). The work's ending
is textured with many ironies, as this evocation of bounty plays against the
child's putrified corpse. This prickly conclusion has consequently provoked
conflicting responses. Park Dixon Goist has written that *Buried Child* taps
into "an American sense of confusion ... an uneasy feeling that somewhere in the past we made a tragic mistake which continues to haunt us."[29]
However, the unearthing of the child may also be interpreted as an image
of hope and redemption. Spurning a pessimistic reading of the work,
Adrian Hall's Yale Repertory production accentuated the lighter features
of the piece and treated the bizarre occurrences of the household as "on-
going family comedy."[30]

Regardless of whether the ending evokes the censorious or the beatific,
one cannot deny Shepard's deployment of one of the most dominant images of our national mythology—America as limitless cornucopia. From
its inception America has been envisaged as a "chosen" land, an idealization that stems in large part from the metaphors purveyed by Puritan
authors who proclaimed the Edenic aspects of the country and its status
as the New Israel. The corn belt context of *Buried Child* and the profusion
of vegetables it spills onto the stage thus activate a nostalgic response.
Even in the face of the pathology that pervades Dodge's household, the
soil of the backyard and its regenerative capacity inspire a sense of awe.

Shepard may to some extent parody the conceptualization of America as the land of the fruited plain; yet his depiction of the heartland betrays an undeniable power and depth. It may be that *Buried Child* presents the country's agrarian roots in a tantalizing fashion, as a reminder of what has been ceded. Still, for many viewers of the play, the idea of the American countryside retains a potency, a balm-like quality, even if only summoned in recollection.

Although *Buried Child* presents a realistic surface, its veneer of normalcy is frequently perforated by surrealistic eruptions and mythic innuendo; *True West*, the third of Shepard's family plays, evidences little of the enigmatic symbology or gothic imagery of its predecessor. Its action remains within a solidly realistic frame, a middle-class kitchen in the suburbs of Los Angeles.

In discussing the conception of *True West*, Shepard shared that he "wanted to write a play about double nature" and asserted his belief that "we're split in a much more devastating way than psychology can ever reveal."[31] This concern with division informs the dramatic action of *True West*, which may be viewed as a sibling rivalry, a contest between Austin, a screenwriter who is housesitting for his mother, and his brother Lee, a drifter and thief who intrudes upon Austin's attempt to land a movie deal.

The play is energized by the stark opposition of the two. Austin appears in a sports shirt and cardigan sweater; Ivy League educated, he has a wife, family, and career—as Lee describes it, "the whole slam."[32] Lee conversely wears Salvation Army apparel; he is virtually illiterate and lives on the desert for months at a time. To some extent the dialectic between the brothers issues from the discordant impulses of the playwright's own sensibility. If the play were to be done cinematically, Shepard once related, he would have one person playing both roles.[33] Now established as a high-profile figure in the theatre and a growing presence in the movie industry, the writer was at this time feeling some uneasiness with his celebrity. Austin thus represents Shepard the legitimate artist; Lee embodies the playwright's asocial, renegade tendencies. John Malkovich, who played Lee in a successful Off-Broadway production of *True West*, described the character as "the side of Shepard that's always been strangled but never quite killed."[34]

Shepard's concern with self-alienation and internal division carries over into the play's social order. As in his previous domestic dramas, *True West* enacts the erosion of belief structures and the duress suffered by the American family. In the play's second scene, Lee tells his brother of his late-night prowling and describes a nearby household: "Like a paradise ... Warm yellow lights. Mexican tile all around. Copper pots hangin' over the stove ... Blonde people movin' in and outa' the rooms, talkin' to each other ... Kinda' place you wish you sorta' grew up in, ya' know" (p. 12). Lee of course speaks from the position of a voyeur. His idealization of this domestic sphere, colored by the imagery of TV commercials and magazine ads, highlights the dysfunction of his own family and reveals in Lee a disappointment, that he and Austin grew up outside the shelter and security of the proverbial nuclear family.

Lee's outlook is understandable given the rupture evident in the family's history. His mother and father have been separated for some time. The alcoholic father figure of the play—modeled on Shepard's own parent—lives as a hermit on the desert. The brothers have not seen each other in years, and the mother is currently on an Alaskan cruise. This sense of familial bifurcation informs the play's geographical imagery, with Austin and his mother associated with the north (Austin lives in Northern California) while Lee and the father are aligned with the south (the Mojave and Mexico). The alienation and animosity that can arise from family discord are emphasized when Lee asks about the country's homicide rate and who most often resorts to violence; he answers his own question: "Family People. Brothers. Brothers-in-law. Cousins. Real American-type people" (p. 24).

The play's dramatic action is initiated when Lee pitches his idea for a "contemporary Western" to Saul, the Hollywood producer, who decides to forgo the project he has been developing with Austin. Saul's negotiations with Lee reverse the brother's societal positions. Now the screenwriter, Lee can garner huge earnings if he can complete his screenplay. Austin conversely plies Lee's trade and proves his talent in burglary by stealing toasters from neighboring homes.

After a series of accusations and confessions, along with an excess of alcohol-induced horseplay, the brothers come to an agreement. Lee will take Austin with him to the desert if Austin helps him write his "true-to-life" Western. The two actually make progress on the story and achieve a fleeting moment of fraternal bonding. Their tenuous collaboration is, however, interrupted by the entry of their mother, who reacts to the household's disheveled condition with a disturbing nonchalance. Her demeanor suggests an emotional imbalance and a dissociative connection to the world around her (she wants the boys to go with her to meet Picasso at the museum). When Lee reneges on his promise to take his brother to the desert, Austin is provoked to violence. The mother observes the struggle with bemusement then exits for a motel. After attempting to choke Lee with a telephone cord, Austin squares off in a face-to-face confrontation with his brother. At this point the play concludes, leaving the audience with an attenuated stage image (and the prospect of an imminent fratricide).

True West conveys a world in which the forces that hold the social fabric intact have been depleted. This impression is evident in the collapse of domestic relations. Just before leaving, the mother complains, "this is worse than being homeless" (p. 58), and as the brothers eye each other with murderous intent, the play's closing confirms the dissolution of the home and the severance of family bonds. The order of the suburban kitchen is torn asunder and emptied; Shepard's closing stage directions, which relate that Lee and Austin seem "caught in a vast desert-like landscape" (p. 59), underscore the brothers' return to a primitive state and suggest that civilization itself has been overthrown.

A very basic question arises in the course of the play: What exactly is the true West? The text provides a range of candidates, from the world of Kirk Douglas cowboy pictures, to the smog-soaked sprawl of Los Angeles, to the desolate aridity of the Mojave. As with *Buried Child*, Shepard is evasive, and the play does not propound any one understanding of the West; still, his career-long fascination with the frontier merits attention (one of the first monographs on the dramatist in fact appeared in a "Western Writers" series[35]). The title itself, *True West*, is drawn from a Western-oriented pulp magazine, a point that alerts us that the playwright understands the mythologized nature of the cowboy experience. Yet, as with *Geography of a Horse Dreamer*, allusion to the Western past engenders strong emotional effect.

Emerson once wrote, "the new yet unapproachable America I have found in the West,"[36] and certainly much of the power of Western iconography draws from this long-lived relation between the West and the idea of America itself. This outlook derives in part from a basic spatial metaphor born of the fact that early settlers moved westward, first from England, then again later from the New World's eastern seaboard. However, beyond physical geography, the country's westward expansion functioned as a leveling dynamic, naturalizing the country's influx of pioneering immigrants. Historian Frederick Jackson Turner called the frontier "the most rapid and effective line of Americanization,"[37] and the West thus emerged as the emblem of those things most American—freedom, opportunity, and limitless open land.

The question *True West* poses is not a superficial one, for it bears upon contemporary American culture's attempt to define itself in a time of shifting expectations. Turner's argument emphasizes the link between the West and the vitalism of the American character, and Shepard's evocation of the West, comparable to his deployment of the fruitful harvest in *Buried Child*, no doubt triggers a dynamic of yearning. While a "true" West may be no more (if it ever was), the emotion and imagery the playwright conjured in this drama spoke to a sense of origins lost, a heritage compromised. It is clear that the concerns of Shepard's family plays found a receptive audience, since these works propelled the writer to a career height enjoyed by a select few American dramatists.

Following its staging at the Royal Court, *Curse of the Starving Class* received the unprecedented distinction of being awarded an Obie for best new play even though it had yet to receive its American premiere. The play's opening at New York's Public Theatre was thus much anticipated. For some time Shepard had been in alliance with Joseph Papp, the savvy producer and astute reader of the public mood who had originally approached Shepard with the idea of writing a family drama; he had even given the playwright a $500 advance (Shepard in turn composed *Curse of the Starving Class*).[38] Papp had spearheaded the New York Shakespeare Festival since the 1950s and assumed control of the Public Theatre upon its inception in 1967. Founded as a nonprofit institution, the Public soon proved itself one of the most influential theatre centers in the country. Housed in the former Astor Library (Papp paid the city of New York one dollar a year for rent), the theatre would launch a number of acclaimed efforts, including the wildly successful *Hair* and *A Chorus Line*. Though Papp produced the occasional blockbuster, his special interest was new writers. He frequently backed work that would not survive in a commercial market, and the careers of many American dramatists—David Rabe, John Guare, and Charles Gordone among them—owe much to Papp's support. In the 1970s Papp's reputation as a producer was unparalleled (he had also taken over direction of the Lincoln Center), and the Public Theatre's production of *Curse of the Starving Class* thus served to promote Shepard's work within one of the nation's chief showcases of American playwriting.

The New York production of *Curse of the Starving Class* utilized Magic Theatre personnel. Robert Woodruff directed the piece; veteran of several Shepard productions, Ebbe Roe Smith performed the role of Wesley. The Public Theatre imprimatur helped legitimize the play, and though the production was not universally praised, the effort drew a number of glowing notices. The *Village Voice* proclaimed the work a "masterpiece."[39] While he did not find the play satisfying on all counts, the eminent Stanley Kauffmann begrudgingly conceded Shepard to be the "best practicing" playwright in America.[40]

While *Curse of the Starving Class* inflated Shepard's stock as an American dramatist, it was *Buried Child* that brought the writer's breakthrough and secured him canonical status in the U.S. theatre. Given the importance of the play, it is curious to trace *Buried Child*'s circuitous route to mainstream visibility. Under the direction of Robert Woodruff, the play was first produced in the protective environment of Shepard's home theatre, the Magic, in June of 1978. The work was then taken to the East Coast and produced at the Theatre for the New City, an Off-Off Broadway outfit run by longtime acquaintances of Shepard. Again with Woodruff as its director (though with a newly assembled cast), *Buried Child* was staged in a "make-shift auditorium"[41] on Second Avenue, where it ran for only sixteen performances. The play was mounted at a cost of $2,000 (with actors receiving a pittance), an amazingly low figure considering that the production budgets of Broadway musicals at this time regularly exceeded a million dollars.[42] The obvious shoestring approach of *Buried Child*'s

New York premiere—with Shepard devotees filling the seats and huddling in the aisleway of the tiny theatre—led Walter Kerr to question Shepard's stature and to label his supporters a "cult audience."[43]

Despite *Buried Child*'s unpretentious beginnings, the work would catapult Shepard into the national limelight. The play was moved up to the commercial arena of Off-Broadway (Shepard's first commercial staging in New York since 1970), where it ran for 152 performances at the Theatre de Lys.[44] At this juncture, Shepard's career—a patchwork of Off-Off Broadway, London fringe, and U.S. regional theatre credits—seemed to gain focus and momentum. Along with the New York production of *Buried Child*, the play also opened in New Haven at Yale Rep. A revival of *Seduced* was soon to begin at the American Place Theatre (March 1979). Shepard was riding a wave of visibility and in *Buried Child* had written a family drama that in a timely manner tapped the impotence and confusion of a nation in decline. Figuratively speaking, Shepard's stars were in alignment, and in the spring of 1979 the playwright received one of the most prestigious honors that can be bestowed upon an American dramatist; *Buried Child* was awarded the Pulitzer Prize.

Under the institutional auspices of Columbia University, the selection process for the Pulitzer Prize has typically reflected a conservative bent and has known frequent controversy. In 1963 *Who's Afraid of Virginia Woolf?*, clearly the most important play of the 1962–63 season, was overlooked because of its alleged indecencies. While the idea itself of selecting one work as the year's best American play has drawn fire, the impact upon the winning playwright and the chosen work cannot be underestimated. The award brings the writer immediate national media attention and sanctifies the play with a cultural seal of approval.

Shepard's welcome into the theatrical mainstream did not come without dissent—editor Otis Guernsey, Jr., for example, excluded *Buried Child*[45] from *The Best Plays of 1978–79* while including *On Golden Pond* and *The First Monday in October*. Shepard's work nonetheless drew attention from artistic directors and theatre companies across the country. Though his plays had received stagings at many of the more illustrious and progressive regional houses, the rank and file resident and community theatres, often bound by restrictive local standards, had not frequently taken on Shepard's brazen theatrics. This point was made by Jane Ann Crum, dramaturge at the Center Stage in Baltimore, when the company decided to produce *Buried Child* just after Shepard had received the Pulitzer and had been in effect declared "respectable."[46] The award opened the floodgates for the playwright, and his work spread throughout the regional and university theatre networks.

The upswell in Shepard's popularity was only magnified with the appearance of *True West*, a work that accelerated the mainstreaming of the playwright. Characterized by one detractor as "middlebrow family entertainment,"[47] the work approximates the familiar conventions of the well-made play. Shepard has spoken of *True West* with pride, that it was the first of his plays he could sit through without embarrassment[48]; having undergone thirteen rewrites, the play indicates the dramatist's move to a more accessible aesthetic and his increased tolerance for the middle-American theatregoer.

As had become a common practice, Shepard oversaw the initial mounting of *True West* at the Magic Theatre though the venue no longer offered the sanctuary it once provided; the small auditorium was filled with reviewers representing publications from around the country.[49] Now a big-name writer, Shepard also experienced complications with the control of his work. Out of financial duress (he received a $1,000 advance), Shepard had signed a deal with Joseph Papp that gave the producer the rights to any new Shepard play written within a five-year period[50]; *True West* was consequently brought to New York and there embroiled in a battle of egos that revealed the power politics of the American theatre at its worst.

True West's move to the Public was beset with problems almost from its inception, and the squabbles between playwright, producer, and director proved fodder for the New York press. Jim Haynie and Peter Coyote, veterans of the San Franciso Mime Troupe, had performed in the Magic Theatre production; however, Papp chose to recast the show, desiring actors with a higher public profile (Peter Boyle was cast as Lee, Tommie Lee Jones as Austin). Shepard resented Papp's decision to go with name actors and complained of having "movie stars shoved down his throat."[51] Recriminations were exchanged, and Shepard publicly renounced all ties with the production. Robert Woodruff, who had directed *True West* at the Magic and had been hired to mount the New York premiere, argued to abort the show. Papp took over the director's responsibilities, and after having had its opening postponed on two separate occasions, *True West* ran to unenthusiastic reviews and an anemic box office. Shepard's agent Lois Berman felt that the script had been made into "mincemeat."[52] Critic Frank Rich remarked that the production looked "as if it hadn't been directed at all."[53] Dispirited by the public bickering, the actors performed in a listless and perfunctory manner. After the play closed, Shepard swore that he would never again give Papp authority to stage his work.

Hoping to mitigate the damage of the Public Theatre debacle, Shepard oversaw a commercial restaging of the Magic production in a large San Francisco venue, the Marine Theatre. The resurrection of *True West*, however, was primarily accomplished by an Off-Broadway revival that originated at Chicago's Steppenwolf Theatre. Having previously staged *Action* and *Curse of the Starving Class* in Chicago, director Gary Sinise displayed a sure command of Shepard's material and emphasized both the broad comedy and eruptive violence of the work. John Malkovich drew rave reviews for his boisterous portrayal of Lee. After a sold-out six-week run, the production moved to a larger theatre for another twelve weeks. Describing the Sinise-Malkovich effort as an "act of theatrical restitution," critic Mel Gussow concluded that the Steppenwolf production had presented "the true *True West*."[54]

Outside of his New York productions, Shepard's remarkable rise in profile owes a significant debt to the American regional theatre. Much is to be said in favor of the regional venues, which (especially in the 1970s) engendered a dispersion of professional performance across the country. Yet, the success and increased institutionalization of the movement also worked to inhibit localism and heterogony. Founded in 1961 by a Ford Foundation grant, the Theatre Communications Group (TCG) developed as a much needed informational service to the regional theatre, acting through the years as a clearinghouse for audition notices, union information, and advice related to the fiscal matters of nonprofit companies. The networks established between theatres proved invaluable in developing what director Alan Schneider noted as a hard "fought for . . . commonality and community."[55] Nevertheless, this impulse toward confederation for some observers served to regularize regional theatre. The TCG's attempt to encourage a common level of professionalism, no doubt an admirable aim, also encouraged uniformity. This tendency has been demonstrated by the repertory itself: quite often, the newest "hot show" of the season would, the following year, populate schedules across the country.

This feature of the regional theatre proved a boon to the playwright during the 1980s. Showered with accolades, his work became increasingly palatable to boards of directors and mainstream audiences. Notice of Shepard productions passed throughout informational networks and in domino fashion spurred productions elsewhere. Many regional theatres each year—or at least biennially—reserve a slot in their seasons for new plays, and Shepard's works became the frequently chosen candidates. Recognized as an eminently "American" playwright, Shepard offered theatregoers avant-garde titillation (without inflammatory or subversive impact) packaged in a homespun idiom and a salt-of-the-earth sensibility. *True West*'s production history exemplifies the proliferation of Shepard's renown. Beginning with the 1983–84 season, the play would be seen in regional theatres across the country, including the Actors Theatre in Louisville, the Alliance Theatre in Atlanta, the Cleveland Playhouse, Gainesville's Hippodrome, the Los Angeles Stage Company, the Missouri Repertory Company, Mississippi's New Stage Theatre, the Pennsylvania Stage Company, and the Virginia Stage Company.[56]

This surge in popularity led one critic to pronounce Shepard the "Dion Boucicault of the avant-garde."[57] Certainly no compliment, this appraisal points toward something real yet paradoxical in Shepard's art. His family dramas produce both shock and solace. They mock, mourn, and revere American life, all at the same time. In *Nationalism, Colonialism, and Lit-*

erature, Seamus Deane points out that nationalistic literature commonly employs the motif of a fall, by which the nation moves "from a state of bliss" into a "modern condition of alienation."[58] It is thus revealing to recall the beginning of *The Tooth of Crime*, when the elder rocker sings "All the heroes is dyin' like flies they say it's a sign a' the times,"[59] for Hoss's appeal to a beseiged, prelapsarian order indicates something characteristic of Shepard's own outlook, a predilection that exposes his playwriting less at the fringe of the American theatre than the heart of a canonical national literature.

One of the foremost scholars in American studies, Sacvan Bercovitch has argued that the jeremiad—a Puritan sermon of reproach—has proven the prototypical form for our country's writers.[60] In the jeremiad, the cleric (or writer) delivers a sort of public admonishment, castigating the congregation (or nation) for its shortcomings. While Shepard has never espoused any particular political platform, his work has often in jeremiad fashion displayed contempt and enmity for the America (and its consumerism) that arose after World War II. In the early work *Cowboys #2*, Stu and Chet recount the changes encroaching upon small-town life and give expression to the nausea born of modernization; *4-H Club* similarly derides the monotonous order of suburbia and middle-class conformism. Shepard's repudiation of "progress" has its origin in the playwright's adolescent experience of California's postwar boom, and his distaste for suburbanization informs the despicable qualities of Taylor, Ella's lawyer friend in *Curse of the Starving Class* who seeks the "development" of the family's property. This antipathy toward modernization is also echoed in *True West*. When Austin states that the area around his mother's home has been "built up," Lee retorts: "Wiped out is more like it" (p. 11). In a rare moment of affection, the brothers reminisce about playing as youths in the nearby hills, yet suburban sprawl has radically altered the environs of their childhood home. Austin recalls: "When we were kids here it was different. There was a life here then" (p. 49).

Consistent in Shepard's work is the presence of a misdirected American culture. His family plays give expression to a basic pessimism and present a dystopian vision, an America of ravaged natural resources, rampant consumerism, and diminished individual freedom. However, it is Bercovitch's conviction that such negativism in American writing belies a fundamental idealism. According to Bercovitch, classic American authors take up the self-anointed role as "keepers of the dream" and thus labor "to defy the false Americanism of their time."[61] This point suggests that the playwright's indictment of consumer culture and its anesthetizing effects stems from his vision of a "true" America that has somehow been betrayed. Bonnie Marranca has written that Shepard "is a romantic, a sentimentalist when it comes to America,"[62] and his plays may indeed serve to "keep" the dream and its implicit faith in American exceptionalism.

Shepard's vision of America is not that of the civic lesson or the history text. In the *Rolling Thunder Logbook*, he scoffs at the country's bicentennial madness. He frequently disparages the landmarks of colonial American history and dismisses New England as "the land of somebody's forefathers."[63] As Robert Coe reminds us, the West for Shepard is "where America has always hidden its promise and its dreams."[64] Like Emerson before him, Shepard sees America and the West as inseparably entwined. He parodies, mimics, recasts and reconstitutes Od West clichés; yet, despite his awareness of its hackneyed depiction, the writer finds something honorable and abiding in the open range. For the playwright the West elicits the concept of "virgin territory" and its premise that open space brings renewal and individual freedom. In *Curse of the Starving Class*, it is telling that Wesley describes Alaska, the last vestige of the American frontier, as a place "full of possibilities" (p. 163). In *True West*, when Saul explains to Austin that Lee's story has "the ring of truth . . . Something about the land" (p. 30), one feels that Saul might as well be describing Shepard's own work. In these dramas, the soil itself seems endowed with a regenerative capacity, one that connects the individual with an "authentic," inner-directed existence. "Of all the contemporary playwrights," John Lahr writes, "he [Shepard] alone still has a romance for the land,"[65] and the land in these plays indeed serves in emblematic fashion, almost as a national repository, for that which the dramatist most values. For Shepard, the enemy is the developer, the politician, the businessman, the bureaucrat—anyone who would despoil and systematize.

Despite the surreality and often shocking theatrics of his plays, Shepard holds a deeply traditional view of America. His comment, that "one of the biggest tragedies" the country has suffered was in "moving [away] from an agricultural society,"[66] underscores his fundamentally agrarian outlook and echoes a Jeffersonian ideology (with its suspicion of centralized authority). For some critics this facet of Shepard's plays masks a darker sort of duplicity. David Savran, for example, argues that the writer's work "appears to be a revolt" against oppression, though at end Shepard "reinforces and even glorifies the American past."[67]

In the late 1970s, punk-rock impressario Malcolm McLaren (former manager of the Sex Pistols), ever attentive to the shifting winds of fashion, broke with the cool formalism that was in ascendance and showcased a most rudimentary material in his New York nightspot—mud.[68] McLaren recognized a shift in cultural mood, and the pervasive urge to return to the basics, in short, to start from scratch. Given his celebration of the American soil, one finds that Shepard's plays exhibit a similiar impetus. And in light of Three Mile Island, Love Canal, and the toxic public mood of the late seventies and early eighties, one can understand the playwright's allure. His works censure the fallen condition of the contemporary moment and rekindle the dream of American bounty.

NOTES

1. The very notion of the Great American Playwright is a vexed issue, and many theatre artists and critics feel that the search for this "figure" places too heavy a burden on every American playwright who shows promise. Some would argue that this is an antiquated idea born of a nationalistic impulse and should be dispensed with altogether.

2. Bruce King, ed., *Contemporary American Theatre* (New York: St. Martin's Press, 1991), 1–11.

3. Shepard, quoted in Jennifer Allen, "The Man on the High Horse," *Esquire*, November 1988, 148.

4. For discussion of the tradition of American domestic realism, see William W. Demastes, *Beyond Naturalism* (Westport, CT: Greenwood Press, 1988).

5. Shepard, quoted in Allen, "The Man on the High Horse," 148.

6. Jack Kroll, "Savage Games People Play," *Newsweek,* 16 December 1985, 85.

7. Arthur Miller, quoted in James Schlatter, "Some Kind of Future: The War for Inheritance in the Works of Three American Playwrights of the 1970s," *South Central Review* 7, no. 1 (1990): 60.

8. Shepard, quoted in Amy Lippman, "Interview: A Conversation with Sam Shepard," *Harvard Advocate* 117, no. 1 (1983): 3.

9. These movie trends are surveyed in Andrew J. Edelstein and Kevin McDonough, *The Seventies from Hot Pants to Hot Tubs* (New York: Dutton, 1990), 35–41.

10. Cited in Jonathan Alter, "The '80s: A Final Reckoning," *Newsweek*, 1 March 1993, 49.

11. Cited in James Gilbert, *Another Chance: Postwar America, 1945–1985* (Chicago: Dorsey Press, 1986), 272.

12. Richard Barnet, *The Lean Years* (New York: Simon & Schuster, 1980), 15.

13. Cited in Rupert Wilkinson, *The Pursuit of American Character* (New York: Harper & Row, 1988), 108.

14. Cited in William E. Leuchtenburg, *A Troubled Feast* (Boston: Little, Brown, 1979), 276.

15. Cited in Matina S. Horner et al., *The Quality of American Life in the Eighties* (Englewood Cliffs, NJ: Prentice-Hall, 1981), 40.

16. Sam Shepard, "American Experimental Theatre—Then and Now," *Performing Arts Journal* 2, no. 2 (1977): 13.

17. Sam Shepard, *Curse of the Starving Class*, in *Seven Plays* (New York: Bantam Books, 1981), 194. Further citations indicated within the text.

18. Shepard, quoted in Lippman, "Interview," 6.

19. Terry Curtis Fox, "Many Deaths in the Family," *Village Voice*, 30 October 1978, 119.

20. Phyllis R. Randall, "Adapting to Reality: Language in Shepard's *Curse of the Starving Class*," in Kimball King, ed., *Sam Shepard: A Casebook* (New York: Garland, 1989), 129.

21. Stanley Kauffmann, "What Price Freedom?" *New Republic*, 8 April 1978, 25.

22. Thomas P. Adler, "Theatre in Review: *Curse of the Starving Class*," *Theatre Journal* 29 (1977): 409.

23. Charles Marowitz, "Is This Shepard or Saroyan?" *New York Times*, 15 May 1977, sec. D, p. 3.

24. Benedict Nightingale, "Only When We Laugh," *New Statesman*, 29 April 1977, 577.

25. Marowitz, "Is This Shepard or Saroyan?" sec. D, p. 3.

26. Otis Geurnsey, Jr., quoted in Gerald Weales, "American Theatre Watch 1979–1980," *Georgia Review* 34, no. 3 (1980): 500.

27. Sam Shepard, *Buried Child*, in *Seven Plays*, 84. Further citations indicated within the text.

28. The title of this unfinished piece is mentioned in Don Shewey, *Sam Shepard* (New York: Dell, 1985), 104.

29. Park Dixon Goist, "Sam Shepard's Child Is Buried Somewhere in Illinois," *MidAmerica* 14 (1987): 123.

30. For discussion of this production, see Michael Feingold, "Seductive," *Village Voice*, 12 February 1979, 93–94.

31. Shepard, quoted in Robert Coe, "Saga of Sam Shepard," *New York Times Magazine*, 23 November 1980, 122.

32. Sam Shepard, *True West*, in *Seven Plays*, 9. Further citations indicated within the text.

33. Cited by Shepard in Ann McFerran, "Poet of Post War Americana," *Time Out*, 4 December 1981, 25.

34. John Malkovich, quoted in Don Shewey, "The True Story of *True West*," *Village Voice*, 30 November 1982, 115.

35. Vivian M. Patraka and Mark Siegel, *Sam Shepard* (Boise, ID: Boise State University Press, 1985).

36. Ralph Waldo Emerson, quoted in Sacvan Bercovitch, *The American Jeremiad* (Madison: University of Wisconsin Press, 1978), 183.

37. Frederick Jackson Turner, *The Frontier in American History* (New York: Henry Holt, 1920), 3.

38. Shewey, *Sam Shepard*, 113.

39. Terry Curtis Fox, "Family Plot," *Village Voice*, 13 March 1978, 77.

40. Kauffmann, "What Price Freedom?" 24.

41. Production conditions described in Walter Kerr, "Sam Shepard—What's the Meaning?" *New York Times*, 10 December 1978, sec. 2, p. 3.

42. Cited in Harold Clurman, review of *Buried Child*, *Nation*, 2 December 1978, 622.

43. Kerr, "Sam Shepard," sec. 2, p. 3.

44. Cited in Peter Kihss, "Shepard Takes Pulitzer for Drama," *New York Times*, 17 April 1979, sec. 1, p. 1.

45. Cited in Weales, "American Theatre Watch," 500.

46. Jane Ann Crum, "Notes on *Buried Child*," in Kimball King, ed., *Sam Shepard: A Casebook* (New York: Garland, 1989), 73.

47. Mimi Kramer, "In Search of the Good Shepard," *New Criterion* 2, no. 2 (October 1983): 55.

48. Shepard discusses his attitude toward the play in Stewart McBride, "Sam

Shepard—Listener and Playwright," *Christian Science Monitor*, 23 December 1980, sec. B, p. 2.

49. Ibid.

50. Cited in Shewey, *Sam Shepard*, 129.

51. Shepard, quoted in Shewey, "The True Story of *True West*," 115.

52. Lois Berman, quoted in John Dark, "The *True West* Interviews," *West Coast Plays* 9 (1981): 55.

53. Frank Rich, "Stage: Shepard's *True West*," *New York Times*, 24 December 1980, sec. C, p. 9.

54. Mel Gussow, "Stage: Shepard's 'West' Revived and Restored," *New York Times*, 18 October 1982, sec. C, p. 18.

55. Alan Schneider, "Introduction: The Whaddaya-Call-It-Theatre," *Theatre Profiles* 5 (1982): x.

56. Production of Shepard's works indexed in *Theatre Profiles* 7 (1986).

57. Charles Marowitz, *Burnt Bridges* (London: Hodder & Stoughton, 1990), 204.

58. Seamus Deane, ed., *Nationalism, Colonialism, and Literature* (Minneapolis: University of Minnesota Press, 1993), 9.

59. Sam Shepard, *The Tooth of Crime*, in *Seven Plays*, 203.

60. For an overview of this viewpoint, see Bercovitch, *The American Jeremiad*, 176–210.

61. Ibid., 180.

62. Bonnie Marranca and Gautam Dasgupta, *American Playwrights: A Critical Survey* (New York: Drama Book Specialists, 1981), 84.

63. Sam Shepard, *Rolling Thunder Logbook* (New York: Viking Press, 1977), 45.

64. Coe, "Saga of Sam Shepard," 122.

65. John Lahr, review of *Curse of the Starving Class*, *Plays and Players*, June 1977, 24.

66. Shepard, quoted in Robert Goldberg, "Sam Shepard, American Original," *Playboy*, March 1984, 192.

67. David Savran, "Sam Shepard's Conceptual Prison: *Action* and the Unseen Hand," *Theatre Journal* 36, no. 1 (1984): 72.

68. Cited in Bevis Hillier, *The Styles of the Century* (London: Herbert Press, 1983), 70.

Chapter 6

Shepard and the America of Reagan

With *Curse of the Starving Class*, *Buried Child*, and *True West*, Shepard tapped the mood of a nation reckoning with lowered expectations and thus gained a new visibility in the American theatre. No longer could the writer be regarded as an artist of the avant-garde, as he emerged as one of the country's most widely produced playwrights. The fluctuations in Shepard's career and the consolidation of his public image have always been closely linked to the ebb and flow of American culture at large, and it is thus interesting to speculate why his acclaim multiplied in the early 1980s (reaching its apogee in 1986), a span of years which marks a high-water point of conservatism in U.S. postwar history.

Seldom does the sentiment of a nation turn on a given moment, and while the periodization of cultural eras does not correspond neatly with calendar measure, one can look to 1980 as a time in which the country—at least through the ballot box—demonstrated a collective shift in attitude. The presidential election presented the electorate with a clear choice of political philosophies and public personae, and the victory of Ronald Reagan would signify a dramatic expression of the nation's uneasy emotion and desire for change.

President Jimmy Carter's Commission for a National Agenda for the Eighties had concluded that the country was between "idea systems,"[1] and certainly the public's frustration with the federal bureaucracy and a flagging economy prompted much reflection upon the proper (and possible) role of government. During his presidency Carter had become recognized as a hands-on administrator, an unassuming technocrat, who rightly or wrongly became identified with traditional Democratic liberalism. His problems were compounded by runaway inflation and a soaring interest rate (in 1980 inflation reached 13 percent; the prime leading rate surpassed 20 percent[2]). When Louis in *Suicide in B-Flat* asks: "Isn't the nation bro-

ken in half? . . . Aren't we leaderless? Jobless? Destitute? Forlorn?"[3] the
character voices an attitude of apprehension common to the late seventies,
and without a doubt Ronald Reagan's candidacy touched something of a
national discontent. Declaring that "government is not the solution but
the problem" (as he would reiterate in his inaugural address[4]), Carter's
challenger called for a revolution that would reorient public policy and
remedy the ills of the welfare state. Reagan preached the fundamental—
promarket, antitax—tenets of Republican conservatism and promised
America a return to its former prosperity.

Almost immediately upon taking office, the Reagan administration began to actualize its agenda, one described by budget director David Stockman as a "frontal assault on the welfare state."[5] Tax rates were slashed
25 percent[6]; by 1986 rates for the highest bracket had been reduced from
50 percent to 28 percent.[7] With utmost confidence in the Laffler Curve, a
theory that linked government revenues with increased productivity in the
private sector (brought by lowering the tax burden and restrictions on
business), Reagan initiated a host of market-friendly initiatives. Vice President George Bush was appointed head of a task force on deregulation
that in its first two years repealed over two hundred measures of the Carter administration.[8] Social services were laid on the chopping block, jeop-
ardizing programs that ranged from student loans, to food stamps, to job
training.[9] The majority of the voting public backed the Reagan revolution,
and, despite suffering a downturn in 1981, the national economy was
booming by 1984, paving Reagan's way to his second term in office.

For many Carter had come to embody the paralysis of a crestfallen
nation, and Reagan's voter appeal in a curious way capitalized upon the
country's desire for a strong masculine presence. Presidents of the seventies had done little to inspire public confidence: Nixon resigned under
a cloud of scandal; Ford drew less attention for his political acumen than
his pratfalls. Perhaps nothing came to represent the Carter administration
in any more damaging a way than the Iran hostage crisis of 1979, when
fifty-three U.S. citizens were held captive in the American embassy in
Teheran. Carter's inability to counter this situation and protect the national honor consolidated his image as a weak and effete leader. By contrast Reagan's paternal presence summoned comparisons to Western film
heroes, a phenomenon enhanced by the many photos taken with Reagan
on horseback at his Santa Barbara Rancho del Cielo, and by his penchant
for quoting Clint Eastwood.[10]

Commentaries on the Reagan years are sure to note the frontier mindset
that informed the president's political and cultural vision. His fiscal policies
rewarded capitalist initiative, inhibited governmental controls, and celebrated the individual entrepreneur. Dominated by mergers, buyouts, and
acquisitions, financial activities described by one commentator as a "rip-
snorting string of shoot-'em-ups like nothing ever seen on Wall Street or

Main Street,"[11] the American business landscape took the semblance of the open range. Moreover, while his administration reduced federal expenditures on social programs, Reagan bolstered military spending, which by 1988 consumed 28 percent of the federal budget.[12] Reagan's jingoism played to a nation dissatisfied with its reduced international stature, and in his dealings with the Soviet Union, Grenada, and Nicaragua, the president often assumed a gunslinger demeanor, one that allowed the country a moment of collective chest thumping.

Reagan's air of assurance merits mention, for the decade of the seventies had proven an unsettling time for conventional notions of American manhood. An unstable job market and stunted earning power, along with the "threat" of an increasingly liberated (and empowered) American woman, had brought questions, confusions, and resentment to many men in American society. The Reagan years, however, saw something of a male resurgence: during this time legislative advancement for women's rights was halted (and at times reversed); traditional values and the sanctity of the nuclear family took a vaunted position in political dialogue. Following a decade that had seen the general slippage of American dominance, the eighties celebrated might and muscle and reaffirmed long-lived views on masculinity; witness the success of Paul Fussell's 1982 work, *The Boy Scout Handbook and Other Observations. Newsweek* magazine in fact credited 1984 as the year that brought "the return of the man."[13]

In the late seventies and early eighties, American masculinity was explored by a number of prominent playwrights.[14] David Rabe, whose Vietnam War plays had dramatized questions of honor, courage, private morality, and public policy, examined the American male in *Hurlyburly*, a work concerning the miasmic lives of men in contemporary Los Angeles. David Mamet also became recognized through "masculine" plays that utilized a strong, profanity-riddled idiom. In works such as *American Buffalo, Sexual Perversity in Chicago*, and *Glengarry Glen Ross* (which won the Pulitzer Prize), Mamet captured the aggressive and competitive energies of American males aiming at some elusive standard of success. Shepard as well gave close attention to the nature of manhood perpetuated in American culture, and in both *Fool for Love* and *A Lie of the Mind* the playwright would examine the dynamism of the male ego and its behavior on the "battlefield" of love.

To analyze Shepard's mature work and his understanding of American masculinity (and perhaps why his fame and repute climaxed in the age of Reagan), one must consider the codes of frontier manhood born of the American West. One must also acknowledge that such codes mask elements that are neither salutary nor humane. The emergence of Western-oriented art in the nineteenth century has been described as "empire building with images,"[15] and certainly the settling of the West and its attendant glorification were fueled by the expansion of U.S. industry in the

1800s. This history includes the subjection of Native Americans, the plunder of natural resources, and an unquestioned assurance of national prerogative.

Historian Frederick Jackson Turner argued in his famous 1893 essay that the American frontier, more than any other factor, had shaped the national character and determined its key identifying traits—coarseness, strength, practicality, individualism, and a "restless, nervous energy."[16] Given the vast expanse and often uninhabitable terrain of the West, such traits were favorable to survival and advantageous to expansionism. The frontier thus placed high value on physical endurance, self-reliance, and emotional durability; it conversely nurtured suspicion of things communal: government, church, education, and marriage. The Western experience in short fostered a competitive, male-oriented social relation based upon a code of work and silence that remains potent even today.

Hailed as "the poet laureate of the American West,"[17] Shepard has throughout his career regarded the cowboy with fascination, and in an early interview the writer acknowledged his fondness for those sixteen- or seventeen-year-old "guys" who "took on this immense country, and didn't have any real rules. Just moving cattle, from Texas to Kansas City, from the North to the South, or wherever it was."[18] Shepard's fast and loose play with history reveals that his understanding of the cowboy, like that of the movie industry, has derived more from myth than fact; still, the image served to codify something in the playwright's dramatic imagination, and the many outlaws, gangsters, rock stars, and visionaries that inhabit his works are indeed cast in the cowboy mold.

An element of the frontier experience that however gives one pause is its validation of violence. Richard Slotkin has traced how America's westward expansion often invoked sacred authority for massacre and extermination,[19] which thereby linked violence in an affirmative way with "regeneration." This dynamic has informed pop-culture representations of the West, and it is thus illuminating that *The Tooth of Crime* would be characterized as a "rock *High Noon.*"[20] Though set in a futuristic landscape, the work recovers features of the Western genre, and the play consequently raises the question of Shepard's general deployment of violence and the extent of its glorification.

Shepard once noted violence as a "tangible presence" felt "everywhere in America,"[21] and in his works we regularly see males who are prone to physical aggression. Described as one who "leads with his cock," Yahoodi in *Mad Dog Blues* "has no control over his primal violence."[22] From the chaotic antics of *4-H Club*, to the thwarted eruptions of *Action*, to the ending of *Buried Child*, where Vince slashes and crashes his way into the family living room, examples of machismo performance abound in Shepard's work. The playwright may believe that his dramas expose and critique American manhood; yet like his characters he himself often seems fascinated by the heat of battle. Early in *The Tooth of Crime*, Shepard orchestrates an uneasy yet intriguing moment when Becky brings forth Hoss's weaponry for inspection. According to the stage directions, "All the weapons should look really beautiful and clean."[23] The pearl-handle revolvers upon the velvet cloth exude a peculiar allure and invite a sort of phenomenological delectation. This infatuation with gun power filters into the violence of Hoss's suicide, which is not treated with censure but granted a degree of valor. The author dictates that the staging of the suicide should not be accomplished through any "jive theatrical gimmicks" but should utilize "the actor's own courage onstage" (p. 249). Shepard's plays, in the estimation of some critics, revel in this realm of experience and in effect wear their violence like a medal.

This aspect of Shepard's writing leads one to question how deeply the playwright himself might be bound to codes of frontier manhood. In the *Rolling Thunder Logbook* he salutes Steve Soles for owning a '52 Ford; for Shepard, this was "credentials enough for any man."[24] The writer's fondness for what might be considered macho behavior has been well documented. He has participated in rodeos, in polo matches; he is an ardent boxing fan. The playwright once declared that he carried a .38 revolver for insurance.

It is moreover revealing that the playwright has called upon frontier terminology to expound upon his art (he has compared writing a character to "getting on a wild horse"[25]). Recalling the artist-pilot in *Icarus's Mother*, Shepard has viewed creation as an exercise in risk taking. He once re-marked: "I feel like there are territories within us that are totally unknown . . . Huge, unknown territories . . . If you don't enter these areas that are deeply mysterious and dangerous, then you're not doing anything so far as I can tell."[26] Such comment suggests that a dynamic of conquest has informed Shepard's aesthetic thinking, one that views playwriting as an act of courage, a test that establishes the writer's mettle both as a man and an artist. This sort of thinking has earned the dramatist title as "the Marlon Brando of writers."[27]

Such an attitude also informs Shepard's regard for conventional stage practice, which the playwright has characterized as moribund and effem-inate. Shepard revolts against theatrical decorum and pursues a testoster-one-soaked performance of power. This in part accounts for the frequency with which critics mention the physicality of his plays—how they "writhe and crackle like high-tension wires."[28] In *Curse of the Starving Class, Buried Child*, and *True West*, we see delight taken in destruction. Door frames are smashed, furniture upended; Lee and Austin virtually demolish their mother's kitchen. Shepard's long-lived interest in the rodeo, which he cites as an important influence on his writing, reveals much about the drama-tist's masculine approach to the stage: "It's the ultimate theatre event; it's got music and pageantry and danger. I do it and it really makes you nervous—one mistake and it's all over."[29]

When asked about the frustrated and eruptive nature of the American male, Shepard answered that "maybe it has something to do with the frontier being systematically taken away."[30] In this remark the playwright clearly subscribes to a salubrious view of the prairie (as virgin land or open range). The romanticization of the frontier has however come under increasing scrutiny and criticism, especially in its regard for women.

As Bonnie Marranca has argued, Shepard's "understanding of women is as old as the frontier principles he celebrates,"[31] and the playwright's work has of late been upbraided for its sexism. His plays exhibit a strikingly limited range of female characters. One notes the emotionless, detached mothers of the family plays. One elsewhere sees women as the prize of male contestation: Oolan in *Forensic & The Navigators* functions in this manner, as does Honey in *Operation Sidewinder*. Even the women in Shepard's plays who manifest a degree of energy and autonomy—Cavale in *Cowboy Mouth* and Shelly in *Buried Child*, for example—activate conflict and function as antagonists to the male heroes. Women typically remain at the periphery in Shepard's plays, while the men act out rituals of assertion and determine their position in the male pecking order.

It is thus curious that female characters should be given greater dramatic focus in *Fool for Love* and *A Lie of the Mind*, Shepard's last two plays of the eighties. During this period, the dramatist grew increasingly cognizant of the violence in his work and began to rethink the codes that had colored his outlook and guided much of his behavior. This rumination was in part triggered by the events of his family life; also, Shepard was by this time no longer a young man. In a 1988 interview, he discussed this point at some length: "I started out when I was 19 . . . full of defenses . . . It's like you're going into battle . . . But there's this whole other territory . . . And that territory becomes more important as you grow older . . . You have to start including that other side or die a horrible death as an artist."[32] In the early eighties Shepard's personal life prompted much soul-searching and brought the playwright a deeper awareness of his vulnerabilities. With *Fool for Love* we thus find something new in his work. In this piece Shepard labored in a self-conscious way to expose the mentality of aggression; he sought to engage the "other side," what he called "the female side."[33]

The playwright in these years attempted to draw closer to his family; this resulted in greater contact with his two sisters, Sandy and Roxanne Rogers (upon her brother's invitation, Roxanne served as assistant director for the New York production of *A Lie of the Mind*). A softening in Shepard's posture can also be attributed to a partial reconciliation with his father. Long estranged, the two had maintained their enmity for many years. In fact, many critics have speculated that the playwright's machismo theatrics stem in some part from his filial insecurity. At this time Shepard renewed efforts to communicate with his father, and in *Motel Chronicles* he tells of visiting his parent's trailer in the desert and confronting his father's alcoholism and solitude. Rather than condemn, Shepard tried to understand his parent's pain and isolation; in the process he would learn much about himself and his own tendencies toward social withdrawal and alienation.

Also at this time Shepard's marriage was collapsing. The writer's long-time womanizing was no secret, yet his wife O-lan had tolerated his behavior. However, while working on the film *Frances*, Shepard met the actress Jessica Lange, and the two became romantically involved. O-lan reconciled with her husband for a brief time, but legal proceedings soon followed. Shepard moved in with Lange on a ranch near Santa Fe (which was not a great distance from his father). In 1984 Shepard's divorce was finalized, and his marriage of fourteen years came to an end.

Written during this time of personal crisis, *Fool for Love* exhibits Shepard's preoccupation with the male ego and its compulsions. The play also exhibits interest in the woman's perspective. Declaring his desire to "take this leap into a female character,"[34] the playwright self-consciously tried to explore the male-female relation in a more balanced manner. The success of this aim is debatable, yet one cannot deny Shepard's growing attention to masculine codes (and their limitations) and his desire to better understand sexual love and its nuances.

Set in the worn confines of a Southwestern roadside motel, *Fool for Love* depicts a volcanic encounter between Eddie and May, longtime lovers who share not only a scarred and tumultuous past but a common biological father. Eddie travels across the country—2,480 miles, he reports—and attempts once again to reclaim his half sister/lover. The Old Man, father of the two, watches the encounter from an imaginative space adjoining the motel room; the text tells us he exists only in the minds of the characters, yet he frequently converses with his children and at times participates in the dramatic action.

Shepard instills in Eddie the full-blown frontier mindset; an aging rodeo rider, Eddie inhabits a world of spurs, shotguns, and tequila. Stage directions call for Eddie's jeans to smell of horse sweat. Threatened by the younger riders on the circuit, he is driven by an intense competitiveness. May mocks his machismo and chides, "Anybody who doesn't half kill themselves falling off horses or jumping on steers is a twerp in your book."[35] It is not surprising that he attempts to win May's affection through manly display (he practices his lariat skills throughout the piece). At other times, however, Eddie employs brute force and believes he can tame May through sheer exertion of will.

It is telling that Eddie ascribes to the dreamscape of the American frontier and its promise of virgin territory. Early in the play Eddie tries to palliate May by detailing an idealized future—the two sharing a "piece of ground" in Wyoming, complete with "a big vegetable garden" and "some chickens maybe" (p. 25). However, Eddie also evinces the frontiersman's fear of domestication, of subjection to the home and hearth. The prospect of emotional commitment (entering the female sphere) and the regulation of behavior it would demand terrifies him. Like his father who led two lives going from one wife to the other, Eddie cannot commit or settle. His affair with the Countess, who hovers in a menacing fashion around the edges of the play, indicates the predatory nature of Eddie's character, which urges conquest and adventure.

Many critics have cited May as the first female in Shepard's writing to display a complexity of character and subtlety of mind: she exhibits both a willfulness and resourcefulness in her dealings with Eddie and proves a worthy combatant in the play's battle of the sexes. Her characterization nonetheless evidences stereotypical elements. She plays the vulnerable female to Eddie's hardened machismo, and when she informs Eddie that she can "smell" his thoughts before he can "even think 'em" (p. 23), we detect the playwright's appeal to a clichéd notion of feminine intuition. Moreover, one sequence deploys May in an egregious manner as an object to be viewed. This comes when she begins to dress for her date with Martin; stage directions call for May to lay her pantyhose, black high heels, and a sleek red dress on her bed and then to dress onstage. The text explains that May "transforms" into a "very sexy woman" (p. 27). Given her frequent visitations to the bathroom, this moment causes one to wonder why May dresses before Eddie (and the audience). A prominent feminist critic has described this sequence as an exercise in "specularization," whereby the woman is held up onstage in fetishlike fashion as an emblem of sexuality, and an instance of the obdurately male nature of Shepard's dramatic imagination.[36]

It should also be observed that *Fool for Love* exhibits extremely volatile emotions and a physicality unsurpassed by any of the author's other plays. The text disallows intermissions and indicates that the piece is to be "performed relentlessly" (p. 19). The intensity of the drama is enhanced by repeated door slams; characters careen into walls (which are amplified electronically—Shepard calls for microphones to be implanted in the set); Eddie and May physically abuse each other on numerous occasions. Ed Harris and Kathy Baker, who played the lovers in both the San Francisco and New York productions, experienced sundry scrapes and bruises during the runs of the show. In view of the play's sexual calisthenics, it is revealing that this play that includes "love" in its title should be so devoid of tenderness. *Fool for Love* is a drama of bondage and escape, expressing Shepard's ambivalent feelings toward the female position, and more often than not the interaction between the play's couple has less to do with affection than libidinal gamesmanship.

While the greater part of *Fool for Love* dramatizes Eddie's attempts to corral May, the play's final moments are given over to recitation. Eddie, May, and the Old Man engage each other in a contest of performance competency. Eddie and May each recount their own story about the Old Man and his treatment of his respective wives. When May discloses that Eddie's mother killed herself due to the Old Man's infidelity, Eddie takes the side of his lover (not his father), adding that his mother shot herself with the Old Man's shotgun. The convergence of stories is accompanied by May and Eddie's embrace. The two lock together in a passionate kiss, evoking a sense of inseparability that is ironically undercut when an explosion occurs offstage. Eddie leaves the room to survey the damage that the Countess has inflicted upon his truck; May begins packing her suitcase, aware that Eddie has again left her, and the piece's ending thus attests to the cyclical pattern of the drama, a feature that suggests male-female relations follow an inevitable oscillation of intimacy and alienation. The possibility of change is muted in *Fool for Love*, and the work leaves the impression that in some wayside motel May and Eddie will one day again enact their battle of irreconcilable passion. For some critics, this is a disturbing feature of the drama, since it conveys a deterministic understanding of gender conflict (and its pugilism), granting it status of a "natural law," beyond any social shaping.[37]

Shepard's next play, *A Lie of the Mind*, also examines the dynamics of sexual violence. Although the writer described it as a "ballad . . . a little legend about love,"[38] *A Lie of the Mind* betrays its epic pretensions with a tale of love and loss that spills across the Western divide and fills its three-act frame to the brim. If nothing else it is by far the playwright's longest work. In rehearsals the piece ran five hours but was cut to three hours and forty-five minutes before opening. Shepard enlisted the services of the Red Clay Ramblers, a bluegrass band from Chapel Hill, North Carolina, for the play's musical accompaniment; he felt that the piece required music "with an American backbone."[39] This demand points to the scope and vision of the work, and we thus see the playwright searching the pains and passion of sexual love as something of an analogue for the yearnings and divided heart of the nation itself.

The action of *A Lie of the Mind* has as its axis the turbulent marital relations of Jake and Beth. At the play's outset, we learn that in a fit of jealousy Jake has beaten his wife almost to the point of death. First performed by Harvey Keitel—an actor described by one reviewer as "our foremost interpreter of wife beaters"[40]—Jake takes flight and seeks refuge in his California childhood home. Under the model airplanes he had built as a boy, he sleeps in the bed of his youth and is fed broccoli soup by Lorraine, his overprotective mother. Beth meanwhile convalesces in Montana under the care of her family. The play's preface cites a passage from the writing of poet César Vallejo which highlights the "slavery" of separation, and the work is pervaded by a motif of rupture. The stage itself is virtually split in half, with Jake's homesite to one side, Beth's to the other. A vast, open space demarcates this division, effecting a stage image with a void at its very core.

Like Shepard's other family plays, *A Lie of the Mind* in one sense functions as a personal exorcism. Jake's biography approximates that of the playwright, and when Lorraine tells of the father's transient military career and the family's many moves, we note parallels with Shepard's own vagrant youth. *A Lie of the Mind* may also be seen as a gesture of bereavement: the artist deals in this play with the 1983 death of his father, a loss which brought the writer great emotional turmoil. At the funeral, Shepard read the work of Lorca and spoke of his father with respect and affection. Like the Old Man of the play, Shepard's father had died drunk on a desert roadside, struck by a passing motorist.

Like *Fool for Love*, *A Lie of the Mind* explores the anxious condition of the modern American male. When Lorraine asks, in Act Three, "Is there any good reason in this Christless world why men leave women?" (p. 86), Shepard acknowledges a malignant urge in the male sensibility. The playwright by this time had become deeply involved with Jessica Lange and had indicated the positive effects of this alliance; however, the malevolence in his father's eyes—"the pure, black hate with no purpose" (p. 93)—Shepard realized often appeared in his own, and in *A Lie of the Mind* the writer sought to confront this element of his psyche, to understand and to allay.

It is in Jake's abuse of his wife that Shepard dramatizes the graphic consequences of an overbearing masculinity. From his childhood, Jake has responded to personal crises with violence. His attack on Beth stems from his own sexual insecurities and his fear that Beth had been having an affair with some "actor jerk." He in fact voices a rationalization common to spousal abuse, that his wife provoked the beating herself.

The men of Beth's family also abide by deeply rooted codes of male behavior. Beth's brother Mike comes to his sister's defense, but his motivation issues from his wounded pride and anger that an outsider has violated his sister—as though she were family property. Beth's father, Baylor, is another personification of the frontier mindset. He longs for life in the "high country," away from civilization—meaning, away from women. Driven by some unconsidered obligation to the rituals of manhood, Baylor hunts deer each season, even though he detests the cold and has no taste for venison. Beth relates to her mother, "he's hiding from us" (p. 48), and later announces that her father "gave up on love" (p. 57). In the domestic relations of both of the play's families, we see that masculine postures have promoted aggression and inhibited intimacy.

Beth's character has been noted as the "most compelling" figure in the play, representing a "new kind of voice in Shepard's work."[41] After her injury Beth rediscovers her powers of speech and to a degree fashions her own language. Her recovery is more correctly a re-creation as she traduces conventional male/female behavior. Beth highlights the constructed nature of gender when she calls her father's hunting shirt a "costume" and engages in a reversal of role play with Frankie, Jake's brother, who has traveled to Montana to check on Beth's health. Beth states: "Pretending fills. Not empty. Other . . . Now, I'm the man . . . Shirt brings me a man" (p. 74). She in turn invites Frankie, who has exhibited an unusual male gentleness, to "be the woman" (p. 74). In calling Frankie a "woman-man," Beth invites the consideration of a new relation, one that eludes the polar oppositions of gender distinctions.

Beth's character represents an innovation in Shepard's writing, for unlike May in *Fool for Love*, Beth embodies sexuality in flux and thus indicates the playwright's effort to rethink gender categories. Nevertheless, the fact that Beth's alternative consciousness has resulted from sexual assault—that she has paid for her "hint of seduction"[42]—should not be trivialized. A number of critics argue that Jake, depicted as the tortured soul whose violence is misunderstood, should gain no audience tolerance whatsoever.

Although Shepard has contended that endings strike him as obligatory and thus often false, the final moments of *A Lie of the Mind* come closest of all his plays to depicting a conclusion that resolves and coheres. If one views the play as the dramatist's would-be masterwork on the American family, we see that Shepard intends a heretofore unseen degree of finality. As a result, the play leaves the audience with a novel sense of closure, resolution, and, for many, optimism.

As *A Lie of the Mind* winds to its conclusion, Lorraine and Sally (Jake's sister) determine to make a clean break; they burn their collection of family mementoes and look to life in the future. Having traveled across the country, Jake comes before Beth on his knees and asks for atonement, confessing: "Everything in me lies. But you. You stay. You are true. I know you now. You are true. I love you more than this life" (p. 129). He renounces all claims to his wife and enjoins her to "stay" with his brother, Frankie. Beth extends a token of propitiation and allows Jake to kiss her gently on the forehead.

The most striking feature of the play's conclusion, however, involves a flag-folding ritual that brings Baylor and his wife Meg together in a moment of rediscovered intimacy. After solemnizing upon the "flag of our nation," Baylor draws close to his wife, who has helped him wrap the flag in the traditional triangle; the two kiss, for the first time, Meg reveals, in twenty years. Shepard here offers a moment of uncharacteristic tenderness, an impression of togetherness capped by Meg's final line. Beth's mother looks across the stage toward the burning mementos Lorraine and Sally ignited in the prior scene and remarks: "Looks like a fire in the snow. How can that be?" (p. 131). This moment exhibits a subtle theatricalism on Shepard's part. The actor playing Meg actually sees a fire on the other side of the stage, and the line thus works to bridge the symbolic gap that traverses the scenic space. Her comment on another level links the divergent homesites of the drama. The snow of Montana and the fire of Southern California are mysteriously wedded, and the play thus leaves one with a note of reconciliation, despite the violence and division that has preceded.

In *A Lie of the Mind* Shepard reaches for the grand scale, what one critic called a "Homeric passion,"[43] and the effort brought a mixed reaction. The work was cited for its unwieldiness and sentimentality. The critic Paul Berman complained that Shepard had "gone long-winded, misty-eyed and soft all at once."[44] The play nonetheless found many advocates. Frank Rich of the *New York Times* described the work as the "unmistakable expression of a major writer nearing the height of his powers."[45] Hailed by William Henry as the "best" of the playwright's "40 odd plays,"[46] *A Lie of the Mind* would indeed mark the peak of Shepard's renown as an American dramatist.

Given his high profile at this time and his success as a film star, the production contexts of *Fool for Love* and *A Lie of the Mind* indicate much about the playwright's theatrical aims. His handling of *Fool for Love's* initial mounting evinces something of a macho ethic in its own right. After *True West's* disastrous run at the Public Theatre, Shepard cut his ties with Joseph Papp and declared his intent always to open his plays in San Francisco, "with no strings attached."[47] Shepard's dismissive regard for New York intimates a can-do spirit that reveals the artist as a rugged individualist of the theatre, one who will do things his way or no way. In the Magic Theatre premiere of *Fool for Love*, Shepard consequently chose to direct the production himself. He cast actors who suited his own outlook and sensibility. John Lion, artistic director of the Magic once stated that Sam was "not looking for actors" but "chance takers."[48] Kathy Baker, who performed the role of May, was a veteran of Shepard's plays, having also appeared in *Seduced* and *Curse of the Starving Class*. Clearly not yet a polished or technically skilled actor, Ed Harris gave the role of Eddie a rough-edged animalism. Harris drew Shepard's praise as "one of the most courageous" actors he had ever known.[49]

The debut of *A Lie of the Mind* ran contrary to the playwright's typical procedure. With *Fool for Love*, Shepard first aired the play in San Francisco before bringing the Magic Theatre production—cast and staging included—to New York's Circle Repertory, a highly reputed nonprofit resident theatre cofounded by Lanford Wilson and director Marshall Mason in the late 1960s. With *A Lie of the Mind*, however, Shepard overstepped the regional and Off-Off Broadway contexts altogether and essayed a mainstream, commercial production. This decision to obviate smaller venues highlights the grandiose nature of *A Lie of the Mind*; it also reveals something about the state of the American theatre in the eighties.

During these years the New York commercial theatre narrowed its horizons while inflating its costs. Though the eighties saw an increase in Broadway's gross receipts, the number of new openings continued to dwindle. The musical gained an almost exclusive foothold, typified by the lavish productions of Andrew Lloyd Webber (*Phantom of the Opera, Cats, Starlight Express*). According to one observer, the fare of the Great White Way was in keeping with the outlook of the Reagan years, reflecting a "conspicuous consumption and ostentatiously public display of wealth."[50] Such glitz caused playwright Christopher Durang to liken Broadway to the Las Vegas strip.[51] The big-money stakes of the commercial theatre in these years were evidenced by the fact that an Off-Broadway staging of a one-set, five character show exceeded costs of $300,000.[52]

The eighties furthermore proved a difficult time for the decentralized U.S. theatre and its nonprofit regional venues. Reaganomics introduced the theatre to a new fiscal era, one of meager means. Though not approaching the massive cuts originally feared, NEA funding for theatre decreased from $10.6 million to $9.3 million in 1985.[53] The tightening of budgets mostly hurt smaller theatres. In 1984 virtually half the TCG theatres showed a fiscal deficit, even though overall attendance had increased.[54] Also affecting the regional theatre was the right wing's increased attention to controversial subject matter—a preoccupation manifest in the Meese commission on pornography—which encouraged theatres to practice a sometimes tacit form of self-censorship. Such factors served to dampen the vitality of the regional theatre, and the optimism it had generated in the seventies had by this time begun to wane.

The playwright Maria Irene Fornés addressed the situation in outspoken terms and declared that regional theatre in the eighties had "betrayed the playwright."[55] Without question provocative projects proved less viable as resident theatres grew more dependent upon corporate sponsorship and season subscription drives (and hence, an increasingly "yuppified" audience). Often utilizing sophisticated marketing techniques, theatres had to vie with symphonies, ballets, and art galleries for audiences and patronage dollars. The entrepreneurial mentality of the eighties upheld the principles of the marketplace, and the nonprofit theatre was all too often regarded as a corporate entity that had to push a product just like any other. One even finds examples of the commmerical theatre utilizing nonprofit venues for try out purposes; note megaproducer Hal Prince's 1987 production of *Roza* at Baltimore's Center Stage.

While the regional theatre had once stirred hope that it might represent the rich diversity of the nation, minority casting in these years would not surpass 10 percent.[56] Other signs, as well, signaled the regional theatre's loss of visionary fire. These changes can partly be explained by a shift in leadership; while many regional theatres in the sixties and seventies were spearheaded by idealistic, charismatic figures, many houses in the eighties were run by "second generation" leaders more geared toward arts administration. The increased involvement of non-theatre professionals also escalated as interest in income planning often overshadowed aesthetic or social concerns. One observer of the nonprofit theatre commented that "managers might be more than equal to the artistic director, and the businessman and the board superior to both."[57]

Given the problems besetting the regional theatre, Shepard's decision to open *A Lie of the Mind* in New York is understandable. Still, one may argue that the speculative germ of the time infected the playwright as well; aiming to capitalize upon his cresting visibility, Shepard cast the dice and played the high-stakes hit-or-miss game of New York commercial theatre.

Even though Shepard had only four years earlier asserted that he would not use New York "as a measure of quality"[58] for his work, *A Lie of the Mind* premiered in New York's Promenade Theatre in December of 1985. He directed the piece himself and led the cast through an exceptionally long and painstaking rehearsal period. Unlike his work with the Magic, this production did not utilize talented though unknown actors; rather, Shepard selected seasoned veterans of the stage and screen, including Harvey Keitel, Aidan Quinn, Amanda Plummer, and Geraldine Page (Rebecca DeMornay was an original cast member but left rehearsals due to "creative differences"[59]). Beyond the play's straightforward narrative line and absence of mythic trappings, one may also recognize a mainstream accommodation in Shepard's decision (evidenced in the text's stage directions) to use a proscenium format, that is, the signature stage configuration of middle-class commercial theatre. *A Lie of the Mind* consequently drew substantial numbers of bourgeois theatregoers, what one writer facetiously described as "a *Newsweek*-toting audience with visions of Sam Shepard himself, matinee idol dancing in their heads."[60]

For some critics, this accessibilty represented a dilution of the dramatist's art. According to David DeRose, *A Lie of the Mind* marked the loss of the nation's "most uncompromising theatrical genius."[61] The centrist nature of the enterprise is reflected by the fact that the Promenade Theatre stands alongside Broadway houses; it bears a Broadway address and "bills" itself as the only Off-Broadway theatre on the Great White Way.[62] Certainly with *A Lie of the Mind* Shepard came as close to becoming a Broadway playwright as he ever would in the first twenty years of his career.

A Lie of the Mind has been termed a "sardonic comedy," and despite the work's predominance of estrangement, the play ends with a surprising optimism. In essence, Shepard deploys sexual division, what he calls the "incredible schism between a man and a woman,"[63] as a metaphor for national fragmentation. *A Lie of the Mind* reveals an expression of reconciliation and redemption not found in his earlier works; the play also evinces a softening of the strident male outlook. The flag-folding ritual executed by Baylor and Meg perhaps best exemplifies this movement, for the enactment is both an expression of intimacy and nationalistic allegiance. The ending of the work has been likened to a homecoming scene in a John Ford Western,[64] and indeed the play, more than any other of Shepard's works, evokes a sweeping view of the American landscape and a hopeful expression of American cohesion.

The implicit patriotism of *A Lie of the Mind* speaks to the renewal of civic optimism evident in the eighties. "It's morning again in America," the sound bite that served as the theme for Reagan's 1984 reelection campaign, trumpeted this upswing in national outlook, and the president would win a second term by the largest electoral vote ever.

When evaluating the impact of the Reagan presidency, proponents will point out that during his administration the economy experienced the longest period of continuous growth in the country's peacetime history. Also, from its record heights in the late seventies, inflation fell to 4.5 percent. In the mid-eighties the prime lending rate dropped to 10 percent.[65] Economic indicators nevertheless cannot convey the sort of sentiment aroused by Ronald Reagan or the implications of his nationalistic idealism. In 1986, the country celebrated Liberty Weekend (July 4th) and the centennial/restoration of the Statue of Liberty, perhaps the most revered of American icons. President Reagan graced the occasion and in his address asserted that what has "made us a people" has been "our love of liberty."[66] Such public performances showcased the Reagan charisma, and, as many pundits have noted, the president's success as a politician owed less to his command of policy detail than to his unwavering faith in the American way of life and his uncommon ability to inspire.

Reagan detractors will argue that the economic vitality of the decade was bought at the expense of the future. Often described as a national shopping spree, these years saw the national deficit grow from $1.2 trillion at the beginning of Reagan's first term to $8 trillion in 1987.[67] The trade deficit in this span rose from $17 billion to $159 billion.[68] Commentators have also noted that the Reagan administration's laissez-faire attitude fomented a mentality of opportunism, one that would tarnish the decade with instances of excess. The Reagan years, a time described as "market culture run amok,"[69] saw a host of figures gain infamy for their epic stories of acquisition, including Ivan Boesky and Michael Milken, who made millions through insider trading. The administration's emphasis on individual initiative and efforts to deregulate moreover contributed to the HUD (Housing and Urban Development) scandal and the Savings and Loan debacle. This managerial laxness culminated in the Iran-Contra affair, which challenged the integrity of leadership and the veracity of the president himself.

Reagan's egalitarian rhetoric notwithstanding, the policies of his presidency often served to narrow rather than include. Economists have shown how the standard of living at this time become like an hourglass in shape, with an ever-widening gap between the richest and the poorest and a decrease in the middle class. During these years the income for citizens on the lower end of the economic spectrum declined, while the the wealth of the top 1 percent of the population doubled.[70] It is signficant that the Reagan administration devalued the multiplicity of communities within the American community. Whereas Democratic liberalism had attempted to maintain a coalition of diverse populations by expanding government services and proffering a rhetoric of accommodation, public policy in the eighties aimed to dismantle social programs and worked to repeal civil rights legislation. In both 1980 and 1984 Reagan found weak voting bases among African Americans, Jews, Asians, Hispanics and women; he later would draw the wrath of the gay community and others for his inattention to the AIDS epidemic.

On a fundamental level the rise of Ronald Reagan corresponds to a watershed swing in American demographics and political alignment. His popularity and consequent electoral strength owe an incalculable debt to the emergence of the Sunbelt. With the shift in population and industry to the South and Southwest, the country felt the stronger impact of conservative political philosophy and fundamentalist religious belief.[71] Numerous historians have illustrated how the seventies rise in multicultural awareness contributed to a reactionary attitude, evident in right-wing Republicanism and evangelical Christianity. These factions promoted a narrowed understanding of American identity, one that required qualifications for belonging—namely, support of the family, pro-market economic philosophy, commitment to traditional values, and a cultural memory informed by America's frontier past. It thus may be contended that the Reagan vision of America (and its much touted moral uplift) issued from and glorified a purist conception of the nation, informed by a white immigrant heritage and Anglo-European custom, a realm described by one Reagan critic as the "America of white privilege."[72]

Political writer Kevin Phillips explains the shift of mentalities from the sixties to the eighties as a move from Woodstock to the Grand Old Opry (which by the early eighties was being seen on public TV).[73] It is thus not surprising that an agrarian sensibility would prove a fascination of the American theatre. One notes, in fact, a surge in country-oriented pieces. In the 1985–86 regional theatre season, for example, only stagings of Dickens's *A Christmas Carol* outpaced productions of *Greater Tuna*, a comedy based on the local character types of Tuna, Texas. This trend was also seen in the popularity of other rural-oriented works, including *Quilters* and *Pump Boys and Dinettes*.[74] Given the fundamentalist turn of culture in America of the eighties, one can begin to understand how Shepard's drama found a reciprocity in this time (during this same 1985–86 season, Shepard plays were scheduled in almost 10 percent of the theatres in TCG listings). His works castigate the shortcomings of the present and stir longing for a bucolic American past, free from government intrusion and the ills of modernity. Shepard's family plays are infused with the pioneer outlook of the West (and Midwest). They display hayseed character types and utilize a language of the common people—that is, of white, rural America. It is revealing that on a 1981 tour to India, Trinity Rep presented two plays in repertory: Shepard's *Buried Child* and Steinbeck's *Of Mice and Men*. Indeed Shepard and Steinbeck share much common ground and for similar reasons are considered quintessential American writers. They both translate the migrant experience of the white farmer and the agrarian values of the American heartland.

It would probably strike Shepard as anathema to view his works according to the political climate of the day. Still, it is curious to consider that the same public concerns that propelled Reagan to the White House may have contributed to Shepard's success as a dramatist. Indeed, the backgrounds of Reagan and the playwright have much in common. The two share a Midwestern heritage (both born in Illinois, to unstable families). Both migrated to California and embraced an individualistic, frontier mindset (the western states have long been Republican strongholds). It is illuminating that Shepard refuses to vote and exhibits an almost libertarian political position. His plays, moreover, give expression to core Republican values, that is, they convey a suspicion of government (Shepard blames the U.S. government for bringing an end to the West's horse culture[75]), an antiintellectualism, a desire for deregulation, and an emphasis on the individual, self-reliant, entrepreneurial spirit. Such an outlook furthermore honors masculine values and finds the realm of women problematic if not threatening. These attitudes clearly had an audience in the eighties, for Reagan, even after the Iran-Contra scandal, held a 70 percent approval rating before leaving office in 1988.[76]

These aspects of Shepard's background should not lead one to equate the playwright's vision of America with that of the New Right. His understanding of the nation, though idealistic at root, is not the naive affirmation of Ronald Reagan. Shepard often betrays a deep cynicism in his outlook and has no facile optimism that the country might actually recover some lost age of innocence. Certainly as the decade unfolded the dramatist grew increasingly suspicious of masculine postures and the militaristic attitudes exhibited by the Republican presidents of the eighties. During the Gulf War Shepard in fact wrote a short play, *States of Shock*, which was staged at the American Place Theatre in 1991; though the piece received harsh reviews, and stands as a minor effort in the playwright's corpus, it is telling that the work takes a strong antiwar position. The drama is set in a middle-America diner into which the Colonel enters with a wheel-chair-bound veteran named Stubbs. We learn that Stubbs may be the officer's son, though the Colonel denies this claim. The emotional devastation experienced by the pair is rendered more profound (and disturbing) by the poignant turn of the drama, when it is reported that the youth's injury was caused by friendly fire.

It is perhaps one of the great ironies of the contemporary American theatre that the wild-boy renegade of the Greenwich Village counterculture should be catapulted to the pinnacle of his acclaim during the height of right-wing conservatism. Shepard's plays may not advocate in any explicit way the Republican agenda; the writer may have indeed found the politics of Ronald Reagan personally distasteful. The imagery, language, locales, and character types of his plays, however, evoke a world and worldview that is not devoid of romanticism, that is not without longing for a pristine American past. Much dark humor may attend Shepard's use of canonical American stories; in the age of Reagan, however, those were the very stories that many Americans held most dear (and wished to have retold).

NOTES

1. Matina S. Horner et al., *The Quality of American Life* (Englewood Cliffs, NJ: Prentice-Hall, 1981), 128.

2. Cited in James Gilbert, *Another Chance: Postwar America, 1945–1985* (Chicago: Dorsey Press, 1986), 315.

3. Sam Shepard, *Suicide in B-Flat*, in *Fool for Love and Other Plays* (New York: Bantam Books, 1984), 206.

4. Ronald Reagan, quoted in Nigel Ashford, "The Conservative Agenda and the Reagan Presidency," in Joseph Hogan, ed., *The Reagan Years* (Manchester: Manchester University Press, 1990), 190.

5. David Stockman, quoted in Walter Karp, *Liberty Under Siege: American Politics, 1976–1988* (New York: Henry Holt, 1988), 129.

6. Cited in Gilbert, *Another Chance*, 315.

7. Cited in Edward Faltermayer, "The Dual Decade: Verdict on the '80s," *Fortune*, 26 August 1991, 65.

8. Cited in Ashford, "The Conservative Agenda," 198.

9. Cited in Gilbert, *Another Chance*, 317.

10. The prospective passage of a Democratic spending bill elicited Reagan's veto threat and the comment, "Make my day"; cited in Michael Schaller, *Reckoning with Reagan: America and Its President in the 1980s* (New York: Oxford University Press, 1992), viii.

11. Faltermeyer, "The Dual Decade," 58.

12. Cited in Cornel West, "Market Culture Run Amok," *Newsweek*, 3 January 1994, 48.

13. Cited in Schaller, *Reckoning with Reagan*, 74.

14. This subject is covered in James Schlatter, "Some Kind of Future: The War for Inheritance in the Works of Three American Playwrights of the 1970s," *South Central Review* 7, no. 1 (1990): 59–75.

15. William H. Truettner, "Ideology and Image: Justifying Westward Expansion," in William H. Truettner, ed., *The West As America* (Washington, DC: Smithsonian Institution Press, 1991), 40.

16. Frederick Jackson Turner, *The Frontier in American History* (New York: Henry Holt, 1920), 35.

17. Robert Coe, "Saga of Sam Shepard," *New York Times Magazine,* 23 November 1980, 122.

18. Shepard, quoted in Kenneth Chubb et al., "Metaphors, Mad Dogs, and Old Time Cowboys," in Bonnie Marranca, ed., *American Dreams: The Imagination of Sam Shepard* (New York: Performing Arts Journal Publications, 1981), 190.

19. See Richard Slotkin, *Fatal Environment* (New York: Atheneum, 1985), 51–80.

20. Charles Marowitz, "Sam Shepard: Sophisticate Abroad," *Village Voice,* 7 September 1972, 59.

21. Shepard, quoted in Stephen Fay, "Renaissance Man Rides out of the West," *Times Sunday Magazine,* 26 August 1984, 19.

22. Sam Shepard, *Mad Dog Blues,* in *The Unseen Hand and Other Plays* (New York: Bantam Books, 1986), 257.

23. Sam Shepard, *The Tooth of Crime,* in *Seven Plays* (New York: Bantam Books, 1981), 204. Further citations indicated within the text.

24. Sam Shepard, *Rolling Thunder Logbook* (New York: Viking Press, 1977), 17.

25. Shepard, quoted in Amy Lippman, "Interview: A Conversation with Sam Shepard," *Harvard Advocate* 117, no. 1 (1983): 5.

26. Shepard, quoted in ibid., 6.

27. Stewart McBride, "Sam Shepard—Listener and Playwright," *Christian Science Monitor,* 23 December 1980, sec. B, p. 3.

28. Jack Kroll, "Crazy Henry," *Newsweek,* 8 May 1978, 94.

29. Shepard, quoted in Ann McFerran, "Poet of Post War Americana," *Time Out,* 4–10 December 1981, 25.

30. Shepard, quoted in Michiko Kakutani, "Myths, Dreams, Realities—Sam Shepard's America," *New York Times,* 29 January 1984, sec. 2, p. 26.

31. Bonnie Marranca and Gautam Dasgupta, *American Playwrights: A Critical Survey* (New York: Drama Book Specialists, 1981), 111.

32. Shepard, quoted in Kevin Sessums, "Geography of a Horse Dreamer," *Interview,* September 1988, 76.

33. Shepard, quoted in ibid.

34. Shepard, quoted in Don Shewey, *Sam Shepard* (New York: Dell, 1985), 150.

35. Sam Shepard, *Fool for Love,* in *Fool for Love and Other Plays* (New York: Bantam Books, 1984), 30. Further citations indicated within the text.

36. Lynda Hart, "Sam Shepard's Spectacle of Impossible Heterosexuality," in June Schlueter, ed., *Feminist Rereadings of Modern America Drama* (London: Associated University Presses, 1989), 220.

37. Rosemarie Bank, "Self As Other: Sam Shepard's *Fool for Love* and *A Lie of the Mind,*" in ibid., 229.

38. Shepard, quoted in Ross Wetzsteon, "Unknown Territory," *Village Voice,* 10 December 1985, 55.

39. Sam Shepard, *A Lie of the Mind and The War in Heaven* (New York: New American Library, 1987), music note. Further citations indicated within the text.

40. Frank Rich, "Theater: *A Lie of the Mind* by Sam Shepard," *New York Times*, 6 December 1985, sec. C, p. 3.

41. Felicia Londre, "Sam Shepard Works Out: The Masculinization of America," *Studies in American Drama, 1945–Present* 2 (1987): 20.

42. Sue-Ellen Case, "Towards a Butch-Femme Aesthetic," in Lynda Hart, ed., *Making a Spectacle: Feminist Readings on Contemporary Women's Theatre* (Ann Arbor: University of Michigan Press, 1989), 297.

43. Gordon Rogoff, "America Screened," *Village Voice*, 17 December 1985, 117.

44. Paul Berman, review of *A Lie of the Mind*, *Nation*, 22 February 1986, 218.

45. Rich, "Theater," sec. C, p. 3.

46. William A Henry, III, "Achieving a Vision of Order," *Time*, 16 December 1985, 83.

47. Shepard, quoted in Barnard Weiner, "The True Story of Shepard's *True West*," *San Francisco Chronicle Datebook*, 12 April 1981, 25.

48. John Lion, quoted in Robert Goldberg, "Sam Shepard, American Original," *Playboy*, March 1984, 112.

49. Shepard, quoted in Chris Peachment, "American Hero," *Time Out*, 23 August 1984, 16.

50. Alan Woods, "Commercial American Theatre in the Reagan Era," in Ron Engle and Tice Miller, eds., *The American Stage* (Cambridge: Cambridge University Press, 1993), 254. Woods provides a general survey of Broadway's status during these years.

51. Christoper Durang, quoted in David Savran, *In Their Own Words* (New York: Theatre Communications Group, 1988), 38.

52. Cited in Esther Harriot, *American Voices: Five Contemporary Playwrights in Essays and Interviews* (London: McFarland, 1988), 94.

53. Cited in Lindsey Zesch, "Stormy Weather," *American Theatre*, June 1984, 29.

54. Cited in Peter Zeisler, "A Growing Chaos," *American Theatre*, March 1985, 3.

55. Maria Irene Fornés, quoted in Savran, *In Their Own Words*, 65.

56. Cited in Kathleen Hulser and Arthur Bartow, "Rehearsal for an Absence of Racism," *American Theatre*, February 1987, 22.

57. W. McNeil Lowery, "Purging the Citadel," *American Theatre*, October 1984, 22.

58. Shepard, quoted in Weiner, "The True Story," 25.

59. An overview of the rehearsal process for *A Lie of the Mind* is given in Nan Robertson, "The Multidimensional Sam Shepard," *New York Times*, 21 January 1986, sec. C, p. 15.

60. Steven Putzel, "Expectation, Confutation, Revelation: Audience Complicity in the Plays of Sam Shepard," *Modern Drama* 30, no. 2 (1987): 148.

61. David DeRose, "Slouching toward Broadway: Shepard's *A Lie of the Mind*," *Theater* 17 (1986): 74. DeRose gives a fine account of the commercialism of the production and its approach to Broadway status.

62. Ibid., 69.

63. Shepard, quoted in Jonathan Cott, "The Rolling Stone Interview," *Rolling Stone*, 18 December 1986, 170.

64. Rich, "Theater," sec. C, p. 3.

65. Cited in Ashford, "The Conservative Agenda," 199.

66. Reagan, quoted in David E. Procter, *Enacting Political Culture* (New York: Praeger, 1991), 25.

67. Adam Smith, *The Roaring 80s* (New York: Summit Books, 1988), 17.

68. Jack Kurtzman, *The Decline and Crash of the American Economy* (New York: W. W. Norton & Company, 1988), 11.

69. West, "Market Culture," 48.

70. Cited in Schaller, *Reckoning with Reagan*, 76.

71. For a discussion of this phenomenon, see Bruce Kuhre, "The Politicalization of the 'Christian Right' and Its Union with the 'New Right,' " in Walter Grunzweig et al., eds., *Constructing the Eighties* (Tubingen, Austria: Gunter Narr Verlag, 1992), 51–66.

72. Joel Kreiger, *Reagan, Thatcher, and the Politics of Decline* (New York: Oxford University Press, 1986), 146.

73. Kevin P. Phillips, *Post-Conservative America* (New York: Random House, 1981), xv.

74. See John Istel, "Less Tragedy, More Tuna," *American Theatre*, October 1985, 18.

75. Shepard argues this point in Sessums, "Geography," 78.

76. Cited in Schaller, *Reckoning with Reagan*, 179.

Chapter 7

Shepard Screened

In 1986 Sam Shepard rose to the pinnacle of his popularity and achieved a mainstream visibility seldom enjoyed by an American writer. With productions of three plays running concurrently in New York, *A Lie of the Mind*, *Fool for Love*, and *Curse of the Starving Class*, Shepard garnered nationwide attention when *Fool for Love* was released as a feature-length motion picture. Under the direction of the acclaimed Robert Altman, the film's cast included the rising star Kim Basinger, Harry Dean Stanton (a veteran character actor with a hip cult following), and the playwright himself in the male lead. Given this flurry of activity and the attendant hype, a cartoon in the *New Yorker* parodied the playwright's phenomenal success, depicting a theatre marquee that read: "Now Playing: the Sam Shepard to Beat All the Other Sam Shepards Now Running."[1]

In the 1980s Shepard became as renowned for his movie work as for his playwriting. Many today recognize him exclusively for his screen roles; for some, his writing if known at all is regarded as a picaresque footnote. During these years, Shepard emerged as a "personality," and the extent of his notoriety reached far into popular culture. *People* magazine recognized the playwright as one of the nation's twenty-five most interesting figures.[2] *Playgirl* noted him as one of America's sexiest men.[3] The writer on the range, Shepard touched a nerve of yearning and desire in the body politic. The playwright found himself idealized not only as a pop star and sex symbol but as an icon of American identity itself.

In retrospect, *Angel City* seems almost prescient, detailing the seduction of its artist-shaman-hero by the moviemaking machinery. Indeed, Shepard now works almost entirely in the film medium; only two new plays have been staged since 1986. His involvement and attendant success in the film industry, however, should come as no surprise. As frequently evidenced in his confessional work, *Motel Chronicles*, the playwright has long exhib-

ited a deeply rooted fascination with the movies. Quoting Sydney Greenstreet, Marlene Dietrich, Humphrey Bogart, and others, his characters
have in many cases parodied, or even simply reproduced, famous film
personalities. As Shepard is a child of the electronic media age, his dramatic vision owes much to the forms, phenomena, and conventions of
cinema. It has been suggested that the fluid, often epic dimension of his
plays comes from a basically filmic imagination; note that *Operation Sidewinder* was conceived by the writer as a "movie for the stage."[4] Certainly
the movies held an almost magical allure for the dramatist long before he
took up the pen.

One might also speculate that the playwright had his sights on stardom
from the beginning of his artistic career. Lacking in stage training and
background in the dramatic tradition, he in a very real sense stumbled into
the theatre. When one imagines him as an adventure-seeking, high-strung
young newcomer to New York, it is understandable how the Off-Off
Broadway scene might have appealed to him, as a ready platform for the
expression of his adolescent angst (and a quick path to recognition). Indeed his rather arbitrary turn to the stage corroborates his more general
indifference to the medium; on numerous occasions, Shepard has admitted
no strong feeling for the theatre per se, has noted its boredom and has
been quick to express his disaffection—"I hate the fucking theatre."[5] As
the playwright confessed early in his career, he wanted to be a rock star,
an assertion that suggests the writer's implicit faith in his inevitable notoriety and his valuation of theatre as a means to an end.

If one somehow sees Shepard's film work as a defection, then a central
culprit must be the economics of the U.S. entertainment industry and the
financial situation of American theatre itself. Throughout the first decades
of his career Shepard struggled emotionally and financially to bring his
works to the stage. Even when he had reached a position of significant
stature, he experienced difficulties in negotiating with producers and in
securing a steady livelihood. The bleak financial prospect for those who
pursue theatre for a living is legendary. In 1993 seventeen thousand of the
twenty thousand New York Equity Actors were employed outside the
theatre.[6] Obviously, the economic stakes of a movie venture dwarf the
budgets of most theatrical productions. The recent Broadway show *Guys
and Dolls* took over $6 million to produce,[7] ranking it as one of the more
costly efforts of the American theatre. Yet, this figure appears embarrass-
ingly paltry when compared to the budgets of American feature films: the
comic actor Jim Carrey can himself command a per-film salary of $20
million.[8] The staggering production costs for Kevin Costner's 1995 action
film *Waterworld*, which was roundly panned by the critics, exceeded $200
million.[9]

For a young writer who is seldom given opportunity (and financial assistance) to develop within the nurturing confines of a theatre company,

the magnetism of Hollywood exerts a powerful influence. The crossover between stage and screen evinces a rich history in American entertainment. Clifford Odets, Arthur Miller, Tennessee Williams, and William Inge, among others, have worked in Hollywood. More recently, John Guare, David Mamet, David Rabe, and Beth Henley (to name a few) have turned to screenwriting. Eric Overmeyer, author of the highly poetic play *On the Verge or The Geography of Yearning*, has for many years worked in television and was formerly a member of the writing team for the medical drama *St. Elsewhere*. In bald mercenary terms, a life in the theatre cannot compete with film and television's financial rewards.

It must also be conceded that the status of American theatre appears minuscule in face of film's market size, the expanding reach of global, multimedia corporations, and the movies' impact on cultural consciousness (and consumerism). In the 1993–94 season, a good year for Broadway, attendance of eight million was cause for celebration. Still, the percentage of the U.S. population that attends theatre remains low, suggesting the coterie (or elitist) nature of theatrical performance. Michael Feingold has opined that "to most Americans today a live stage performance is a marginal and exotic phenomenon,"[10] and without question the audience drawn by all of American theatre combined, from community playhouses to the Great White Way, cannot measure up to the box-office figures generated by any Steven Spielberg or Disney production.

In *True West*, Lee parrots the views of the producer Saul and declares, "In this business we make movies. American movies. Leave the films to the French."[11] Lee's pronouncement draws attention to Hollywood's blockbuster mentality and the sensationalist tastes of its audience. It also says something nationalistic about the movies themselves, that the American movie is perhaps the most cherished and dominant art form in American culture. For many theatre artists, this has lead increasingly to the belief that legitimacy only comes when one has "made it" on the screen (and at the box office). Hosts of our country's upcoming writers, even when they pursue work in poetry, fiction, or playwriting, labor in the shadow of the film industry. A writer indifferent to media opportunities faces likely obscurity (and poverty). Success in film or TV not only often serves to consolidate an artist's public reputation, it allows the individual to become involved in one of most influential institutions of the public or private sector—the machine that shapes the very stuff of American dreams.

A survey of Shepard's work in film includes a number of projects that date from his New York days. In these early years he cowrote *Me and My Brother* with Frank Rich. He scripted the unproduced screenplay *Maxagasm*, which had been commissioned by the Rolling Stones. Certainly, the major effort of his early career came with *Zabriskie Point*. Although he had acted in *Brand X*, a cult film directed by Win Chamberlain (a Warhol associate), it was not until many years after his New York residency that Shepard gained attention as a film actor, in *Days of Heaven* (1978). Since that time, Shepard has worked regularly as a screen performer and has amassed a sizable list of credits: *Resurrection* (1980), *Raggedy Man* (1981), *Frances* (1982), *The Right Stuff* (1983), *Country* (1984), *Fool for Love* (1985), *Crimes of the Heart* (1986), *Baby Boom* (1987), *Steel Magnolias* (1989), *Defenseless* (1991), *The Voyager* (1991), *Thunderheart* (1992), *The Pelican Brief* (1993), and *Safe Passage* (1994).

Shepard's repute has often fed and framed his on-screen performances. The majority of his film roles capitalize on his image as a renegade, the uncompromising nonconformist who eschews convention (and often "city ways") and retains an inner, private vision. In *Resurrection* Shepard plays the obsessed son of a small-town minister. He brings a manic intensity to the role, and in *Motel Chronicles* he recounts shooting an action scene for the film in which he rode a motorcyle at eighty-five miles per hour; in the rush of the moment and its exhilaration, Shepard discovered that whatever confusions he felt about playing this character evaporated—he only had to be himself.[12]

In both *Raggedy Man* and *Frances* Shepard also plays an outsider. In the former, he appears in the film's opening moments, his character shown womanizing in a beer joint; this behavior we understand to cause a breakup of his family and the relocation of his wife (played by Sissy Spacek) and children. His character experiences some sort of disfiguring trauma and thereafter lurks around the edges of the movie, as the raggedy man. In an ending that perhaps served as wish fulfillment for the dramatist given his own personal history and obsession with family dysfunction, the raggedy man gains redemption by foiling a rape attempt upon his wife; though he is killed in the process, he provides his children with an assurance of protection and a guarantee of paternal love.

In *Frances* Shepard plays an unconventional journalist who befriends Frances Farmer, the precociously talented yet wildly independent actress who is promoted, then punished, by movie-industry moguls. His character stands outside the system and functions as support to Farmer, a fellow loner and outcast. This film is significant not only because it provided the writer his largest role thus far, but also because it brought Shepard and Jessica Lange together romantically.

The deployment of Shepard as a renegade has more recently informed his work in the action/thriller genre. In *Defenseless* he plays a police detective who bucks the system and solves an incest/porn/murder mystery, winning the affections of Barbara Hershey's character in the process. Set in the Arizona desert, *Thunderheart* displays the playwright as another irascible lawman, one who lives by his own code and commands status as a living-legend. And, in the 1993 film, *The Pelican Brief* Shepard plays a nonconformist (and rather dissolute) law professor; the character works at his own discretion and avows a legal philosophy that privileges individual rights.

When German director Volker Schlondorff chose Shepard for the 1950s hero of his film *The Voyager* he termed the playwright the perfect cast, the perfect "intellectual loner."[13] This sort of thinking has influenced the majority of Shepard's film work; he typically plays roles that align with (and market) his offscreen persona. This pattern held true to form in his most heralded film role to date, that of Chuck Yeager in *The Right Stuff*, a role that would earn him an Oscar nomination in 1983.

A major American film with a considerable production budget, *The Right Stuff* envisioned itself as an American epic about the U.S. space program. Director Phil Kaufman sought a special performer to play the role of Chuck Yeager, the maverick test pilot who broke the sound barrier. Serving as a contrast to the Mercury 7 astronauts, Yeager was depicted as the cowboy-pilot, the loner who stretched the boundaries of aviation and rode the skies for glory's sake. The Mercury 7 flyers were conversely portrayed as corporate men, NASA's ambassadors, who were lionized by a celebrity-hunger media machine. In *The Right Stuff* the Yeager character is, of course, the film's true hero, the lean, laconic American flyer.

Kaufman pursued Shepard for this role, and his reasons for doing so are telling.[14] The director was fully aware of Shepard's repute as a playwright and discerned parallels between the writer and Yeager the test pilot. In essence, Kaufman wanted a rebel to play the role of rebel. Moreover, he saw in Shepard a sort of natural charisma; the playwright brought an untutored approach to the part, one devoid of affectation and artifice, and the casting decision proved a stroke of genius. His portrayal was widely praised; as one prominent film critic astutely noted, the playwright "was the right iconic choice for the part."[15]

In addition to the irony and amusement of watching the playwright displayed as a movie actor, one recognizes another facet of Shepard's celebrity that extends beyond his portrayal of outsiders, that is, the more general fascination aroused by his face and body, as that of an American body. It is not insignificant that the writer's rise as a film personality coincided with the election of a film personality to the U.S. presidency. Emphasizing the easy intercourse between the realities of politics and the conventions of film, Michael Rogin has examined how Reagan frequently appealed to movies in portentous moments of his presidency.[16] A veteran of jingoistic war pictures and grade-B Westerns, Reagan—the former host of *Death Valley Days*—saw his screen credits instill in his political life an uncanny potency. In essence, his all-American persona translated into political capital. In similar manner Shepard's very face and gait have helped usher him before the public eye. When Chris Peachment writes that the playwright "belongs in the era of John Ford or Howard Hawkes,"[17] he highlights a key feature of Shepard's popularity; like the president of this time, the playwright profited from a cultural nostalgia, one informed by vaunted media images of the American frontier.

A number of media constructs in these years confirm the reactionary temper of the times and the nation's desire for assurance, certitude, and stories of American muscle. The early 1980s witnessed a boom of chauvinistic action pictures, a phenomenon dominated by the Sylvester Stallone character Rambo, an indomitable killing machine who returned to Vietnam and through his single-handed heroics restored America's tarnished national honor. A similar dynamic can be found in a number of Chuck Norris's *Missing in Action* movies. While the cowboy genre experienced no great rise, science fiction became a popular form, evidenced in the *Star Wars* series, which, as has been observed, packaged the Western formula in sci-fi decor.[18]

The restoration of American pride, frequently cited as a hallmark of the eighties, triggered renewed interest in the country's rural legacy. The eighties also brought an epidemic of bankruptcies and foreclosures, causing many to wonder if corporate farming would displace the family farm altogether. Celebrities rallied to the cause: showcasing musicians as diverse in appeal as George Jones and Neil Young. Willie Nelson's Farm Aid concerts, inaugurated in 1985, brought in millions of dollars for the relief of beleaguered farmers. Also at this time a spate of "save-the-farm" films played the nation's moviehouses, a trend best exemplified by *Places in the Heart*, the award-winning film that brought Sally Field an Oscar for best actress. Given his rugged features and homespun manner, it is not surprising that Shepard also starred in a farm movie of this formula—*Country*. Playing opposite Jessica Lange, a native of Minnesota and herself an offspring of agrarian stock, Shepard gave a strong performance as a despondent farmer facing the imminent loss of his land. In the early eighties, Western wear and country music flourished, and one might rightfully argue that what fueled Shepard's rise to screen stardom were the same forces that brought us J. R. Ewing and the mechanical bull.

The film success of Sam Shepard stands as a most fascinating dimension of his career, for the art and persona of no American playwright have ever been so intertwined. Certainly, at no time in the history of the American theatre has a playwright's physique been so valued. Imagine if you will (or can) the faces of Christopher Durang, Maria Irene Fornés, David Mamet, or August Wilson, all American playwrights of significant accomplishment and stature. None can begin to match the visibility of Sam Shepard, whose features, for many admirers, would as easily suit Mount Rushmore as the movie screen.

Throughout his career as a playwright, critics have commented upon the writer's physical appearance with inordinate frequency. Early on reviewers mentioned his lean and ascetic features: Stewart McBride, for example, noted Shepard as "a handsomely rangy fellow in dark aviator glasses and tooled cowboy boots."[19] Such observations indicate a preoccupation not just with Shepard's authorship but with his looks and bearing; these remarks also invite the fundamental question begged by the writer's ascendance in American popular culture—to what extent has his fame derived from his very visage? Importantly, Shepard has never claimed to be an actor; he readily confesses that he lacks "the chops" and attributes his success to posturing and the close-up camera shot.[20] This admission corroborates the fact that viewers see in Shepard a rare physical charisma. His face and figure evoke a train of connotative metaphors and emotions, triggering something powerful in the nation's collective consciousness.

Days of Heaven director Terrence Malick offered Shepard his first role in a feature film after having only seen a brief profile shot of the writer in *Reynaldo and Clara*,[21] the unwieldy film that documented Bob Dylan's Rolling Thunder Tour. For Malick, Shepard's features compelled attention and conveyed something of the great American prairie; he would remark that the writer "looked great" on horseback.[22] Shepard's physical presence was similarly deployed in *The Right Stuff*. The playwright speaks little in the film and is typically shown in profile, solemn, brooding, against the backdrop of desert expanse (director Philip Kaufman praised Shepard for the way he filled his leather jacket). Time and again, Shepard's look and its earthy appeal have been instrumental in his film work and the types of roles he has undertaken: in *Baby Boom* he plays a soft-spoken country veterinarian to Diane Keaton's frazzled, urbanite businesswoman; in *Crimes of the Heart* he plays yet another "horse doctor"; and in *Steel Magnolias* Shepard performs as the rough-edged car mechanic married to a small-town beautician (played, significantly, by Dolly Parton).

Marshall McLuhan gained fame in the 1960s by forecasting a paradigmatic shift in cultural consciousness. For McLuhan, the rise of the media and its technologies threatened a profound restructuring of knowledge and perception.[23] He stressed that American society had shifted from a reading public to a viewing public and underscored the media's increasing influence in the shaping of public opinion and political reality. The insights in his book *The Medium is the Message* have to a large extent been verified, for TV and film have gained unprecedented power in American culture and have contributed heavily to the promulgation of cultural values. If national solidarity comes from a general accedence to communal myths and privileged narratives, one may conclude that the movies have become the repository of America's stories (and their depiction of an American identity); in short, it is Hollywood that now guards and purveys the "parables" of the nation.

A list of the various American icons to whom Shepard has been compared is enlightening: Ernest Hemingway, Huck Finn, Audie Murphy, and John Wayne, among others; it has even been written that the playwright seems "locked in the body of Jimmy Stewart."[24] Such comparisons confirm that Shepard's power as a film presence comes in large measure from the way in which his image and body recall a deeply ingrained American outlook, one that is endlessly recycled in the movie industry. In book-cover photos and publicity shots, Shepard is almost always shown in Western wear, often in a cowboy hat. The writer rarely smiles in his photos, and in many instances his eyes are averted from the camera, suggesting an unpracticed rural modesty. His gaze often seems fixed upon an outward point of focus, as though looking to the horizon. An untamed spirit, pictured in flannel shirt, boots, and worn jeans, Shepard exudes a frontier appeal and intimates a secretive understanding of the soil itself.

The cowboy imagery in cigarette advertising sheds light on the Shepard persona and the chord it has struck in the American movie audiences. After having tested a number of male types, from the athlete, to the sailor, to the man-about-town, the Philip Morris Company found that the cattleman proved most popular in appeal and best served as a marketing tool.[25] Shepard satirizes this advertisement image when May in *Fool for Love* ridicules Eddie as a wanna-be Marlboro Man. Still, the playwright's movie personae have frequently tapped into the mythology of Western masculinity and the magnetism it exerts on the viewing public. Like the tobacco industry, movie studios are profit driven, and we thus note how the man in the saddle has endured as a bankable film commodity.

At the end of *Suicide in B-Flat*, we learn that the unknown murder victim had suffered the ignominy of having his face "blown off." That Shepard would cite such a gruesome detail is revealing, since the writer's film career owes much to the lineaments and contours of his own countenance. In a genuine sense, Shepard has become his face. Arthur Schlesinger, Jr., has commented that Hollywood is "an industry that lives by stereotypes,"[26] and without question Shepard's visage has become iconic. The movies in chief use his features in decorative, even formulaic fashion, almost as an item of Americana, and it is always surprising when Shepard speaks, because his voice—rather nasal and high-pitched—belies his rugged, chiseled appearance. According to Wynn Handman, Shepard possesses a "face that is itself an American landscape"[27]; such comment alerts us to how Shepard has become a cipher, a distillation of frontier nostalgia and churning male emotion. In a contemporary era of racial, sexual, and ethnic renegotiation, where the conception of an America community has come under radical critique (along with the question, What does an American look like?), the playwright's face on the silver screen conjures for many in the American public a pristine cultural memory, that born of the prairie and the mesa, which palliates the viewer with its aura of agrarian innocence and evocation of an unsullied American past.

Shepard has never been incognizant of the mythologizing propensity of film; indeed the dream-weaving power of the medium has proven a recurrent subject of investigation in his dramatic writing. He is fully aware of the types that reappear in the American cinema and their often manipulative usage. Yet, though Shepard has expressed a frequent dislike of the film industry and has characterized Los Angeles as "degenerate and depraved,"[28] he has to some degree submitted himself to Hollywood's operations (and economics). His on-screen performances have of late reflected a relaxation of aesthetic standards. The playwright appears to have grown comfortable with the notion of appearing in movies that seek simply to entertain (and make money). This is evident in *Baby Boom*, a movie described by one reviewer as "a bland piece of comic pap."[29] *Crimes of the Heart* also confirms this trend: though the film drew upon Beth Henley's award-winning play, the project took the semblance of a blockbuster, and Shepard joined the star-studded cast of Sissy Spacek, Jessica Lange, Diane Keaton, and Tess Harper.

Many of Shepard's recent film roles have come in mainstream action pictures: *Defenseless* and *Thunderheart* are both rather run-of-the-mill murder mysteries; in the latter, he was paired with the young actor (and hot property) Val Kilmer, who had just come off his breakthrough performance as Jim Morrison in *The Doors*. Based on John Grisham's best-selling novel, *The Pelican Brief* is a cinematic rendition of "page-turner" fiction—chiefly plot driven and slight on intellectual content. Shepard has been seen most recently costarring with Susan Sarandon in the family drama *Safe Passage*.

While Shepard has emerged as a salable Hollywood commodity and has to some extent consented to his promotion and deployment as a film personality, his career reveals a paradoxical relation to the cinematic medium. Efforts such as *Baby Boom* may speak to the compromises he has made vis-à-vis the studio machine; still, as is the case with many artists in the professional theatre, Shepard's participation in unremarkable movie fare has afforded him the opportunity to pursue more personal and challenging projects. His work in film thus presents a divided picture. In many instances he has acquiesced before the dictates and demands of the movie industry; he has on other occasions exhibited an unremitting aesthetic integrity.

For the better part of his career, Shepard has been judicious in his working relationships. He has collaborated with a number of unconventional film artists, Terrence Malick, Robert Altman, and Wim Wenders among them. The playwright has voiced a genuine admiration for Malick, an artist considered by Shepard a "real director, not a Hollywood director,"[30] whose aesthetic perfectionism kept *Days of Heaven* two years in the editing process. The playwright accepted a role in *Resurrection* chiefly out of respect for and desire to act alongside the talented Ellen Burstyn. Two of Shepard's film roles, in *Raggedy Man* and *Crimes of the Heart*, issued from a personal relationship with Sissy Spacek and her husband, director Jim Fisk. Importantly, Shepard has not jumped at every role offered. He declined the part of Eugene O'Neill in *Reds* and turned down the male lead in *Urban Cowboy*, parts filled by Jack Nicholson and John Travolta, respectively.[31]

Shepard has furthermore developed a film career outside of his on-screen performances, and in a number of projects his artistic imprimatur can be discerned in a more informing way. German director Wim Wenders read and enjoyed Shepard's quasi-autobiographical writings in *Motel Chronicles* and approached the playwright about a possible collaboration. Shepard agreed and authored the screenplay that would become *Paris, Texas* (1984), a work that explores many of the issues that had dominated his recent stage writing—the dissolution of the family, the power of paranoia (the lies of the mind), and the possible redemption found in sacrifice and surrender. Against the vast and desolate beauty of the American Southwest, the film's action depicts a broken family and its tenuous mending. Travis, the movie's central character (played by Harry Dean Stanton) emerges from his ascetic, desert-rat existence and is reunited with his young son, whom he gives over to his estranged wife (played by Natassia Kinski). Before yielding the child, Travis appears before his wife, and in a scene that presages Jake's suppliance in *A Lie of the Mind* he confesses his brutal jealousies and seeks an end to the familial and marital sorrow. Praised for its stark emotion and panoramic evocation of the Southwestern landscape, *Paris, Texas* was presented at the 1984 Cannes Film Festival and won the prestigious Palm d'Or.

In his dealings with Antonioni on *Zabriskie Point* Shepard learned early in his career that the director is the chief artistic force in the production hierarchy of feature films. Never one to refuse a challenge, the playwright has recently tried his hand in this arena. Even as he was performing (often in subordinate roles) as a screen actor, we see Shepard's increasing hunger to gain greater authority in his film work. Taking steps to ensure the artistic and financial control of his projects, he has of late attempted himself to assume the position of the director. In short, the playwright has emerged as a would-be auteur of the American cinema.

Shepard received his baptism as a movie director with the 1988 film *Far North*. He has commented upon the rigors of the work's filming and how the technical matters of selecting shots, lenses, and camera angles proved especially demanding.[32] He has always been reluctant to turn his plays over to directors and producers, and in *Far North* the writer maintained control over his work by mastering the filmmaking apparatus himself. The enterprise moreover exhibited a nepotistic aspect and emerged as something of a family affair. Set in Duluth, Minnesota, home of Jessica Lange, *Far North* starred Lange and also presented a number of her actual family members. Ann Wedgeworth and Tess Harper, friends who had worked with Shepard on other projects, were also granted significant roles. The film's soundtrack was provided by the Red Clay Ramblers, the band enlisted for the New York production of *A Lie of the Mind.*

The drama of *Far North* portrays the ineffectual attempts of the family patriarch—a figure cut in the Baylor mold—to control his household and its many wayward females (from wife to daughter to granddaughter). Though the film is at heart a comedy and suggests that men and women can live together peaceably, the work acknowledges the confusions men face and their inability to keep up with the changing times.

While Shepard termed *Far North* a "domestic film," his latest work *Silent Tongue* explores broader subject matter and assumes a more expansive canvas. Shepard explained the film in succinct terms: "big screen, animals, land, epic scenes, bigger, more dramatic . . . more wides, the possibilities with this have to do with the land itself."[33] In the vein of *Dances with Wolves*, *Silent Tongue* tells the story of a snake oil salesman (and his family) as his medicine show travels across the West. With a cast that includes a number of colorful, offbeat performers (Alan Bates, Richard Harris, and River Phoenix) the film celebrates the Western landscape, the "innocence" of Native Americans, and serves as a master expression of Shepard's vision of the American frontier and its vast expanse. Writing in the *New York Times*, Caryn James describes *Silent Tongue* as "daringly different" from Hollywood fare and declares that with this film Shepard "truly becomes a film maker."[34]

Shepard's screen career curiously exhibits the play of oppositional impulses. The artist's rise to fame in mainstream studio productions runs counter to his emergence as an imaginative and willful director of his own film projects. This experience has brought a degree of pragmatism, even cynicism, to his outlook. Discussing greyhound racing in his London days, Shepard once remarked, "Greyhound racing is great because you can breed your own dog, raise it, take it to the track, and race it, which is unheard of in horse racing because it's too expensive."[35] The playwright has realized that moviemaking, like dog or horse racing, is basically dependent on money and that artistic prerogative corresponds in a direct way to financial independence: it is telling that the film *Country*, starring Shepard and Lange, was coproduced by Lange herself.[36] The writer has sought capital for his directorial projects outside of major studios. *Far North* was funded by a consortium of independent investors. It is ironic that *Silent Tongue*, a film about the American frontier in the late nineteenth century, was bankrolled by producers from France.[37]

Shepard's efforts as a film auteur have gained the artist limited attention, and his prominence in the film industry remains tied to his on-screen performances. *Far North* was at best a modest success and received little national exposure; *Silent Tongue* was in a state of dormancy for several years, waiting for an American distribution company to take up the film's marketing and promotion[38] (it was screened at the 1993 Sundance Film

Festival and gained national release early in 1994). Shepard currently is experiencing the frustration of many independent filmmakers who struggle to raise capital and bring their projects to completion, only to find limited opportunities for screenings and media attention; nonetheless, he remains undeterred. Commenting upon the production of *Far North*, the writer remarked, "It took me 20 years to learn how to write a play . . . I don't know how long it's going to take me to learn how to make a movie."[39] It appears that Shepard acknowledges and welcomes the novel challenges of the film medium. We also note something of an evolutionary process in the his career, that his work in theatre may have paved the way for his future as a cinematic artist. Film for Shepard may prove the final frontier, and American audiences may find that the writer regarded as the pre-eminent playwright of his generation may conceive the master works of his maturity not for the stage but the silver screen.

Shepard's career again and again reveals the artist in a symbiotic relation with the forces and figures that regulate the American entertainment industry. Film and theatre largely remain business ventures in America, and unlike many European countries, the United States fails to regard the arts as cultural necessities; performance is at best subsidized at modest levels. Basic economic realities thus breed an inherent conservatism in American entertainment forms—especially those aimed at a mass audience, since unconventional or iconoclastic artworks only rarely seize the popular imagination and translate into economic profit. Shepard has long struggled against the strictures of American theatre and film and has become rather jaded through the years. When recently asked about artistic freedom in America, the writer flatly responded: "It certainly doesn't exist in this country."[40]

Despite such cynicism, the playwright must admit a degree of complicity. While he has maintained a guarded relationship with the studio machine—keeping a Garbo-like seclusion—and has not maximized his media exposure (when the film version of *Fool for Love* was initially released he declined a photo shoot that would have put his face on the cover of a national publication), Shepard has demonstrated a wily opportunism in his film career. His flight from publicity hounds notwithstanding, Shepard has always been fascinated by his own celebrity and has played a game of hide-and-seek with the American public. He has earned a comfortable living as a movie actor and currently draws a handsome salary for each screen appearance. He has moreover agreed to perform in movies with questionable artistic merit. And his face has in fact found its way to the covers of many national weeklies. One finds that the playwright has in many cases courted celebrity and has colluded with the very forces he often assails.

Perhaps the most intriguing insight that derives from an examination of Shepard's film career concerns the way in which the artist has been relegated to a pose. Shepard has been described as "a man of few words, most of them mumbled,"[41] and it is highly ironic that after having worked as a wordsmith for over thirty years he has achieved greater recognition for his "look" than his "voice." This phenomenon is evidenced even in his first feature film, when, as director Malick would later confess, most of Shepard's speaking scenes in *Days of Heaven* ended up on the editing room floor. While the film itself was panned, Shepard's performance was lauded for its "monolithic taciturnity."[42] The title of his latest directorial effort, *Silent Tongue*, reveals an unintended irony, for one may argue that Shepard screened is Shepard silenced. The playwright of the manic monologue has been subjected to the freeze-frame; he has become a facial shot. He has thus experienced on some level the very dilemma of his artist-hero-outlaws, from Duke Durgens to Hoss to Henry Hackamore, who find themselves transfigured into media/myth constructs, marketed for the tastes and yearnings of a mass national audience.

It has been argued that the movies support in America a "common dream life,"[43] and indeed one recognizes that Shepard's screen image often resubstantiates a fundamental persona central to American culture's self-perception. It may thus be argued that Sam Shepard, whose classic American features have often been compared to those of Gary Cooper, has served a vision or version of national identity that aims to solidify consensus (while unwittingly excluding competing visions or visages). With a face that exudes a strong, silent manhood and frontier resolve, Shepard, shown so often in close-up, by his very looks stirs a nationalistic remembrance and prompts hope for the recovery of American will and spirit.

The career of Sam Shepard is a model case study in the paradoxes of the avant-garde artist in American culture. In his early works we note eruptive energies, destabilized framing, and an adolescent delight in subversion. However, as the insights of Bakhtinian theory remind us, the cultural process often works to countervail iconoclastic urges, to draw the wayward into the fold of sanctioned culture. Shepard's rise as a film personality represents a mainstreaming of the artist and a tempering of his anarchic inclination. The two-dimensional space of the screen has in some measure corralled the bucking bronco of the avant-garde. In his journey from the coffeehouses of Greenwich Village to the shopping mall multiplex cinemas, it may be thought that the playwright has been party to a sort of Faustian bargain. For fame and monetary gain Shepard has retreated from the heteroglossic; his work and person now tell the tales of a canonical American narrative. In Shepard's early one-act *Up to Thursday*, a youth sits in his jockey shorts, draped irreverently in an American flag. Today it is Shepard's countenance itself that is hoisted up and unfurled, a contemporary answer to J. Hector St. John Crevecoeur's famous 1830s question: "What then is the American, this new man?"[44]

NOTES

1. Cited in Esther Harriott, *American Voices: Five Contemporary Playwrights in Essays and Interviews* (London: McFarland, 1988), 15.

2. Cited in John Glore, "The Canonization of Mojo Rootface: Sam Shepard Live at the Pantheon," *Theatre* 12, no. 3 (1981): 53.

3. Cited in Don Shewey, *Sam Shepard* (New York: Dell, 1985), 143.

4. Shepard, quoted in Mel Gussow, "Sam Shepard: Writer on the Way Up," *New York Times*, 12 November 1969, 42.

5. Shepard, quoted in John Dark, "The *True West* Interviews," *West Coast Plays* 9 (1981): 57.

6. Cited in Mike Dorning, "Soaring Prices Cut Broadway's Power," *Baton Rouge Morning Advocate*, 21 December 1993, sec. D, p. 10.

7. Ibid.

8. Cited in "Sticker Shocks," *U.S. News and World Report*, 25 December 1995, 84.

9. Cited in Charles Fleming, "That Sinking Feeling," *Vanity Fair*, August 1995, 111.

10. Michael Feingold, quoted in *Grove's New American Theater* (New York: Grove Press, 1992), xv.

11. Sam Shepard, *True West*, in *Seven Plays* (New York: Bantam Books, 1981), 28.

12. See Sam Shepard, *Motel Chronicles* (San Francisco: City Lights Books, 1982), 13.

13. Volker Schlondorff, quoted in Chris Peachment, "Lonesome Cowboy," *Independent*, 12 April 1992, 22.

14. Phil Kaufman's casting decision explained in David Thomson, "Shepard," *Film Comment* 19 (December 1983): 49–50.

15. Stanley Kauffmann, "True to Life, True to Film," *New Republic*, 14 November 1983, 25.

16. Michael Rogin, *Ronald Reagan, The Movie* (Berkeley: University of California Press, 1987), 1–43.

17. Peachment, "Lonesome Cowboy," 22.

18. Dean McWilliams, "The Search for an Icon: Values in American Popular Films of the 1980s," in Walter Grunzweig et al., eds., *Constructing the Eighties* (Tubingen, Austria: Gunter Narr Verlag, 1992), 86–87.

19. Stewart McBride, "Sam Shepard—Listener and Playwright," *Christian Science Monitor*, 23 December 1980, sec. B, p. 2.

20. For Shepard's views on film acting see Chris Peachment, "American Hero," *Time Out*, 23–29 August 1994, 17; and Ross Wetzsteon, "Unknown Territory," *Village Voice*, 10 December 1985, 55.

21. Cited in Ellen Oumana, *Sam Shepard: The Life and Work of an American Dreamer* (New York: St. Martin's Press, 1986), 108.

22. Cited in Jack Kroll, Constance Guthrie, and Janet Huck, "Who's That Tall Dark Stranger?" *Newsweek*, 11 November 1985, 71.

23. See Marshall McLuhan, *The Medium is the Massage* (New York: Bantam Books, 1967).

24. Michael Feingold, "Seductive," *Village Voice*, 12 February 1979, 93.

25. See Bruce Lohof, "The Higher Meaning of Marlboro Cigarettes," in Christopher Geist and Jack Nachbar, eds., *The Popular Culture Reader* (Bowling Green, OH: Bowling Green University Popular Press, 1983), 115.

26. Arthur Schlesinger, Jr., quoted in John O'Connor and Martin A. Jackson, eds., "Foreword," in *American History/American Film* (New York: Continuum, 1988), xiv.

27. Wynn Handman, quoted in Kroll, Guthrie, and Huck, "Who's That Tall Stranger?" 70.

28. Shepard, quoted in Peachment, "American Hero," 16.

29. Peachment, "Lonesome Cowboy," 22.

30. Shepard, quoted in Peachment, "American Hero," 16.

31. Cited in Lynda Hart, *Sam Shepard's Metaphorical Stages* (Westport, CT: Greenwood Press, 1987), 119.

32. Cited in Jennifer Allen, "The Man on the High Horse," *Esquire*, November 1988, 146.

33. Shepard, quoted in Elgy Gillespie, "Say It Again, Sam," *Weekend Guardian Supplement*, 8 August 1992, 26.

34. Caryn James, "Sam Shepard's Spiritual, Imagistic Vision of the Old West," *New York Times*, 25 February 1994, sec. C, p. 3.

35. Shepard, quoted in Stephen Fay, "Renaissance Man Rides out of the West," *Times Sunday Magazine*, 26 August 1984, 19.

36. Financial aspects of *Far North* cited in Allen, "The Man on the High Horse," 144.

37. Cited in Gillespie, "Say It Again, Sam," 12.

38. Cited in Don Shewey, "Fools for Sam," *Village Voice*, 14 September 1993, 103.

39. Shepard, quoted in W. J. Weatherby, "Rile 'em, Cowboy," *The Guardian*, 4 June 1991, n.p.

40. Shepard, quoted in Gillespie, "Say It Again, Sam," 26.

41. John Lahr, *Automatic Vaudeville: Essays on Star Turns* (New York: Alfred A. Knopf, 1984), 41.

42. Cited in Peachment, "Lonesome Cowboy," 21.

43. Schlesinger, *American History/American Film*, xiv.

44. J. Hector St. John Crevecoeur, cited in Arthur Schlesinger, *The Disuniting of America* (New York: W. W. Norton, 1992), 12.

Chapter 8

The End of the Trail?

Sam Shepard's image as the rodeo rider of the American theatre has helped consolidate his position as a major American dramatist. He has been hailed for the rough-edged sensibility of his works, their vibratory quality, and their evocation of uncharted territory—that is, the open range of the national imagination. His participation in the avant-garde and his inveterate distrust of the institutions controlling American entertainment have moreover contributed to his status as an American original, an artist loath to compromise his vision or surrender his work to the dictates of committee. Though frequently regarded as the primitivist without peer— an impression Shepard has both valued and cultivated—his repute as a visionary on the edge of American civilization has helped render him a consummate insider, an icon of America itself.

From the outset of his career Shepard's plays have denounced stricture, the oppressive nature of the group, and any imposition brought by affiliation, doctrine, or ideology. The iconoclastic energy of his work has abated in his later career, yet the idiosyncratic path of the playwright (and his status as a rule breaker, loner, and nonconformist) has curiously evinced positions and postures elemental to the national character: rugged individualism, emphasis on self-taught skills, suspicion of authority and antiintellectualism. This feature of Shepard's career underscores the deep irony of American consensus, that the right to pursue one's own path operates as a shared, group belief. In essence individualism in the United States serves as a very cornerstone of community.

Rupert Wilkinson has identified four fears elemental to the American outlook:

1. the fear of being owned (including fear of dependence and being controlled and shaped by others)

2. the fear of falling apart

3. the fear of winding down (losing energy, dynamism, forward motion)

4. the fear of falling away from a past virtue and promise[1]

Examination of Shepard's corpus of work reveals how these noted preoccupations recur throughout his writing. His early plays are on one level case studies in paranoia, venting the young writer's "fear of being owned" or controlled by parental authority or the conformist mentality of post–World War II American society. Certainly Shepard's later family plays draw much of their dramatic power from their often enigmatic though penetrating expression of a cultural malaise, one evident in the dismantling of the domestic order and the depletion of America's moral capital (and phsycial resources).[2] Strong strands of nostalgia can be found in Shepard's writing and film work, and one might further speculate that a "fear of falling away" from a halcyon past has not only inspired Shepard's aesthetic efforts but has in large part fostered the audience appeal he has enjoyed, both as playwright and screen personality.

Such observations suggest that Shepard—despite his critique of American conformism and bureaucracy, despite his irregular and transgressive theatrics—holds to principles and viewpoints central to the American heritage. In his analysis of *Action*, David Savran uses Shepard's own metaphor of the "unseen hand" to examine the ideological premises, the "conceptual prison," of the playwright's outlook.[3] If one views the "unseen hand" in a Bakhtinian sense, we can see that Shepard's individualistic art utterances carry the consciousness of community, and his idiosyncratic insights, often conveyed through the deconstruction of folklore and pop-culture imagery, reconfigure and recover a traditional American ethos. A fascinating dialectic thus resides at the heart of Shepard's career as a dramatist and film artist. His works have frequently been multivalent in voice and stylistically irregular. Yet, even as his art has often contested the status quo and utilized venues at the fringes of American theatre, the writer and the anarchic energies of his work have met counterbalancing forces and have in a sense been enveloped, brought under the umbrella of artistic legitimization. The mainstreaming of the artist gives evidence to how the institutional forces of American culture (and the economic organization of the entertainment industry) have on some level defused, funneled, and transfigured the dangerous or unlicensed aspects of Shepard's work. Still, and this point cannot be underestimated, the implicit outlook of his art and the attitudes it suggests have expedited—perhaps even on some level predestined—his canonization as a Great American Playwright.

Beyond issues of production hierarchies, the boundaries of the canon, and the commodification of American art, Shepard's rise to fame invites a basic reconsideration of national identity itself. If the writer is viewed as the country's most American playwright, what does that tell us about America of the contemporary moment? To what America does Sam Shepard speak?

Sheldon Hackney, head of the National Endowment for the Humanities, in 1994 drew attention to the country's shifting sense of self when he outlined a series of "conversation projects" focused on the commmon values and differences of the American citizenry. Call for such discussion highlights the issue of American consensus and how it has been problematized by the surge of identity politics in the last three decades. Assimilationist conceptions have been further strained by recent demographic patterns. During the 1980s, the country experienced a massive influx of immigrants, over 40 percent of whom were Asian.[4] By the turn of the century it is projected that more than a third of the U.S. population will be of a "minority" background.[5] A number of metaphors have been popularized which convey the new disposition of American culture; the melting pot has been displaced by the salad bowl, the gumbo, and the kaleidoscope. This climate contributed to the election of Bill Clinton, who capitalized upon the inattention given to issues of diversity in the Reagan/Bush era and promised a government of mixed representation, one that would "look like" today's America.

Visions of the country's future (and the possibility of diverse communities acting cooperatively) have however produced numerous and often adversarial political agendas. With rather increasing frequency, American society has of late exhibited the schisms that divide its population, and rancor, not reconciliation, seems the order of the day. Commonly regarded as the revenge of the "angry white male," a phenomenon born of decreasing economic opportunity and resentment against minorities, the election in November of 1994 brought a profound change in the orientation of the government's legislative branch as Republicans assumed majority status in both the House of Representatives and the Senate. Supported by the conservative Christian Coalition, the party issued its "Contract with America" and called for a return to traditional values, a reverence for textbook American history, and a complete rethinking of the welfare state. Opposed to affirmative action, immigration, and multicultural education, the Republican Revolution has signaled the rising frustration and increased polarization of the electorate. The results of the 1994 election no doubt indicate the exhaustion of the liberal-Left agenda, which, in the words of one critic, has now been "left for dead."[6]

Some years ago a scholar attributed Shepard's success to the manner in which his plays "flush out the hidden yearnings and terrors of the American collective unconscious."[7] Given the growing diversification of American society and the polarities manifest in the currently raging "culture wars," it is questionable that the playwright can continue (if ever he did) to fulfill such "collective" service. Certainly, in a time when matters of political correctness have become issues of national debate, Shepard seems awkwardly out of step. One sees that Shepard's plays have almost exclusively been concerned with the male experience, the European immigrant past, and the heritage of the West. It is illuminating to note Shepard's uneasiness with the "foreign." Few African American figures populate his plays—the drunken Negro in *Dog*, the black radicals in *Operation Sidewinder*. Mrs. Cherry's valet (Wong) in *Shaved Splits* is derived from less than flattering Asian stereotypes. The playwright has been accused of homophobia,[8] and the ire Shepard has aroused in many feminist circles has already been mentioned. Seen against such recent work as Suzan-Lori Parks's *The America Play*, which views American history as a hole in which the lives of the disenfranchised have been interred and forgotten, Shepard's plays can appear sentimental, mournful of a lost American plenitude.

It must be admitted that Shepard's vision is chiefly retrospective. His plays seldom consider utopian possibilities or envision a reconfigured (or reenlivened) American culture that holds promise for all. A striking image is deployed near the conclusion of his film *Far North*; in this sequence the beleaguered patriarch stands on a backwoods highway and turns to see his two daughters and granddaughter dressed in skins and war paint and riding on horseback, bearing down upon him with scowls, yelps, and sharpened weapons. A hallucinatory vision fueled by male anxiety, the scene is indicative of Shepard's outlook and, in face of a shifting American landscape, perhaps suggests a current image of the playwright—Shepard standing as the lone cowboy, the last embattled American male, while forces of otherness assail and threaten.

In contemporary America, one wonders if a center can in fact be discerned, if the notion of a center should not be discarded altogether. In Tony Kushner's recent play *Angels in America*, the character Harper observes the world in upheaval and speaks of systems collapsing and old orders coming undone. Kushner's play, which won the 1993 Pulitzer Prize, reflects the decentering of American culture; it also indicates the U.S. theatre's increased attention to nontraditional voices. Pulitzer Prize winners over the last few years include a woman (Wendy Wasserstein), an African American (August Wilson), and a gay man (Tony Kushner). Many regarded the appointment of George C. Wolfe, an African American director, to the top position of New York's Public Theatre as another signal of the theatre's diversification. Wolfe replaced JoAnne Akalaitas, a figure renowned as an avant-garde experimenter in the sixties and seventies; in a capsule the change in personnel documents a watershed moment, a move from the counterculture to the multicultural. Wolfe recently spoke about *Angels in America* in a rather prophetic manner, declaring that there is no Other in America today, meaning, there is no one outlook, no one history, no one "story" that determines who belongs and who does not. According to the director, the American theatre has become the "watering hole of survival," where we all gather for replenishment and tell each other our many stories.[9]

Megan Terry, who made her fame with the Open Theatre and who now serves as the Omaha Magic Theatre's playwright-in-residence, has made a similar point. Terry argues that no one can be the Great American Playwright in today's theatre, because there are too many American audiences.[10] In a recent interview, Shepard confessed that the current state of the American theatre has given him pause, as he can "no longer ... figure out who the audience is."[11] Unlike his Off-Off Broadway days, when he was in effect preaching to the converted, Shepard as an American playwright of the nineties seems somewhat adrift. This situation perhaps illuminates the writer's increased involvement in the movies, a form geared to the American public's lowest common denominator.

To facilitate the work of his biographer, Shepard should have ended his career with *A Lie of the Mind*; its epic scope and lofty ambition would have served well as a point of closure for the writer's life in the theatre. The piece may arguably be regarded as a "great" American play, a work about the nation that acknowledges tension and rupture while simultaneously promoting understanding and unity—the folded flag, the fire in the snow. Shepard has not since that time equaled *A Lie of the Mind*, either in quality of writing or in intensity of audience response.

In 1987 Shepard and Lange became the parents of a baby boy (named Samuel) and a year later moved their household to a Virginia farm, where Shepard raised horses and settled into the life of the gentry. As the decade drew to its end, many of the playwright's admirers wondered openly if Shepard had not entered a state of semiretirement, if he had not in fact relinquished his office as America's preeminent living dramatist.

Indeed, only three years after the New York premiere of *A Lie of the Mind*, a Chicago group, Theatre Oobleck, staged a send-up of Shepard's family plays entitled *The Slow, Painful Death of Sam Shepard*.[12] The reported demise of Shepard as a vibrant force in the American theatre received little evidence to the contrary with his 1991 play, *States of Shock*, a small-scale piece that seemed an overly self-conscious, mannered exercise in the Shepardian style (perhaps aimed at recapturing the verve and vitality of his earlier work). Labeled "states of schlock" by one critic,[13] the piece experienced a short, undistinguished, and disappointing run at the American Place Theatre.

Shepard has reclaimed some repute with his latest stage effort, *Simpatico*, which premiered at the Public Theatre in the fall of 1994. Returning to a wider canvas, the playwright stretches the dramatic action of the play from Cucamonga, California to the bluegrass, horse country of Kentucky. The three-act work—the original manuscript numbered over two hundred pages[14]—focuses on the complex relationship between the play's two male leads: Carter, a burned-out loner living in a small-town desert locale, and Vinnie, a cocksure con artist who supports Carter (and has taken up with Carter's former wife in Kentucky). In film noir fashion, the work untangles the mystery of a past scam executed by the play's central characters. Against the backdrop of this intrigue, *Simpatico* conveys a strong sense of dissatisfaction in the lives of its characters, who have in varying ways sought the promise of American bounty; references to the Kentucky Derby, in fact, invoke commentary (often with sarcasm) from the principals upon the nature of the American soil, the heartland, and the country's present-day disquietude.

The Public Theatre's production of *Simpatico*, which was directed by Shepard himself, initially drew a polite though lukewarm reception from the critics (harsher reviews followed). Vincent Canby's review in the *New York Times* indicates the mixed impressions generated by the play; while Canby lauded *Simpatico* as a "fine" piece, he went on to describe the play's ending as one that "seems more theoretically correct than emotionally fulfilling."[15] Recalling the criticisms of *States of Shock*, another reviewer noted the "pallid" aspect of the play and found an almost imitative quality to the work: "it feels less like a Shepard play than a B-movie script by someone who's read a lot of Shepard."[16]

While the question remains as to whether Shepard can again summon the creative fire that propelled his work to a position of prominence in the U.S. theatre, one must grant the playwright respect for what he has accomplished in his thirty-year (and counting) career as an American dramatist. He has taken the vernacular strains of the American idiom and forged a compelling dramatic voice, one that echoes the rhythms of the cornbelt and the desert Southwest. With an imaginative flair surpassed by no other playwright in our country, Shepard has infused the American family play with a brooding lyricism, an often disturbing sense of depth and mystery, and a visceral urgency conveyed through riveting character confrontations and uncanny stage imagery. He has moreover touched a yearning in his audience, one born of the aspirations and disappointments that come with being an American in the latter half of the twentieth century. One critic's assessment of Vinnie in *Simpatico* not only illuminates the disaffected disposition of the character but in an incisive way captures the outlook and identity that define Shepard himself:

He's a last, bewildered son of those once vital, hardworking, often lawless and repressed God-fearing folk, the restless pioneers who moved from east to west to open this land. Now at the end of their cycle, with no plains or mountain ranges to cross, the sons of these pioneers are disconnected from any sense of purpose or community. They hustle and scheme without moral compass, trying to survive by making accommodations that are at best temporary, more often delusional.[17]

Shepard has succeeded as few American writers in capturing the mood and sensibility of American society as it has evolved in the post–World War II era. His plays have reveled in the flotsam of popular culture while simultaneously recalling time-honored outlooks and narratives from America's past. Still, even as Shepard has taken his place among the most revered of our country's dramatists, his plays have achieved limited commercial success. It is not insignificant that the playwright intended *Simpatico* to be his first Broadway show but could not raise the $800,000 necessary for its production.[18] That Shepard was unable to realize this Broadway staging speaks volumes about the current state of the American theatre; it perhaps also intimates something about the momentum of Shepard's career. It thus remains to be seen if "the American theatre's great white hope,"[19] who burst upon the scene in the counterculture days of the sixties, will thrive and prosper in the multicultural America of the next millineum.

POSTSCRIPT

In the spring of 1996, Sam Shepard rebounded into the public eye with the first Broadway production of his thirty-year career. Originating at Chicago's Steppenwolf Theatre under the direction of Gary Sinise, where the text of the play underwent substantial revisions, a revival of *Buried Child* opened in New York on April 30 at the Brooks Atkinson Theatre. With the Steppenwolf cast largely intact, the show drew lavish praise, was labeled a "hit," and rekindled discussion of Shepard's stature and importance as an American dramatist.

This interest in Shepard's work reflects a curious trend in the last two years—that is, the elder statesmen of the American theatre have found themselves appreciated anew. Edward Albee, after suffering years of abuse from theatre critics, restored his reputation with *Three Tall Women*, winning the 1994 Pulitzer Prize; the spring of 1996 saw a New York revival of his 1966 play *A Delicate Balance*. At the age of seventy-nine, Horton Foote won the 1995 Pulitzer Prize for his drama *The Young Man from Atlanta*. Having lately showcased the works of both Albee and Foote, New York's Signature Theatre Company is dedicating its entire upcoming season to Shepard plays.

Still, the question lingers as to what extent Shepard will remain a visible force in the American theatre. He has moved to Minnesota with Jessica Lange and is raising cattle.[20] Much of his energy in these last years has been given to short-story writing; his collection, *Cruising Paradise*, was published in May of 1996. Much of the playwright's recent press coverage has treated Shepard as a historical figure, suggesting that *Buried Child* exists as a classic text of the modern American stage. And the new success of Shepard, Foote, and Albee may indicate something about the reactionary temper of the mid-nineties, a time that embraces Shepard almost as an item of cultural nostalgia. Now himself the representative of the American dramatic tradition, Sam Shepard has become a grand old man of the theatre.

NOTES

1. Rupert Wilkinson, *The Pursuit of American Character* (New York: Harper & Row, 1988), 2.

2. David J. DeRose argues that the guiding motif of Shepard's plays is that of "a world that has come unfixed." See *Sam Shepard* (New York: Twayne, 1992), 4.

3. David Savran, "Sam Shepard's Conceptual Prison: *Action* and the Unseen Hand," *Theatre Journal* 36, no. 1 (1984): 57–73. This essay remains one of the most important works in Shepard scholarship.

4. Cited in Lawrence H. Fuchs, *The American Kaleidoscope* (Middletown, CT: Wesleyan University Press, 1990), 278.

5. Cited in Crawford Young, "The Dialectics of Cultural Pluralism," in Crawford Young, ed., *The Rising Tide of Cultural Pluralism* (Madison: University of Wisconsin Press, 1993), 5.

6. Michael Tomasky, "The Left Lost Touch," *Village Voice*, 22 November 1994, 19–20; "Left for Dead" headline on front cover.

7. John Lahr, "Playing Fast and Loose," *Times Literary Supplement*, 24 November 1978, 136.

8. Alan Shepard, "The Ominous 'Bulgarian Threat' in Sam Shepard's Plays," *Theatre Journal* 44, no. 1 (1992): 60.

9. George C. Wolfe, quoted on Tom Bywaters, "In the Wings: *Angels in America* on Broadway," PBS Great Performances Series (May, 1993).

10. Megan Terry, quoted in David Savran, *In Their Own Words* (New York: Theatre Communications Group, 1988), 254.

11. Shepard, quoted in Elgy Gillespie, "Say It Again, Sam," *Weekend Guardian Supplement*, 8 August 1992, 13.

12. Production recounted in Loren Kruger, "The Slow and Painful Death of Sam Shepard," *Theatre Journal* 41, no. 4 (1989): 538–39.

13. John Simon, "States of Schlock," *New York*, 27 May 1991, 71.

14. Mel Gussow, "A Play Lies Fallow," *New York Times*, 27 December 1993, sec. C, p. 11.

15. Vincent Canby, "Sam Shepard Goes to the Races and Wins," *New York Times*, 20 November 1994, sec. H, p. 8.

16. Michael Feingold, "Loner Stars," *Village Voice*, 22 November 1994, 77.

17. Canby, "Sam Shepard Goes to the Races," sec. H, p. 5.

18. Gussow, "A Play Lies Fallow," sec. C, p. 11.

19. Ann McFerran, "Poet of Post War Americana," *Time Out*, 4 December 1981, 24.

20. Cited in Stephen Schiff, "Shepard on Broadway," *New Yorker*, 22 April 1996, 84.

Chronology

Date	Events in Shepard's Life	Art and Entertainment	Public Life
1943	November 5, born Sam Shepard Rogers VII in Fort Sheridan, Illinois	Humphrey Bogart appears in *Casablanca*	U.S. troops lead Allied conquest of Sicily
1944		Aaron Copland debuts *Appalachian Spring*	Allied forces stage Normandy invasion
1945		Jackie Robinson signs with the Dodgers	Germany surrenders; United States drops atom bombs on Hiroshima and Nagasaki
1946		O'Neill's *The Iceman Cometh* premieres	United Nations holds first session
1947		Motion picture industry blacklists the Hollywood 10; *A Streetcar Named Desire* opens in New York	Death of industrialist Henry Ford
1948		Jackson Pollock exhibits *Composition No. 1*	Republicans nominate Thomas E. Dewey
1949		Miller wins Pulitzer for *Death of a Salesman*	General Motors earns record net profits
1950		RCA introduces the color TV tube	U.S. troops sent to Korea
1951		Salinger publishes *Catcher in the Rye*	Rosenbergs found guilty of espionage
1952		Gary Cooper stars in *High Noon*	Eisenhower/Nixon ticket wins
1953		Death of Eugene O'Neill; 20th Century Fox introduces Cinemascope	Statistics note dramatic rise in surburban population

1954		Newport Jazz Festival begins; *On the Waterfront* wins best picture Oscar	Supreme Court orders school desegregation
1955	Rogers family moves to California	Death of James Dean; Disneyland opens	AFL and CIO merge
1956		Arthur Miller weds Marilyn Monroe	Rosa Parks challenges racist bus ordinances in Montgomery
1957		*Long Day's Journey Into Night* wins Pulitzer; Jack Kerouac publishes *On the Road*	USSR launches Sputnik
1958		Paul Robeson receives passport after seven-year suspension	United States sends first satellite into space
1959		Death of Buddy Holly; *A Raisin in the Sun* opens on Broadway	Alaska becomes the forty-ninth state; Ford discontinues the Edsel
1960		Harper Lee publishes *To Kill a Mockingbird*; *The Fantasticks* begins run in New York	Kennedy/Nixon debate airs on national TV; FDA approves the birth control pill
1961	Enrolls in Mount San Antonio Junior College	Death of Gary Cooper	Formation of the Peace Corps; Bay of Pigs invasion
1962	Tours with Bishop's Company Repertory Players	Steinbeck wins Nobel Prize; Albee's *Who's Afraid of Virginia Woolf?* premieres; federal government funds public TV	Cuban missile crisis; first African American enrolls at University of Mississippi

Date	Events in Shepard's Life	Art and Entertainment	Public Life
1963	Settles in New York's East Village; meets Ralph Cook at the Village Gate	Death of Clifford Odets; Guggenheim Museum exhibits Pop Art; Peter Sellers stars in *Dr. Strangelove*	Martin Luther King delivers "I Have a Dream" speech; JFK assassinated in Dallas
1964	*Cowboys* and *The Rock Garden* at Theatre Genesis	The Beatles appear on U.S. TV; Lenny Bruce is tried for obscenity	LBJ signs Civil Rights Act; Goldwater runs on GOP ticket
1965	*Dog* and *Rocking Chair* at La MaMa; *Up to Thursday* and *4-H Club* staged by Albee's Playwrights Unit; *Chicago* at Theatre Genesis; *Icarus's Mother* at Caffe Cino	Luis Valdez founds El Teatro Campesino	Malcolm X assassinated in Harlem; United States commits first combat troops to Vietnam; LBJ advances Medicare bill
1966	*Red Cross* at Judson Poets' Theatre; wins three Obies; *Fourteen Hundred Thousand* at Firehouse Theatre in Minneapolis	Open Theatre presents *Viet Rock*; NEA receives first funds	California elects Reagan governor; Timothy Leary arrested for narcotics possession; N.O.W. founded
1967	*La Turista* at the American Place Theatre; *Melodrama Play* at La MaMa; one-acts toured by La MaMa in Europe; *Cowboys #2* at Mark Taper Forum in Los Angeles; *Forensic & the Navigators* at Theatre Genesis; receives grants from University of Minnesota, Yale, and Rockefeller Foundation	Death of Woody Guthrie; Dustin Hoffman appears in *The Graduate*; death of Joe Cino; founding of Negro Ensemble Company	50,000 protestors converge on the Pentagon; Thurgood Marshall becomes first black Supreme Court justice

1968	Cowrites screenplay for *Me and My Brother*; contributes to script for *Zabriskie Point*; receives Guggenheim Fellowship; performs with rock band Holy Modal Rounders	*Hair* opens on Broadway; Peformance Group presents *Dionysus in 69*	Assassinations of Robert Kennedy and Martin Luther King; U.S. soldiers involved in Mylai massacre; street violence erupts in Chicago during Democratic National Convention
1969	La MaMa tours *The Holy Ghostly*; weds O-lan Johnson; *The Unseen Hand* at La MaMa; *La Turista* at London's Royal Court Theatre	Beckett wins Nobel Prize; rock festivals at Woodstock and Altamont; Dennis Hopper appears in *Easy Rider*; Circle Repertory founded	534,000 U.S. troops stationed in Vietnam; first U.S. astronaut walks on the moon; Stonewall riots unite gay and lesbian community
1970	*Zabriskie Point* released; son Jesse Mojo born; *Operation Sidewinder* at Lincoln Center; *Shaved Splits* at La MaMa; appears in *Brand X*	Monday Night Football debuts on ABC; Hendrix and Joplin die of drug overdoses; Mabou Mines stage *The Red Horse Animation*	National Guardsmen fire on students at Kent State; first celebration of Earth Day; U.S. troops invade Cambodia
1971	*Mad Dog Blues* at Theatre Genesis; affair with Patti Smith; *Cowboy Mouth* and *Back Bog Beast Bait* at the American Place Theatre; moves to London	*Fiddler on the Roof* becomes longest-running musical on Broadway; Dance Theatre of Harlem established; *Patton* wins Oscar for best picture	26th ammendment lowers the voting age to 18; Charles Manson sentenced to gas chamber
1972	*The Tooth of Crime* at Open Space Theatre	Helen Reddy sings "I Am Woman"; Playwrights Horizons founded	Nixon visits China; George Wallace runs for presidency

Date	Events in Shepard's Life	Art and Entertainment	Public Life
1973	Publishes book of poetry, *Hawk Moon*; *Blue Bitch* on BBC; *Nightwalk* for Open Theatre; *The Tooth of Crime* receives an Obie	Death of John Ford; Charles Ludlam stars in Ridiculous Theatre Company's *Camille*; George Lucas directs *American Graffiti*	OPEC stages oil embargo; Court rules on *Roe v. Wade*; Senate conducts Watergate hearings; members of AIM seize Wounded Knee
1974	*Geography of a Horse Dreamer* at Royal Court; *Little Ocean* at Hampstead Theatre Club; *The Tooth of Crime* at the Royal Court; *Action* at the Royal Court; returns with family to California	Hank Aaron breaks Babe Ruth's homerun record; Evel Kneivel fails in leap across Snake River Canyon; At the Foot of the Mountain opens	Nixon resigns; racial violence disrupts Boston public schools
1975	*Action* and *Killer's Head* at American Place Theatre; *Action* at Magic Theatre; tours with Rolling Thunder Review	Bruce Springstein releases *Born to Run*; Mamet's *American Buffalo* premieres; Robert Altman directs *Nashville*	Saigon falls to Viet Cong; Gerald Ford survives two assassination attempts; unemployment rate reaches highest mark since 1941
1976	Joins Magic Theatre Company; *Angel City* at Magic Theatre; *Suicide in B-Flat* at Yale Repertory; receives Creative Arts Medal from Brandeis University; receives Rockefeller Grant	Robert Wilson's *Einstein on the Beach* staged in New York; Sylvester Stallone stars in *Rocky*	Patty Hearst stands trial; nation celebrates the bicentennial; Sunbelt leads U.S. in population growth; Carter wins presidential election

168

1977	*Inacoma* at Magic Theatre; *Curse of the Starving Class* at Royal Court; publishes *Rolling Thunder Logbook*	Michael Christofer's *The Shadow Box* wins Pulitzer; Death of Elvis Presley; The Eagles release *Hotel California*	Protestors gather at Seabrook nuclear plant; Ernest Morial becomes first black mayor of New Orleans; Department of Energy created
1978	*Curse of the Starving Class* at Public Theatre; *Seduced* at Trinity Square Repertory; *Buried Child* at Magic Theatre; *Tongues* at Magic Theatre; appears in *Days of Heaven*	"Dallas" becomes a hit prime-time soap; Valdez's *Zoot Suit* opens at the Mark Taper Forum	California approves Proposition 13; Panama Canal Treaty ratified; assassination of Harvey Milk, San Francisco city councilman
1979	Wins Pulitzer Prize; *Savage/Love* at Magic Theatre; writes libretto for *Jacaranda*	Death of John Wayne; *The Deerhunter* and *Coming Home* dominate the Oscars; Lloyd Richards becomes head of Yale Rep	Islamic fundamentalists seize U.S. Embassy in Teheran; atomic leak discovered at Three Mile Island nuclear plant
1980	*True West* at Magic Theatre; appears in *Resurrection*	Sissy Spacek stars in *Coal Miner's Daughter*; Lanford Wilson wins Pulitzer	United States boycotts Moscow Olympics; Reagan wins presidency
1981	Appears in *Raggedy Man*; meets Jessica Lange	Wooster Group's *Routes 1 & 9* opens in New York; Spielberg directs *Raiders of the Lost Ark*	Sandra Day O'Connor becomes first woman Supreme Court justice; House of Representatives approves a 25 percent tax cut; AIDS virus identified
1982	Publishes *Motel Chronicles*; appears in *Frances*	Fierstein's *Torch Song Trilogy* opens on Broadway; death of Henry Fonda	AT&T loses antitrust suit; Nicaraguan junta denounces United States

Date	Events in Shepard's Life	Art and Entertainment	Public Life
1983	*Fool for Love* at Magic Theatre; appears in *The Right Stuff*; receives Academy Award Nomination; father dies; divorce proceedings begin; after divorce lives with Lange in New Mexico	Brooklyn Academy of Music hosts its first Next Wave Festival; TV viewers see last episode of *M*A*S*H*; Robert Duvall stars in Horton Foote's *Tender Mercies*	Reagan proposes "Star Wars" defense plan; terrorists kill 216 U.S. Marines in Beirut; U.S. troops invade Grenada
1984	Writes screenplay for *Paris, Texas*; appears in *Country*; PBS broadcasts *True West*	Death of Lillian Hellman; Mamet's *Glengarry Glen Ross* wins Pulitzer	Mondale chooses Geraldine Ferraro as running-mate; Reagan wins landslide victory
1985	*The War in Heaven* airs on radio; *A Lie of the Mind* opens Off-Broadway; appears in *Fool for Love*	Rock Hudson dies of AIDS; Spalding Gray debuts *Swimming to Cambodia*	GE buys RCA, largest non-oil corporate merger in U.S. history; United States becomes a debtor nation for the first time since 1914
1986	Has daughter Hannah with Lange; appears in *Crimes of the Heart*	Paul Simon releases *Graceland*; *Joe Turner's Come and Gone* staged at Yale Rep	Nation watches space shuttle Challenger disaster; Clint Eastwood wins mayoral election in Carmel, CA; Statue of Liberty celebrates its hundredth birthday
1987	Has son Samuel with Lange; publishes "True Dylan" in *Esquire*; appears in *Baby Boom*	Death of Andy Warhol; *Les Misérables* opens on Broadway	Oliver North testifies before Congress; Robert Bork's nomination to Supreme Court denied; stock market plunges a record 508 points
1988	Releases *Far North*	*Phantom of the Opera* enjoys record revenues on Broadway	Jesse Jackson seeks Democratic nomination; Bush/Quayle ticket wins election

1989	Appears in *Steel Magnolias*	*Oh, Calcutta!* closes in New York after 5,595 performances; death of Samuel Beckett	Racial tensions spark riots in Miami; U.S. troops invade Panama; the Exxon Valdez spills oil on Alaskan coast
1990		Kevin Costner stars in *Dances with Wolves*	U.S. hostages freed in Beirut; Bush concedes to tax increases
1991	*States of Shock* at American Place Theatre; appears in *The Voyager*; appears in *Defenseless*	Geena Davis and Susan Sarandon star in *Thelma and Louise*; death of Joseph Papp; Circle Rep stages *The Baltimore Waltz*	U.S. forces launch Operation Desert Storm; Supreme Court nominee Clarence Thomas gains Senate approval
1992	Appears in *Thunderheart*	Mamet's *Oleanna* runs in New York	Bill Clinton wins presidential election; Rodney King verdict triggers riots in Los Angeles
1993	Appears in *The Pelican Brief*	Kushner's *Angels in America* wins Pulitzer	Democrats fail to pass national health care
1994	*Simpatico* at Public Theatre; appears in *Safe Passage*; releases *Silent Tongue*	Tarantino directs *Pulp Fiction*	Republicans win control of both congressional houses
1995	*Buried Child* at the Steppenwolf	Tom Hanks wins Oscar for *Forrest Gump*	Balanced budget amendment fails to gain passage; Federal Building bombed in Oklahoma City
1996	*Buried Child* on Broadway; publishes *Cruising Paradise*; season of Shepard plays at the Signature Theatre	*Rent* wins Tony award	Republicans nominate Bob Dole; Bill Clinton is reelected

Further Reading

AMERICAN HISTORY AND CULTURE

Berman, Ronald. *America in the Sixties*. New York: The Free Press, 1968.

Bookbinder, Robert. *The Films of the Seventies*. Secaucus, NJ: Citadel Press, 1982.

Cagin, Seth, and Philip Dray. *Hollywood Films of the Seventies: Sex, Drugs, Violence, Rock 'n' Roll, and Politics*. New York: Harper & Row, 1984.

Combs, James. *The Reagan Range: The Nostalgic Myth in American Politics*. Bowling Green, OH: Bowling Green State University Popular Press, 1993.

Daniel, Clifton, ed. *Chronicle of the 20th Century*. Liberty, MO: J. L. International Publishing, 1992.

Edelstein, Andrew J., and Kevin McDonough. *The Seventies from Hot Pants to Hot Tubs*. New York: Dutton, 1990.

Gilbert, James. *Another Chance: Postwar America, 1945–1985*. Chicago: Dorsey Press, 1986.

Girgus, Sam B., ed. *The American Self*. Albuquerque: University of New Mexico Press, 1981.

Grunzweig, Walter, Roberta Maierhofer, and Adi Wimmer, eds. *Constructing the Eighties*. Tubingen, Austria: Gunter Narr Verlag, 1992.

Hogan, Joseph, ed. *The Reagan Years*. Manchester: Manchester University Press, 1990.

Horner, Matina S., et al. *The Quality of American Life in the Eighties*. Englewood Cliffs, NJ: Prentice-Hall, 1981.

Kaiser, Charles. *1968 in America*. New York: Weidenfeld & Nicolson, 1988.

Karp, Walter. *Liberty Under Siege: American Politics, 1976–1988*. New York: Henry Holt, 1988.

Kreiger, Joel. *Reagan, Thatcher, and the Politics of Decline*. New York: Oxford University Press, 1986.

Leuchtenburg, William E. *A Troubled Feast: American Society Since 1945*. Boston: Little, Brown, 1979.

Miller, Nathan. *Stealing from America: A History of Corruption from Jamestown to Reagan*. New York: Paragon House, 1992.

Morgan, Edward P. *The 60s Experience: Hard Lessons About Modern America*. Philadelphia: Temple University Press, 1991.

Oakley, J. Ronald. *God's Country: America in the Fifties*. New York: Dembner Books, 1986.

Palmer, John L., and Isabel V. Sawhill, eds. *The Reagan Record*. Cambridge, MA: Ballinger, 1984.

Palmer, William J. *The Films of the Eighties: A Social History*. Carbondale, IL: Southern Illinois University Press, 1993.

Phillips, Kevin P. *Post-Conservative America: People, Politics, and Ideology in a Time of Crisis*. New York: Random House, 1981.

Rotundo, E. Anthony. *American Manhood: Transformations in Masculinity from the Revolution to the Modern Era*. New York: Basic Books, 1993.

Schaller, Michael. *Reckoning with Reagan: America and Its President in the 1980s*. New York: Oxford University Press, 1992.

Slotkin, Richard. *Fatal Environment*. New York: Atheneum, 1985.

——. *Gunfighter Nation: The Myth of the Frontier in Twentieth-Century America*. New York: Atheneum, 1992.

Smith, Adam. *The Roaring 80s*. New York: Summit Books, 1988.

Stein, Arthur. *Seeds of the Seventies: Values, Work, and Commitment in Post-Vietnam America*. Hanover, NH: University Press of New England, 1985.

Taylor, Joshua C. *America as Art*. New York: Harper and Row, 1978.

Truettner, William H., ed. *The West as America: Reinterpreting Images of the Frontier, 1820–1920*. Washington: Smithsonian Institution Press, 1991.

Walzer, Michael. *What It Means to Be an American*. New York: Marsilio, 1992.

Wilkinson, Rupert. *The Pursuit of American Character*. New York: Harper & Row, 1988.

AMERICAN DRAMA AND THEATRE

Adler, Thomas P. *Mirror on the Stage: The Pulitzer Plays as an Approach to American Drama*. West Lafayette, IN: Purdue University Press, 1987.

Atkinson, Brooks. *Broadway*. Revised ed. New York: Macmillan, 1974.

Bigsby, C.W.E. *Modern American Drama, 1945–1990*. New York; Cambridge: Cambridge University Press, 1992.

——. *A Critical Introduction to Twentieth-Century American Drama*. Vol. 3; Beyond Broadway. New York; Cambridge: Cambridge University Press, 1985.

Blum, Daniel. *A Pictorial History of the American Theatre: 1860–1985*. New York: Crown, 1986.

Brustein, Robert. *The Third Theatre*. New York: Alfred A. Knopf, 1969.

Chinoy, Helen Krich, and Linda Walsh Jenkins, eds. *Women in American Theatre*. Revised ed. New York: Theatre Communications Group, 1987.

Cohn, Ruby. *New American Dramatists 1960–1990*. New York: St. Martin's Press, 1991.

Demastes, William W. *Beyond Naturalism: A New Realism in American Theatre*. Westport, CT: Greenwood Press, 1988.

Durham, Weldon B. *American Theatre Companies, 1931–1986*. Westport, CT: Greenwood Press, 1989.

Engle, Ron, and Tice Miller, eds. *The American Stage: Social and Economic Issues from the Colonial Period to the Present*. New York; Cambridge: Cambridge University Press, 1993.

Farber, Donald C. *From Option to Opening*. New York: Drama Book Specialists, 1977.

Gard, Robert E., Marston Balch, and Pauline B. Temkin. *Theater in America*. Madison, WI: Dembar Educational Research Services, Inc., 1968.

Gardner, R. H. *The Splintered Stage: The Decline of the American Theater*. New York: Macmillan, 1965.

Greenberger, Howard. *The Off-Broadway Experience*. Englewood Cliffs, NJ: Prentice-Hall, 1971.

Harriot, Esther. *American Voices: Five Contemporary Playwrights in Essays and Interviews*. London: McFarland, 1988.

Henderson, Mary C. *Theater in America*. New York: Harry N. Abrams, 1986.

Herman, William. *Understanding Contemporary American Drama*. Columbia, SC: University of South Carolina Press, 1987.

Hill, Errol. *The Theatre of Black Americans*. 2 vols. Englewood Cliffs, NJ: Prentice-Hall, 1980.

Hughes, Catherine. *American Playwrights 1945–75*. London: Pitman, 1976.

King, Bruce, ed. *Contemporary American Theatre*. New York: St. Martin's Press, 1991.

Lahr, John. *Up Against the Fourth Wall*. New York: Grove Press, 1970.

Langley, Stephen. *Theatre Management in America*. New York: Drama Book Publishers, 1980.

Leiter, Samuel L. *Ten Seasons: New York Theatre in the Seventies*. Westport, CT: Greenwood Press, 1986.

Little, Stuart. *Off-Broadway: The Prophetic Theatre*. New York: Coward, McCann & Geoghegan, 1972.

Marranca, Bonnie, and Gautam Dasgupta. *American Playwrights: A Critical Survey*. New York: Drama Book Specialists, 1981.

Mordden, Ethan. *The American Theatre*. New York: Oxford University Press, 1981.

Novick, Julius. *Beyond Broadway: The Quest for Permanent Theatres*. New York: Hill and Wang, 1968.

Poggi, Jack. *Theater in America: The Impact of Economic Forces, 1870–1967*. Ithaca, NY: Cornell University Press, 1968.

Poland, Albert, and Bruce Mailman, eds. *The Off-Off-Broadway Book*. New York: Bobbs-Merrill, 1972.

Scharine, Richard. *From Class to Caste in American Drama*. Westport, CT: Greenwood Press, 1991.

Schlueter, June, ed. *Feminist Rereadings of Modern American Drama*. London: Associated University Presses, 1989.

Schlueter, June, ed. *Modern American Drama: The Female Canon*. London: Associated University Presses, 1990.

Seller, Maxine Schwartz, ed. *Ethnic Theatre in the United States*. Westport, CT: Greenwood Press, 1983.

Shank, Theodore. *American Alternative Theatre*. New York: Grove Press, 1982.

Szilessy, Zoltan. *American Theater of the 1960s*. Carbondale, IL: Southern Illinois University Press, 1986.

Weales, Gerald. *The Jumping-off Place: American Drama in the 1960s*. New York: Macmillan, 1969.

Williams, Mance. *Black Theatre in the 1960s and 1970s: A Historical-Critical Analysis of the Movement*. Westport, CT: Greenwood Press, 1985.

Zeigler, Joseph Wesley. *Regional Theatre: The Revolutionary Stage*. Minneapolis: University of Minnesota Press, 1973.

COLLECTIONS OF SHEPARD'S PLAYS

A Lie of the Mind and The War in Heaven. New York: New American Library, 1987.

Fool for Love and Other Plays. New York: Bantam Books, 1984 (includes *Angel City*, *Geography of a Horse Dreamer*, *Action*, *Cowboy Mouth*, *Melodrama Play*, *Seduced*, and *Suicide in B-Flat*).

Fool for Love and The Sad Lament of Pecos Bill on the Eve of Killing His Wife. San Francisco: City Lights Press, 1983.

Mad Dog Blues and Other Plays. New York: Winter House, 1972 (includes *The Rock Garden*, *Cowboys No. 2*, *Cowboy Mouth*, *Blue Bitch*, and *Nightwalk*).

Seven Plays. New York: Bantam Books, 1981 (includes *Buried Child*, *Curse of the Starving Class*, *The Tooth of Crime*, *La Turista*, *True West*, *Tongues*, and *Savage/Love*).

States of Shock, Far North, Silent Tongue. New York: Vintage Books, 1993.

The Unseen Hand and Other Plays. New York: Bantam Books, 1986. Reprint ed. New York: Vintage Books, 1996 (includes *The Rock Garden*, *Chicago*, *Icarus's Mother*, *4-H Club*, *Fourteen Hundred Thousand*, *Red Cross*, *Cowboys #2*, *Forensic & the Navigators*, *The Holy Ghostly*, *Operation Sidewinder*, *Mad Dog Blues*, *Back Bog Beast Bait*, and *Killer's Head*).

SHEPARD'S NONDRAMATIC WRITING

Cruising Paradise. New York: Knopf, 1996.

Hawk Moon. Los Angeles: Black Sparrow Press, 1973. Reprint ed. New York: Performing Arts Journal Publications, 1981.

Joseph Chaikin and Sam Shepard: Letters and Texts, 1972–1984. Edited by Barry Daniels. New York: New American Library, 1989.

Motel Chronicles. San Francisco: City Lights Books, 1982.

Rolling Thunder Logbook. New York: Viking Press, 1977.

BOOKS ON SHEPARD

Auerbach, Doris. *Sam Shepard, Arthur Kopit, and the Off-Broadway Theatre*. Boston: Twayne, 1982.

Benet, Carol. *Sam Shepard on the German Stage: Critics, Politics, Myths*. New York: Peter Lang, 1993.

DeRose, David J. *Sam Shepard*. New York: Twayne, 1992.

Hart, Lynda. *Sam Shepard's Metaphorical Stages*. Westport, CT: Greenwood Press, 1987.

King, Kimball, ed. *Sam Shepard: A Casebook*. New York: Garland, 1989.

Marranca, Bonnie, ed. *American Dreams*. New York: Performing Arts Journal Publications, 1981.

McGhee, Jim. *True Lies: The Architecture of the Fantastic in the Plays of Sam Shepard*. New York: Peter Lang, 1993.

Mottram, Ron. *Inner Landscapes*. Columbia: University of Missouri Press, 1984.

Oumano, Ellen. *Sam Shepard: The Life and Work of an American Dreamer*. New York: St. Martin's Press, 1986.

Patraka, Vivian M., and Mark Siegel. *Sam Shepard*. Boise, ID: Boise State University Press, 1985.

Shewey, Don. *Sam Shepard*. New York: Dell, 1985.

Tucker, Martin. *Sam Shepard*. New York: Continuum, 1992.

Wilcox, Leonard, ed. *Rereading Shepard*. New York: St. Martin's Press, 1993.

INTERVIEWS WITH SHEPARD

Allen, Jennifer. "The Man on the High Horse." *Esquire*, November 1988, 141–44, 146, 148, 150–51.

Blumenthal, Eileen. "Chaikin and Shepard Speak in Tongues." *Village Voice*, 26 November 1979, 103, 109.

Chubb, Kenneth, et al. "Metaphors, Mad Dog Blues, and Old Time Cowboys." *Theatre Quarterly* 4 (1974): 3–16.

Coe, Robert. "Saga of Sam Shepard." *New York Times Magazine*, 23 November 1980, 56–59, 118, 120, 122, 124.

Cott, Jonathan. "The Rolling Stone Interview: Sam Shepard." *Rolling Stone*, 18 December 1986, 166–72, 178, 200.

Dark, John. "The *True West* Interviews." *West Coast Plays* 9 (1981): 51–71.

Fay, Stephen. "The Silent Type." *Vogue*, 4 February 1985, 213, 216, 218.

Goldberg, Robert. "Sam Shepard, American Original." *Playboy*, March 1984, 90, 112, 192–93.

Gussow, Mel. "Sam Shepard: Writer on the Way Up." *New York Times*, 12 November 1969, 42.

Kakutani, Michiko. "Myths, Dreams, Realities—Sam Shepard's America." *New York Times*, 29 January 1984, sec. 2, pp. 1, 26–28.

Kroll, Jack, with Constance Guthrie and Janet Huck. "Who's That Tall Dark Stranger?" *Newsweek*, 11 November 1985, 68–74.

Lippman, Amy. "Interview: A Conversation with Sam Shepard." *Harvard Advocate* 117, no. 1 (1983): 2–6, 44–46.

Rosen, Carol. "Emotional Territory: An Interview with Sam Shepard." *Modern Drama* 36, no. 1 (1993): 1–11.

Sessums, Kevin. "Geography of a Horse Dreamer." *Interview*, September 1988, 79–81, 85–86.

ARTICLES AND ESSAYS ON SHEPARD

Bachman, Charles R. "Defusion of Menace in the Plays of Sam Shepard." *Modern Drama* 19, no. 4 (1976): 405–16.

Blau, Herbert. "The American Dream in American Gothic: The Plays of Sam Shepard and Adrienne Kennedy." *Modern Drama* 27, no. 4 (1984): 520–39.

Brater, Enoch. "American Clocks: Sam Shepard's Time Plays." *Modern Drama* 37, no. 4 (1994): 603–12.

Callens, Johan. "Inter/National Stages." In Marc Maufort, ed. *Staging Difference: Cultural Pluralism in American Theatre and Drama*. New York: Peter Lang, 1995.

Chubb, Kenneth. "Fruitful Difficulties of Directing Shepard." *Theatre Quarterly* 15, no. 4 (1974): 17–25.

Cima, Gay Gibson. "Shifting Perspectives: Combining Shepard and Rauschenberg." *Theatre Journal* 38 (1986): 67–81.

Demastes, William W. "Understanding Sam Shepard's Realism." *Comparative Drama* 21, no. 3 (1987): 229–48.

DeRose, David. "Slouching toward Broadway: Shepard's *A Lie of the Mind*." *Theater* 17 (1986): 69–74.

Falk, Florence. "The Role of Performance in Sam Shepard's Plays." *Theatre Journal* 33, no. 2 (1981): 182–92.

Freedman, Samuel G. "Sam Shepard's Mythic Vision of the Family." *New York Times*, 1 December 1985, sec. 2, pp. 1, 20.

Goist, Park Dixon. "Sam Shepard's Child Is Buried Somewhere in Illinois." *MidAmerica* 14 (1987): 113–25.

Hart, Lynda. "Sam Shepard's Pornographic Visions." *Studies in the Literary Imagination* 21, no. 2 (1988): 69–82.

Heilman, Robert B. "Shepard's Plays: Stylistic and Thematic Ties." *Sewanee Review* 100 (1992): 630–44.

Kleb, William. "Sam Shepard's *Inacoma* at the Magic Theatre." *Theater* 9 (1977): 59–64.

———. "Creating the California Playwright." *Performing Arts Journal* 4, no. 3 (1980): 60–71.

Kramer, Mimi. "In Search of the Good Shepard." *New Criterion* 2, no. 2 (1983): 51–57.

Lanier, Gregory W. "Two Opposite Animals: Structural Pairing in Sam Shepard's *A Lie of the Mind*." *Modern Drama* 34, no. 3 (1991): 410–21.

Londre, Felicia. "Sam Shepard Works Out: The Masculinization of America." *Studies in American Drama, 1945–Present* 2 (1987): 19–27.

Madden, David. "The Theatre of Assault: Four Off-Off Broadway Plays." *Massachusetts Review* 8, no. 4 (1967): 713–25.

Mazzocco, Robert. "Heading for the Last Roundup." *New York Review of Books*, 9 May 1985, 21–27.

McBride, Stewart. "Sam Shepard—Listener and Playwright." *Christian Science Monitor*, 23 December 1980, sec. B, pp. 1–3.

McDonough, Carla J. "The Politics of Stage Space: Women and Male Identity in

Sam Shepard's Family Plays." *Journal of Dramatic Theory and Criticism* 9, no. 2 (1995): 65–83.

Nash, Thomas. "Sam Shepard's *Buried Child*: The Ironic Use of Folklore." *Modern Drama* 26, no. 4 (1983): 486–91.

Oppenheim, Irene, and Victor Fascio. "The Most Promising Playwright in America Today Is Sam Shepard." *Village Voice*, 27 October 1975, 9.

Podol, Peter. "Dimensions of Violence in the Theatre of Sam Shepard: *True West* and *Fool for Love*." *Essays in Theatre* 7, no. 2 (1989): 149–58.

Putzel, Steven. "Expectation, Confutation, Revelation: Audience Complicity in the Plays of Sam Shepard." *Modern Drama* 30, no. 2 (1987) 147–60.

———. "An American Cowboy on the English Fringe." *Modern Drama* 36, no. 1 (1993): 131–46.

Rabillard, Sheila. "Destabilizing Plot, Displacing the Status of Narrative: Local Order in the Plays of Pinter and Shepard." *Theatre Journal* 43, no. 1 (1991): 41–58.

Rosen, Carol. "Sam Shepard's *Angel City*: A Movie for the Stage." *Modern Drama* 22, no. 1 (1979): 39–46.

Savran, David. "Sam Shepard's Conceptual Prison: *Action* and the Unseen Hand." *Theatre Journal* 36, no. 1 (1984): 57–73.

Schlatter, James. "Some Kind of Future: The War for Inheritance in the Works of Three American Playwrights of the 1970s." *South Central Review* 7, no. 1 (1990): 59–75.

Schvey, Henry. "The Master and His Double: Eugene O'Neill and Sam Shepard." *Journal of Dramatic Theory and Criticism* 5, no. 2 (1991): 49–60.

Shepard, Alan. "The Ominous 'Bulgarian Threat' in Sam Shepard's Plays." *Theatre Journal* 44, no. 1 (1992): 59–66

Simard, Rodney. "American Gothic: Sam Shepard's Family Trilogy." *Theatre Annual* 41 (1986): 21–36.

Stambolian, George. "Sam Shepard's *Mad Dog Blues*: A Trip through Popular Culture." *Journal of Popular Culture* 7, no. 4 (1974): 776–86.

Thomson, David. "Shepard." *Film Comment* 19 (1983): 49–56.

Wetzsteon, Ross. "Sam Shepard: Escape Artist." *Partisan Review* 49, no. 2 (1982): 253–61.

Whiting, Charles G. "Images of Women in Shepard's Theatre." *Modern Drama* 33, no. 4 (1990): 494–506.

Wilcox, Leonard. "Modernism vs. Postmodernism: Shepard's *The Tooth of Crime* and the Discourse of Popular Culture." *Modern Drama* 30, no. 4 (1987): 560–73.

Wilson, Ann. "Fool of Desire: The Spectator to the Plays of Sam Shepard." *Modern Drama* 30, no. 1 (1987): 560–73.

Zinman, Toby Silverman. "Visual Histrionics: Shepard's Theatre of the First Wall." *Theatre Journal* 40, no. 4 (1988): 509–18.

———. "Sam Shepard and Super-Realism."*Modern Drama* 29.3 (1986): 423–30.

For further bibliographical information on Shepard, see William Kleb, "Sam Shepard," in Philip Kolin, ed., *American Playwrights Since 1945: A Guide to Scholarship, Criticism, and Performance* (Westport, CT: Greenwood Press, 1989), 387–419.

Index

About the Author

LESLIE A. WADE is an Associate Professor in the Louisiana State University Department of Theatre. He received his Ph.D. from the University of California at Santa Barbara. Wade has presented his work at national and international conferences and has published essays on American theatre and popular culture. Also a dramatist, Wade has had several of his works produced and has won numerous awards for his plays.

ISBN 0-313-28944-1